HUNYADI:
LEGEND AND REALITY

Joseph Held

EAST EUROPEAN MONOGRAPHS, BOULDER
DISTRIBUTED BY COLUMBIA UNIVERSITY PRESS, NEW YORK

1985

EAST EUROPEAN MONOGRAPHS, NO. CLXXVIII

Copyright © 1985 by Joseph Held
Library of Congress Card Catalog Number 84-82224
ISBN 0-88033-070-8

Printed in the United States of America

TABLE OF CONTENTS

	Acknowledgments	v
	Introduction	vii
	List of Illustrations	x
	Historical Place Names	xi
I.	Origins	1
II.	Hunyadi's Hungary: The Privileged Orders	17
III.	Hunyadi's Hungary: The Church	42
IV.	Hunyadi's Hungary: The People	56
V.	Lord and Commander	80
VI.	From Victory to Defeat	91
VII.	Regent	113
VIII.	Struggle for Survival	135
IX.	The Phoenix	155
X.	Epilogue	170
XI.	Note on the Sources	174
	Notes	176
	Index	246

ACKNOWLEDGMENTS

I have spent many years thinking about and working on this volume, often being forced to set it aside while my other duties at Rutgers University claimed my attention. Yet all this time it has never been completely out of my mind. The hope of one day being able to complete it was a purpose worth working for.

As it has been the case with other such studies, this was not intended to become a book. As I began my research into the ways of fifteenth-century society in the Kingdom of Hungary, I was more attracted to the least known area of scholarship, the exploration of the everyday life of the rural population. I hoped to complete an article about the life of simple folks in a particular village during an agricultural cycle. However, I could not proceed in a vacuum; the rest of society kept intruding at every point of my work and the figure of János Hunyadi loomed ever larger over its horizon. Eventually, I decided on a compromise. This book is, therefore, a study of the life of János Hunyadi and an examination of the ways of various segments of society in the Kingdom during his time.

I have received a great deal of help and encouragement from many scholars and friends while I struggled with my ideas and the scarce resources available for such a study. I spent a year at the Haus-Hof-und Staatsarchiv in Vienna, where my friend, Herr Anton Nemeth, provided gudiance for my initial research. I owe him a gratitude and many thanks. Peter Hanák, a member of the Hungarian Academy of Sciences and of the Historical Institute at Budapest, helped me to focus my attention on Hunyadi as a pivotal force in early fifteenth-century Hungary. Academician

György Ránki, the Deputy Director of the Historical Institute at Budapest and Visiting Professor at the University of Indiana, Bloomington, stimulated my thinking in the same direction. I want to acknowledge their contribution to my thinking. Professors Traian Stoianovich and James Muldoon, my colleagues at Rutgers University, provided detailed criticism of the manuscript. They are, of course, in no way responsible for the errors and mistakes that I may have made in this study. The friendship that I have received from Professor Iván Völgyes all these years greatly encouraged me in my work, and this volume is dedicated to him with greatfulness.

Mrs. Barbara Metzger spent many hours editing the manuscript and her contribution to the final version of the book was indispensable. The illustrations, maps and the cover of the volume are the work of my artist wife, and no words can express my gratitude for her endurance and patience during the long years of my labors.

Finally, my secretaries, Elizabeth Ann Skyta and Roberta Diamondstein, have typed and proofread several versions of this work, and I owe both of them a special gratitude for their supreme effort.

Joseph Held
Rutgers University
Camden, N. J.

INTRODUCTION

Few periods in Hungarian history present a richer variety of events and personalities than the fifteenth century. Straddling two distinct historical periods (the last part of the Middle Ages and the early Renaissance), this century brought forth such colorful characters as that irrascible king of Hungary, Sigismund of Luxemburg, the magnates Miklós Ujlaki and László Garai, the Counts Cilli and the Serbian despot (king) Djurdj Branković, and not the least the soldiers János Hunyadi, Jan Jiškraz of Brandiši and Mihály Szilágyi. It has often been said that the second half of the century was dominated by the younger son of János Hunyadi, Mátyás, elected king of Hungary in 1458. However, his rise to the throne would not have been possible without the groundwork laid down by his father.

Hungary was one of the great powers of Europe during much of the fifteenth century. Its sphere of interests extended from the Carpathian Basin into the northern Balkans and included Moldavia and Wallachia, Serbia, Bosnia, and the Dalmatian seacoast. A great continental power, Hungary controlled part of the land routes leading to the east and the south from Germany and Austria to the Middle East. As such, Hungary participated in great power politics. King Sigismund, elected Holy Roman emperor in 1411, was instrumental in encouraging the prelates of the Roman Catholic church to assemble in the great conciliar movement of the early fifteenth century trying to end the schism in the church. King Mátyás, in turn, established a modern state by contemporary standards with a secular bureaucracy and a standing army, both firsts in the history of the Kingdom of Hungary. His court was a glittering center of Renaissance culture, and his library was one of the most famous of its kind in his time.

Society in the Kingdom of Hungary was equally varied and richly shaded. The various social strata were not yet rigidly defined, and there was considerable upward mobility for the ambitious and lucky members of the lower ranks. Membership in the upper social strata was not guaranteed even for sons of the richest aristocrats. One characteristics factor operating among the aristocrats was the rapid turnover of office holders —both secular and clerical—few of whom had been able to hold office for more than a decade. Aristocratic families had died out with dreary frequency, providing room for upwardly mobile lesser noblemen.

Society in fifteenth-century Hungary had been held together not so much by the power of the king—he was usually sharing his power with the secular and clerical lords—as by the moral force of the Roman Catholic church. As an institution, the church provided the glue of communication among individuals and social strata. The church, being the single richest landholding institution in the country, also provided the intellectual underpinnings, the moral and even physical support, and the ideological justification for the rule of the upper strata.

The lowest social stratum, that of the peasants, had no say in the affairs of the realm at all. Living in small villages or market towns, they tilled the soil, raised animals or managed the floodplains. However, the peasants were not isolated from the "outside" world. They traded their produce, often traveling great distances even as far as Silesia. Regularly visiting the markets of nearby towns and cities, they led an active and productive life. They were certainly better fed and clothed than many of their Western European counterparts. Even the serfs among them had rights and freedoms, and upward mobility was possible for them.

In Hunyadi's time, the overriding problem in the Kingdom of Hungary were the continuous struggles among aristocratic alliances (the so-called "leagues"), sapping the internal strength of the realm, and the increasingly greater threat represented by an aggressive, expansive Ottoman Empire in the south. The Ottomans gradually extended their control over much of the Balkan Peninsula, subjugating the diverse peoples of the region one by one, pushing ever closer to the borders of the Kingdom of Hungary. Hunyadi spent a great part of his adult life fighting against both the internal and external enemies of the Kingdom. Yet, by the time of his death in 1456, most of the fortifications and strong points of the Balkans,

Introduction

a system that previously provided the bases of forward defenses against the Ottoman menace, were lost. Western Europe, whose monarchs were busy in consolidating their holds on their respective kingdoms, was no longer able or willing to unite with Hungary in opposing the Ottomans. Hunyadi's Hungary, left alone to do the best it could, was the last bastion shielding Western Europe from the great Muslim power during much of the first half of the fifteenth century. This struggle and Hunyadi's role in it is the central theme of this study.

LIST OF ILLUSTRATIONS

1.	János Hunyadi in Thuroczi's Chronicle	7
2.	The "Holy Crown" of St. István	21
3.	Hunyadi's Properties in 1456	35
4.	"Disorganized" Village	66
5.	"Long" Village	66
6.	The Three-field System in 15th Century Hungary	69
7.	The Medieval Village of Móric	75
8.	Peasant Implements	77
9.	Hunyadi's and Wladislaw I's Route during the Long Campaign	93
10.	Hunyadi's Road to Varna	107
11.	The Road to Kosovo-Polje	131
12.	Belgrade in July, 1456	158

The historical place names listed below, mostly Hungarian, have been changed in the surrounding states after World War I. To the right of each name the new name is given in this list.

Bábolna	Bobilna
Bártfa	Bardejov
Besztercebánya	Banska Bistrica
Brassó	Braşov
Eperjes	Prešov
Galambóc	Golubac
Gyulafehérvár	Alba Iulia
Hunyadvár	Hunedoara
Karánsebes	Caransebeş
Kolozsmonostor	Cluj-Manastur
Kolozsvár	Cluj-Napoca
Lőcse	Levoča
Macsó	Mačva
Marosvásárhely	Tirgu Mureş
Nagyszeben (Szeben)	Sibiu
Nagyvárad (Várad)	Oradea
Nicopolis	Nikopol
Pozsony	Bratislava
Ragusa	Dubrovnik
Szabadka	Subotica
Szalánkemén	Slankamen
Szatmár	Şatu Mare
Szentimre	Sintimbru
Szörény	Severin
Trencsén	Trenčin
Temesvár	Timişoara
Zimony	Zemun

I

ORIGINS

> "Hudianisch gar mächtiglich, zu streiten ist im niemant geleich, wider die Türken unverzagt, gar grosse ere er bejagt, sein lob wil ich preisen...."*

In the spring of 1457, conspiracy was brewing at the court of King László V of Hungary. The king was only seventeen and highly impressionable, but a true Habsburg. He was also cunning and fond of intrigue. He had received a good foundation in politics from the kinsmen who had reared him, the Holy Roman emperor Friedrich III of Habsburg and the wily Ulrich von Cilli, Count of Zagoria.[1] Nevertheless, he was a worried young man. Count Cilli, military governor of Croatia, Slavonia and Dalmatia, and chief captain of the armies of the Kingdom of Hungary, had been murdered in Nándor-Alba (Belgrade) by László Hunyadi, son of the great general János Hunyadi, the previous November, while the king and Cilli had been visiting that fortress, and for sometime afterwards the king himself had feared for his life.[2] In fact, he had no need to worry; Cilli's death had been the outcome of a long-standing enmity between him and the Hunyadis, and in any case he had been a treacherous man and fully deserved his fate.[3]

---

* Mandelreis, "Türkenschrei," Robert von Lilienkron, *Die Historische Volkslieder der Deutschen* (Leipzig, 1876), 1:461.

By the time of the murder, János Hunyadi, the former regent of Hungary and perpetual count of Beszterce, was also dead, having been carried off by the plague in August shortly after his successful defense of Belgrade against the armies of Mehemed II. His sons László and Mátyás had been stunned by his death, but László had quickly moved in to fill the vacuum left by his father's passing. This was to be expected; he had been active in Hungarian politics from an early age, especially during the last years of his father's regency, and he had his uncle, the renowned general Mihály Szilágyi to provide him with counsel and support.[4]

The Hunyadi family had long been a thorn in the side of the haughty aristocrats of the Kingdom of Hungary. Not only did the Hunyadies lack an ancient (and therefore respectable) family tree, but they had the audacity and, what is more, the ability to achieve high social status and great political power in the realm. János Hunyadi had become regent in 1446, while the king was still an infant and his succession to the throne of Hungary was uncertain. When László had finally ascended the throne, he had appointed Hunyadi chief captain of the armies of Hungary and manager of the royal revenues. Hunyadi's *banderium* (private army) had been the strongest in Hungary. Thus, he had been much too powerful for the liking of the king and the envious aristocrats who surrounded him. With his death, the appetite of the court, and especially Cilli, for his family's wealth had only increased.

László Hunyadi then in his early twenties, had an impressive physical presence;

> he had a manly constitution, a broad chest, a sunburned face and happy eyes. He was mild by nature but he was easily excitable. His mind was sharp and was usually of a friendly disposition. He was brave and knew how to use arms. But his proud demeanor often aroused the envy and scorn of the barons of the realm....[5]

This, of course, meant trouble, because he was no match in intrigue for the palatine, László Garai, who had succeeded Cilli in the king's favor.[6] Garai belonged to an envious group of aristocrats who were eager to see the sons of the general out of the way. The cabal formed at the royal court included, among others, Miklós Ujlaki, a duplicitous, conceited man, formerly a close ally of János Hunyadi and now the military governor of Transylvania; Pál Bánfi, and the king's German advisers.[7]

The conspirators suggested to the king that László Hunyadi was plotting in order to capture the inheritance of the now extinct Cilli family. They also appealed to the king's mysticism by arguing that the murdered favorite's soul would not find rest until his death was avenged.[8] Despite having sworn at Temesvár not to punish the Hunyadis for the murder, the king was not entirely opposed to their elimination. He was receptive to the conspirators' suggestion that his oath had been forced out of him and was therefore null and void. In addition, the royal treasury was practically empty and the quickest way of filling it was by confiscating the wealth of others. The Hunyadis, the single richest family in the realm, were obvious candidates for despoliation.

When László Hunyadi arrived at court that spring, the king had not yet been entirely won over by the conspirators. In fact, he proceeded to appoint the young Hunyadi his treasurer and to entrust him with the defense of the fortress of Belgrade. Although it is unlikely that the young king originally perceived it as such, this appointment eventually proved to have been a trap. Hunyadi could fulfill his task only by raising a sizable army, and in doing so he unwittingly played into the hands of the conspirators. On their prompting, the king asked Hunyadi to deliver his younger brother Mátyás to Buda "as a sign of his good will" (in reality as a hostage) when he left for Belgrade. Hunyadi agreed, despite his father's admonition never to appear at court with his brother.[9] As a precaution, however, he sent some of his soldiers, until then stationed at Pest, across the Danube to Buda, where they took up quarters near the palace. Once again, his enemies could point to this as proof of his sinister intentions.

Hunyadi was aware of the danger, but he believed that the best way to allay the rumors was to depart immediately for Belgrade. Garai dissuaded him, arguing that a hasty departure would arouse suspicion and would be considered an insult to royalty.[10] The conspirators now received the king's approval for their plans. Their hand was strengthened by the arrival of Jan Jišrkaz of Brandiša, a former Hussite general and a strong supporter of the king.

On March 14, Hunyadi was invited to a meeting on the pretext of preparations for his departure for Belgrade. On his arrival at the gates of the palace, he was seized and taken prisoner. At the same time, Mátyás Hunyadi and several friends of the House of Hunyad, including the humanist bishop of Nagyvárad, János Vitéz of Zredna, were also captured.[11]

The next day, a hastily convened "court of justice" consisting mostly of enemies of the Hunyadis pronounced the two brothers and their friends guilty of treason and sentenced them all to death. The king, however, recoiled from the proposed bloodbath (in this he was not yet a true Habsburg) and agreed only to the execution of László Hunyadi for the murder of Cilli.[12]

In the evening of March 16 "while the burghers of Buda were still laboring in their vineyards," László Hunyadi was led, surrounded by heavily armed guards, to the square of St. George in front of the royal palace. A black flag was carried before him. His long, blond hair flowed over his shoulders. Though he was dressed in a richly embroidered gown, his hands were tied behind his back like those of a common criminal. Arriving at the square, he was ordered to kneel before the executioner's block. He asked the masked man to tie his hair out of the way of the sword. Then he was struck three times on the neck, without, however, being mortally wounded.[13] Legend would later say that the executioner was so moved by Hunyadi's youth and bravery that he did not have the heart to kill him. After the third stroke, Hunyadi jumped to his feet, loudly exclaiming that he had endured as much punishment as custom demanded, and started to run toward a small crowd of spectators. But his feet became entangled in his gown—or, perhaps, the effects of the sword began to be manifest—and he fell to the ground. Then he was seized anew and, at a command from a window of the palace, the fourth stroke separated his head from his body.[14]

The news of the execution quickly spread throughout the realm, where it caused unrest and consternation. Conrad Mesner, a merchant from Constance who happened to be in Buda, hastened to notify the prince of Milan, an acquaintance of the Hunyadis since the 1430s, attributing the execution to the desire of the king for revenge for the murder of Cilli.[15] The king, seeking to justify the deed, issued a statement calling the conspirators the saviors of his rule and condemning the entire Hunyadi family for alleged wrongs against the crown.[16]

Some of Hunyadi's friends escaped from Buda and began organizing resistance to the ruler. Hunyadi's mother, Erzsébet Szilágyi, incited friends of the Hunyadis to take up arms.[17] Within a month, probably fearing for his life, the king left Hungary for Vienna and then Prague, where he announced his planned marriage to the daughter of Charles VII of France. He took Mátyás Hunyadi with him as a prisoner. The Hunyadis' power and influence in the Kingdom of Hungary appeared to have been effectively destroyed. Yet, the story does not end here. Within a year, László V was dead. Rumor had it that he had been poisoned by George of Podiebrad, the regent of Bohemia.[18] His former prisoner, Mátyás Hunyadi, was elected king by the diet. He was to inaugurate a brilliant phase of Renaissance culture in East Central Europe. Not only did he prove to be an able statesman, but he can be regarded as one of the first of a long line of kings of the region intent upon establishing a centralized pre-modern state.

Whatever his character, Mátyás Hunyadi (Corvinus) could hardly have achieved what he did without the political and financial groundwork laid down by his father. Although János Hunyadi was to be remembered for centuries as a military genius, he was much more than that. Rising from an obscure lesser noble family of immigrants to Hungary, he became regent in 1446 and a perpetual baron in 1453, the richest, most powerful aristocrat of his time. As if these achievements were not enough, he was also a feared enemy of the Ottoman Empire, an *athleta Christi* of the Roman Catholic church.[19]

But the military aspects of János Hunyadi's career have always been overemphasized. The legend of Hunyadi as the simple soldier who had singlehandedly stopped Ottoman expansion into the Danube basin emerged soon after his death. The chronicler Joannis Thuróczi, writing in the 1470s, and Antonius Bonfini, composing his Renaissance-inspired history of the Hungarians in the 1490s, portrayed him as the only conscientious patriot in the realm threatened by the Ottoman Turks in the south and the Holy Roman Emperor in the west and beset by internal struggles among its great lords. According to his legend, Hunyadi used his own resources in winning his resounding victories in the Balkans, and every one of his many failures was caused by misfortune or betrayal. Although critics of Hunyadi existed even during his lifetime (the most severe being a Polish historian, Joannis Dlugosz) their criticism has been attributed to national envy or personal bias.

To argue that Hunyadi was nothing if not a politician is not in any way to denigrate his military successes; legends, after all, do tend to have their bases in fact. It is undeniable that Hunyadi's daring actions transformed the atmosphere of gloom and defeatism fueled by half a century of uninterrupted Ottoman successes against European armies in the Balkans into one of confidence and the hope of victory. His military prowess seems, however, to have had its limits; for instance, he was never able to defeat Jan Jiškraz, who controlled virtually all of the northern regions of Hungary (today, Slovakia) at the time, nor was he any more successful in dealing with other internal opponents.

János Hunyadi was a complex man at once unselfish and egotistical, a military genius and a blunderer, ardent pursurer of wealth, position, and political power, and equally ardent defender of the faith and the frontiers of the Kingdom of Hungary. His legend needs to be placed in a new perspective. What emerges is the achievement of the political man, one of the most eminent in the annals of East Central Europe.

* * *

In an age when family trees and long lines of ancestry were important ingredients of a successful political career, Hunyadi's origins were obscure indeed. Beyond the names of his parental grandfather, Serba or Sorba, and his father, Voyk or Woyk, we know next to nothing of his ancestry. Legend has him the offspring of an illicit affair between king Sigismund and a Transylvanian woman of the Morzsinai family,[20] and of one between Stepan Lazarevič, the despot of Serbia and a Hungarian woman from Nagyszeben.[21] A document issued by László V in January 1453 at Pozsony, summarizing Hunyadi's career, mentions his lowly origin; "he spent his youth under the reign of King Sigismund . . . and he strove hard to achieve by his own hard work, through hardship and personal heroism that which others gained through their ancestry and titles. . . ."[22] Laonikos Chalconcondylas mistakenly argued that Hunyadi's birthplace was a Transylvanian city.[23] His ancestry was disputed for centuries by Hungarian, Romanian and South Slavic historians, each claiming him for their own.[24]

The first document mentioning the Hunyadis is a patent issued in 1409 by king Signismund granting them the castle of Vajdahunyad, in Hunyad county, Transylvania. The patent mentions Voyk, his brothers Radul and Magos, Voyk's son János, and his nephew, also called Radul.[25] The contemporary chronicler Thuróczi explained that the family had come to Transylvania from Wallachia,[26] and the chronicle of the counts Cilli

Origins

János Hunyadi

in Thuróczi's Chonicle

remarked, "it is know that this János Hunyadi was born in Wallachia...."[27]

Hungarian historians have sometimes attempted to deny Hunyadi's Wallachian origin.[28] The fact that king Sigismund mentioned the young János in the original patent and that his successors, Albert I and Wladislaw I granted large landed estates to the Hunyadis has been considered evidence for their Hungarian and royal ancestry. It is likely, however, that Voyk came to Hungary—perhaps a refugee from the fratricidal Wallachian wars—during the late 1390s and that he was of the Orthodox religion. Once in Hungary, he probably married a Hungarian lesser noblewoman whose name we do not know,[30] and through this marriage came to be accepted as a lesser nobleman of the realm. More than this, he became a *miles aulae*, a soldier and counselor of the king. It is possible that he had converted to Roman Catholicism before his marriage; his children were reared as Roman Catholics.

The family of Voyk had no direct ties to the aristocracy of the Kingdom of Hungary in 1409. Its social status and advancement depended solely upon the good will of the king. Unflagging loyalty to the sovereign, an ability to procure mercenaries for the king's *banderium* and, above all, willingness to lend the king money were the requirements for advancement.[31] The story of the Hunyadis shows that social and political prominence did not depend entirely upon ethnic or social origins, although an aristocratic background and good family connections were certainly no hindrance to an upwardly mobile man.[32] In the case of men of exceptional ability, apparently not even noble status was absolutely necessary for an appointment to so important a position as membership in the royal retinue.[33] Voyk himself did not (could not) use the designation "de Hunyad," a sign of noble status, until 1414,[34] and the family received its coat of arms only from the hands of László V in 1453.[35] Valor in battle was an important means of upward social mobility, and Voyk must have been an excellent soldier indeed.[36] He also seems to have been the right man in the right place at the right time. King Sigismund, seeking to lessen his dependence upon the feudal armies of the aristocrats, increasingly resorted to the use of mercenaries, and Voyk appears to have been an excellent recruiter. Further, the king was also frequently in need of money and the Hunyadis often provided it.

Origins

Voyk sired three sons János, János Jr. (!) and Voyk Jr.—and perhaps one or two daughters of whom only one is known to us by name.[37] He appears to have died while his sons were still young; they requested the confirmation of their possession of Vajdahunyad in their own names in 1419, something that would have been unthinkable if he had still been alive.[38] The elder János was probably born at court around 1407.[39] The birthdates of his siblings are unknown. It is most likely, however, that they were all brought up in the recently acquired family castle. We know next to nothing about the fate of the youngest, Voyk Jr. He probably died at an early age, since no trace of him can be found in documents after 1419. János Jr., on the other hand, accompanied his elder brother on his early campaigns and died of wounds received in battle in 1441 or 1442.[40]

The Hunyadi children were probably taught reading and writing by the local priest and the nearby Franciscan friars of Hátszeg, but their teachers may not have been well-educated. They apparently did not—probably could not—teach the children Latin, the universal language of the age, but the evidence on this is ambiguous to say the least. Hunyadi himself certainly spoke several other languages. He knew Wallachian and understood Serbian and perhaps even Turkish. He learned Italian as a young man when he spent some time in Milan in the 1430s. He was also acquainted with military history.[41] As a self-made man, he absorbed the elements of the culture of the social stratum to which he wanted to belong, and he was fascinated by the world of the Italian Renaissance, which he observed at first hand.

If the formal education of the Hunyadi children was sketchy, there can be no doubt about the thoroughgoingness of the military training the boys received. They were obviously intended to grow up as soldiers. Their instruction in the use of arms and in field-generalship included harsh physical exercises. According to Thuróczi, "János Hunyadi became accustomed to all extremes of weather in his early life and consciously practiced exposure to all sorts of hardships."[42]

In asserting that Hunyadi began his career as a herald in the house of Stepan Lazarević,[43] Chalcocondylas was misinformed; it was probably Lazarević's successor, Djuradj Branković whom Hunyadi served in one of his Hungarian fortresses.[44] Chalcocondylas also mentioned a rumor that Hunyadi may have served the Ottoman Ali, son of Evrenos, as a groom, but this is unlikely. From the service of Branković, Hunyadi probably moved to the private army of the Székely count, György Csáki and then to Péter Ungor, Ferenc Csanádi, and the father of Miklós Ujlaki, whose son later became Hunyadi's ally and rival. By that time, Hunyadi commanded six lancers. Around 1428, he bcame a *miles aulae* of King Sigismund, and never again was to serve anyone other than the king of Hungary.[45]

It is possible that somewhere along the line Hunyadi received military instruction from Philippo degli Scolari, who was count of Temes and Ozora during the 1420s. A favorite of King Sigismund, Scolari was a descendant of a Florentine merchant family and a powerful lord in southern Hungary. Hunyadi may have learned basic methods of warfare from him, and he could also have been introduced to Renaissance culture at Scolari's court.[46]

Before becoming the king's soldier, Hunyadi had married Erzsébet Szilágyi, a woman about his age. Their elder son, László, was born around 1430 or 1431 and their younger, the future King Mátyás (Corvinus), about eight years later.[47] Erzsébet came from an upwardly mobile family of lesser noble soldiers. Her father, László Szilágyi, served the military governor of the district of Macsó (Mačva), János Maróti, and eventually became count of Bács county in the early 1440s. He must have been an educated man, since he held the title of *magister*. The Szilágyis had a wide network of family-relations in Transylvania, including the respected lesser noble families of Vingárts and Garázdas. Erzsébet's older brother Mihály was to become Hunyadi's most important comrade-in-arms, the much feared Kara Mihail of the Ottoman wars.[48]

We possess several descriptions of the young Hunyadi as he entered the service of the king. Bonfini described him as a man of medium height with a thick neck and chestnut-brown hair, large, serious-looking eyes, and a well-proportioned body.[49] Thuróczi stated that "he was a man of war, born to bear arms: . . . War was, for him, what water is for the fish, or a shady forest is for a stag: . . . He liked to fight the Turks more than to go dancing."[50] Here Thuróczi had been carried away by his own rhetoric; we know that Hunyadi was admired at court for his magnificent dancing.[51]

The young Hunyadi had already acquired some of the characteristics that were to be typical of him in later life. He was accustomed to do nothing without first calculating its possible consequences,[52] and practiced his military skills constantly.[53] Raised as a soldier, Hunyadi was favored by fate in being able to use his skill to his advantage, but he was also a tenacious, cautious, calculating man, a born politician. He was, above all, prudent in foreseeing the need to amass the personal resources without which he could not advance in society—first and foremost a private army. But he was also willing to listen to advice and learn from others. "He argued," noted Andreas Pannonius, one of his soldiers during the 1440s, that

> experience provided a secure basis on which the more general knowledge of a commander, acquired through diligent study, should rest. He believed that the acquisition of military know-how should not depend upon accidental information and that it was a serious matter that had to be learned. He insisted that such knowledge consisted of many rules that had to be mastered through a long and arduous process. . . .[54]

Hunyadi also believed that without discipline no soldier or politician could hope to succeed. Thus, he insisted upon strict discipline both for himself and for his men, and they seem to have respected him the more for practicing what he preached.

The early 1430s brought an important change in the life of the young *miles aulae*. In the fall of 1431 he accompanied his sovereign to Italy. For the next two years Hunyadi remained in Milan, where he served Philippo Visconti as a mercenary.[55] While there he became acquainted with some of the leading Italian *condottiere,* including Nicola Piccinnino and Francesco Sforza, the latter a captain of the Visconti at that time. Thus, Hunyadi had a golden opportunity to learn from these professional soldiers as a participant in Milan's Venetian wars. In the fall of 1433, he rejoined King Sigismund, who was on his way to the Council of Basel. He must have served his Italian patron well, for he left bearing rich rewards.[56] In Basel he met János Vitéz of Zredna, a man destined to become the bishop of Nagyvárad through Hunyadi's patronage and a close friend and adviser of the young commander.[57]

From this point until 1436 we simply do not know what János Hunyadi was doing. Once source maintained that immediately after his return from

Italy he began his struggle with the Ottomans, "gaining immense booty and wealth,"[58] but this is not likely. More probably he lived the life of a court soldier, lending money to the king and thus enhancing his standing at court. What we do know is that he and his brother, János Jr., assumed joint command of fifty armored knights in 1436 and went to Bohemia in the king's entourage.[59] The trip gave them an opportunity to experience first-hand the tactics of the Hussite armies, especially in their use of the battle wagons. Upon Sigismund's death on December 9, 1437, the Hunyadis joined the retinue of his successor, Prince Albrecht II of Austria, as he was crowned King Albert I of Hungary on December 18.[60]

Albert I, Sigismund's son-in-law, was elected king by a small group of aristocrats. A courageous man, he faced a difficult task. His wife Erzsébet was a power-hungry, domineering woman who chafed under the role of queen. His mother-in-law, the former Barbara von Cilli, was no less resentful over her exclusion from power. The Hungarian aristocrats, in turn, were anxious to curb the prerogatives of their new king and extracted an oath from him to this effect upon his coronation.[61] A great peasant revolt in Transylvania had been all but suppressed when Albert I came to the throne, but in May 1439 he had to subdue his riotous subjects in the capital city of Buda. Finally, the Ottoman threat continued undiminished in the south. As if these problems were not enough, Bohemia once again proved reluctant to accept a king not elected by all of its high nobles. The opposition to Albert's rule in Bohemia was led by Henry Ptoczek, the Steinbergs, and George of Podiebrad, the future regent and eventual king of Bohemia. They invited Kasimir, brother of the king of Poland, to assume the throne of Bohemia.

Albert turned first to the north; he went with three thousand soldiers to Prague and had himself crowned king. By early August 1439 his army had grown to twenty thousand men, mostly from Austria, the Holy Roman Empire, and Hungary, and the Hungarians included the Hunyadi brothers. This army defeated a Hussite contingent of fifteen thousand whose fleeing soldiers sought refuge at Tabor. Albert besieged and ultimately took the mountain fortress though meanwhile he was forced to dispatch part of his forces to Silesia to confront a Polish army led by Kasimir and drive it back to Poland.

While the king was preoccupied with the affairs of Bohemia, the Ottomans made a large-scale surprise raid on southern Hungary and Transylvania.

Ali Pasha, son of Evrenos, the commander of the European army of the Ottoman Empire, crossed the Danube River near Szendrő (Smederevo) and reached Transylvania in mid-July. Although the military governor of the province, Dezső Losonci, ordered a general mobilization of the nobility, there was little response to his call. The peasant rebellion that had ended only a few months before had taken its toll among the nobles, and the Ottomans had the run of the province. In rapid succession they took the cities of Szászsebes and Medgyes and burned and looted the villages of the Barcaság, including the Brassó area. Although their eight day siege of the city of Nagyszeben failed, they eventually recrossed the Carpathians unmolested with immense amounts of booty and thousands of slaves.[62]

The calamity forced the king to act quickly. The Hunyadi brothers were dispatched to the south on May 9, 1439,[63] entrusted with the defense of the fortresses of the military district of Szörény. One may be justifiably sceptical about the assertion of latter-day historians according to whom this was an appropriate response to the disaster. Why were the Hunyadis sent to Szörény instead of to Transylvania? One explanation may be that he was reluctant to create the impreesion that he did not trust Losonci. In any case, János Hunyadi's struggle with the Ottomans began at an auspicious time. In September, the two Hunyadis were appointed joint military governors of the same district. At that point, as a historian recently remarked, the immigrants from Wallachia became true Hungarian nobles. It is possible that, having escaped from Ottoman domination, they saw the defense of their new homeland as a necessity, and this hastened their assimilation. As the historian added, however, "the Hunyadis' concept of the *patria* was different from that of the nobility. It was mainly expressed in action, and it encompassed the people as a whole."[64] This should not come as any surprise. Immigrants, especially those fleeing oppression, have exhibited similar behavior throughout history. This was undoubtedly true in the late Middle Ages, when national identities were not yet fully formed and religious allegiances were stronger than ethnic ones as in our own time. While one must be wary of too modernist an interpretation of Hunyadi's patriotism, it is certainly true that he was ready to act decisively when the Kingdom of Hungary was threatened.

In making them joint governors of Szörény, King Albert gave the Hunyadi brothers a free hand to defend the fortresses of the district as best they could, but the funds that he provided for them were to last only for a period of three months. They needed over 6,000 gold florins to pay the mercenaries and he could give them only about 4,000. He therefore pawned the town of Szabadka (Subotica), Halas, and Továnkut to them for 2,757 florins. This was enough to hire about a hundred armored knights and auxiliary troops for the three months in question. Thus, if the Hunyadis wanted to succeed, they had to augment their forces by using their own funds and this they proceeded to do. By September 1439 their little army had swelled to two hundred knights.[65] The pattern was set; the royal grants that Hunyadi was to receive in the future would be used partly to strengthen his private army and, incidentally, his personal political power.

The troops of the Hunyadi brothers already included their own *familiares* (retainers), mostly impoverished lesser nobles who sought their fortunes with the young commanders. They also hired mercenaries and used a few peasants from their own estates to augment their forces. Though the distinction between *familiares* and mercenaries was not a sharp one, the former were tied to their patrons by concepts of feudal loyalty. Although in a few short years the number of Hunyadi's soldiers was to increase many times over the original few hundred, the composition of his army remained basically the same. The one exception was Hunyadi's last great battle, the defense of Belgrade in 1456, in which peasants outnumbered all others in his army.

Most of the retainers were lesser noblemen, probably attracted through the family connections of the Szilágyis. Hunyadi himself had begun his career in a similar way. At first, neither Hunyadi had the reputation to attract many such soldiers. At the time of their joint appointment as governors of Szörény, the Hunyadis possessed only the forty villages of their original estate, but they soon added eighty villages in Temes County a few towns in Bodrog, and a large estate centering on Marosvásárhely in Transylvania. Their aggregate holdings came to about 700,000 acres. There were salt and gold mines on the estate of Hunyadvár, and the income from them, although in normal times reserved for the royal treasury, was probably used by the Hunyadis for their own purposes. As military governors they were now among the barons of the realm, and János Hunyadi had begun his climb to the top of the political structure of the Hungarian state.

A strange part of this story is that of Hunyadi's younger brother. We actually know very little about him. We do not know if he were as talented as his older sibling in military matters, or if he had similar organizing and political abilities. However, one cannot but wonder at fate which ended the life of János Hunyadi Jr. at an early age, while his brother went on to achieve fame and fortune. He later spoke of his younger brother as a brave soldier who sacrificed his life in the Ottoman wars. But we do not even know the exact date or circumstances of his death. His figure merges with countless thousands of others who died in these turbulent decades in the defense of their *patria* and whose fate was never truly appreciated by the luckier survivors—or History.

In June 1439, Sultan Murad II laid siege to the fortress of Szendrő (Smederevo), defended by the troops of Branković under the command of the despot's two sons. Branković did not wait for the sultan's army; he fled to Hungary with the rest of his family. Since they did not have sufficient forces to challenge the sultan in open battle, the Hunyadis led a series of raids into the district of Viddin, "mercilessly exterminating the Ottomans, putting their abodes to the torch, and mutilating and killing these robbers," as László V's patent was to recall these events fourteen years later.[66]

In response to the Ottoman attack on Serbia, King Albert called the nobility to arms. At the end of June he established a camp at Titel where there was a ford on the Danube. The nobles, however, were in no great hurry to join their king. By early August, fewer than twenty thousand soldiers had gathered; they had no commanders, and their discipline was slack. On August 27 Szendrő fell; Branković's sons were captured and sent to Edirne, then the Ottoman capital, where they were blinded by order of the sultan.[67] The Hungarian king and the few lords who had joined him at Titel could do nothing. They were lucky that the sultan did not turn on Hungary next. Instead, Murad led his army to Bosnia, forcing its king, Stepan Twartko, to pay a huge sum of money, and then returned to Edirne for the winter. The Hungarian king declared that next year he would lead a large army against the Ottomans, but this was no more than an attempt to save face.[68] In any case, Albert I was never again to lead an army; he contracted dysentery that was epidemic in the camp and died on his way to Vienna on October 27, 1439.

In the chaotic period that followed the king's death, the Hunyadi brothers were to play an important role. The king's widow was expecting a child. She was understandably anxious to delay the election of another king at least until she had given birth, hoping for a son who could be presented as a rightful heir to his father's throne. Her supporters included the Holy Roman emperor Frederick III of Habsburg, her other relatives in Austria, including the Counts von Cilli, and the Hungarian Dénes Széchi the bishops of Veszprém and Győr, Bertalan Frangepán, Tamás Széchi, the Kanizsai family and other lords. But Hungarian customs were ambiguous in matters of succession. The small but well-organized army of the Hunyadi brothers was therefore an important instrument in the hands of a candidate for the throne.

II

HUNYADI'S HUNGARY: THE PRIVILEGED ORDERS

Hunyadi was not a political or social reformer; most of all he was an entrepreneur and a soldier concentrating on the accumulation of wealth as a means to his military success and political power.[1] It is, therefore, a valid exercise to examine the governing institutions of the fifteenth-century Kingdom of Hungary as if they were frozen in his time.

The Kingdom of Hungary, surrounded by the Carpathians in the north, east, and southeast, the Danube on the south, and the Leithe and the Lower Austrian Alps on the west, was a great power in late-fourteenth century Europe.[2] The principalities of Moldavia, Wallachia, Croatia, and Slavonia, the Serbian despot, and even Ragusa, the great trading center of the Dalmatian coast, all owed feudal loyalty to the king of Hungary. As the Ottomans appeared in the northern Balkans,[3] as Venice increased its influence in the remnants of the once mighty Byzantine Empire, and as the Czech Hussites intruded more and more into northern Hungary (today's Slovakia), the security of its more than 300,000 square kilometers of territory was threatened.

The Hungarian *regnum* was characterized by a particular form of feudalism.[4] As described by Max Weber, it was based on the voluntary association of free, vertically stratified ruling strata standing above the rest of the population, whose own freedoms were regulated by various customs and laws.[5] Lords and vassals were all members of a privileged political "nation" whose ideology was partly created, partly supported by the Roman Catholic church. The association of lords and noble vassals was cemented by concepts of voluntarism and mutual loyalty. Their relations were mostly based on the institution of the lord's *familia*, which included his retainers and officials.

The *familiares* were members of a king's, a great lord's, or a prelate's retinue (though sometimes a richer nobleman had his own retainers). Their contracts of service had definite time limits and specified not only the obligations of retainers toward their lord but also the lord's duties —payments and services—toward his men.[6] Many *familiares* received a small estate or part of an estate for the duration of their services. Some estates were permanently designated for retainers and, consequently, often changed hands as one *familiaris* replaced another.[7]

The retainers fulfilled all sorts of functions. They were soldiers first of all but they also acted as managers of estates, collectors of serf obligations and judges of the serfs living on their lord's estates. Many of them established the bases of their future careers while serving a lord. The Hunyadis were a prime example but their case was certainly not unique. The relation of the *familares* to their lord was often the means by which lower-ranking members of the privileged orders achieved upward mobility. The Thuróczis, Szapolyais, Marótis, and Kanizsais all started their careers as retainers.

A fundamental difference between Western-style feudalism and Hungarian vassalage was that in the latter non-nobles were also admitted to the lord's *familia*.[8] However, while noble retainers were judged in criminal cases by the king's representative, the non-noble *familiares* were under the jurisdiction of their lords just as his serfs were.

A noble *familiaris* did not lose his personal freedom in serving his lord. He lived on his own estate (maintaining a miniature replica of his lord's court), and this was the base from which he performed the tasks assigned to him by his superior. His lord had the right to call him to arms whenever he needed him but not to tax him. Nor could he be drawn directly into his lord's court of justice, since his person was ultimately subject only to the king. Furthermore, his personal property was not subject to the jurisdiction of the lord he served and could not be confiscated except upon orders of one or another of the royal courts of justice.

One of the major duties of a *familiaris* was to render justice to serfs on his lord's estate. The non-noble *familiares* usually judged only minor cases; more serious crimes such as murder, arson, and robbery, belonged to the jurisdiction of noble retainers. According to István Sinkovics, the captains of fortresses and the overseers of the lord's estates visited the villages under their jurisdiction three times a year and, together with the village judges and jurors, rendered decisions in civil and criminal cases.

The retainers were also responsible for the collection of various levies, taxes, and serf-obligations. These were first collected by the village judges and given to the *familiares*. The funds thus collected were often used by the retainers and never reached the lord's treasury. Custom dictated that in the case of the collection of the *lucrum camerae*, the levy collected in lieu of the subjects' obligation to exchange worn-out gold coins for newly minted ones, the king's men counted the collected revenues on each estate and came to an agreement with the lord about the amount to be turned over to the royal treasury. The rest was the task of the lord's retainers; the king's men had no other reason to visit the estates and this meant that they were effectively exempt from royal scrutiny.[9]

Only retainers who had no land of their own lived in their lord's castle or in a village or estate belonging to him. They were the ones who performed minor tasks such as being messengers or servants for their lord.

The more important *familiares* acted as their lord's representatives at the royal court or in the county seat. If he were a baron, his retainers were the judges when he was called on to render judicial decisions. The position of a retainer was not inheritable. If a retainer died, his sons had to conclude their own contract with the lord. Conversely, if a lord died, his retainers were free either to serve his son or widow or search for another position.

At the top of the pyramid stood the king. Kingship in Hungary, as in the other European monarchies at the time, was considered to have been blessed by God, and the king was viewed as the special representative of the godhead in society. He was crowned by the highest-ranking members of the church's hierarchy, usually the archbishop of Esztergom, the primate of Hungary. The coronation took place at the ancient city of Székesfehervár, where Hungary's first Christian king, St. István, had been crowned. Through the coronation ceremony the king became God's secular viceroy, the defender of the faith and, of course, of the prerogatives of the church. But if he broke the bond of mutual loyalty with the highest-ranking members of the aristocracy and the clergy, he could expect to be punished.[10]

The king was a symbol of order and the continuity of social and political relations. Although he was obviously mortal, kingship was considered eternal through inheritance and various symbols of continuity. Thus, the concept of "the king's two bodies" described by Kantorovicz,[11] that is, an organic view of kingship and the state, had already become the theory of political life.

Rule by inheritance was not yet firmly established. On the basis of the legend of the elevation of Árpád upon the shields of the seven tribal chieftains when the Hungarians embarked upon the conquest of the Danube Basin in the ninth century, the highest dignitaries of the state claimed the right to approve the selection of each king. However, even during the reign of the Árpád dynasty (1000-1302) there were no clear rules of succession. There were frequent conflicts over the kingship between the first-born of a king and the oldest male member of the royal family.[12]

In the fifteenth century, the king had to be approved by the aristocrats and the clergy before his coronation could take place. He was also required to affirm their rights and privileges (included in the Golden Bull of András II in 1222), which included the right to resist the king who threatened their liberties. He was required to issue a decree confirming his coronation oath; the oath of Albert I, elected in 1437, for example, promised among other things not only his respect for the "liberties" of the nobles but also the restoration of "rights" that allegedly had been taken away from them by his predecessor.[13] Albert's son, László V, had a difficult time being accepted as king even though according to some of the rules of inheritance his succession should not have been questioned.[14] Thus, kingship in Hungary stood midway between the purely hereditary monarchy of England and France and the fully elective office of the Holy Roman emperor.

The alleged crown of St. István was a major symbol of the continuity of the office of kingship in fifteenth-century Hungary. It was widely, if erroneously, believed that this crown had been sent to the king by Pope Sylvester II in the year 1000 and that its subsequent wearer had acquired the qualities of the first Hungarian saint. We know, of course, that the crown in question was not the original diadem. That one was captured in the Battle of Ménfő in 1044 by the Holy Roman emperor Henry III and subsequently returned to Rome; its later history is unknown.[15] When András I (raised in Kiev) came to the throne in 1047, he turned to the Byzantine emperor Constantine Monomachus for a crown, and the emperor sent him one whose frontpiece bore his own portrait together with those of the empresses Augusta and Theodora. This crown was also lost, only to be turned out by a peasant's plow in 1860. King Géza I turned once more to Byzantium. The emperor Michael Dukas sent him a new crown in 1074, and this became the lower part of the so-called Holy Crown of St. István. The upper part may have been made of gold leaf from the cover of a Bible that may or may not have belonged to the first Hungarian king.[16] This crown became the property of each subsequent king for the duration of his reign. In time, it developed into the symbol of the body politic of the "nation," that is, the privileged orders, and as such was separated from the person of the king. This concept developed gradually, gaining impetus during each interregnum, especially those that spanned the years between Lajos I the Great's death and the accession of Sigismund (1382-87) and during the infancy of László V after the death of Wladislaw I (1444-52). During these periods the highest dignitaries of the state, the prelates and the great lords, governed the *regnum* (in the second instance together with the regent, János Hunyadi) in the name not of the king but of the Holy Crown.

This concept conferred political power on the "political nation," the *regnum*.[17] Upon the consent (election) of the privileged orders, royal prerogatives were transferred to the king when he was crowned. That this consent was essential became clear in the case of the coronation of László V which, though performed with the Holy Crown, was declared nvalid because the *regnum* had not approved it.[18] Thus, the crown came ɔ symbolize not only kingship, but also the continuity of the *regnum*. ings came and went, but the crown to which all royal prerogatives were ınsferred by the consent of the *regnum* "connected" all of them in a ′stical unity.

As a logical development of this concept, the alleged Holy Crown itbecame the symbol of Hungarian nationhood in later times, coning all segments of society in a theoretical unity. In the fifteenth

The "Holy Crown of St. István"

That was probably never even seen by the first Hungarian King.

century, the crown already possessed "rights" that were exercised in its name by the lawful ruler, be he king, or regent, or the royal council. In this sense the Holy Crown was the "owner" of all the lands and revenues of the realm. The king could and did grant properties to members of the privileged orders but only temporarily. If one of those died without leaving an appropriate heir or committed an offense against the crown (such as treason), the properties reverted to their original owner.

The king, once crowned, was entitled to exercise all royal prerogatives, circumscribed only by his oath. He was the patron of the church; he had the sole right to appoint officials of state and remove them at will. He granted land to "deserving men" and created nobles out of commoners. He concluded peace or declared war and sent and received ambassadors. He was, above all, the supreme judge of the realm, and all judges exercised their authority by his leave. He was, therefore, both the executive and the single most important legislator of the realm.

In order to fulfill all these functions, the king should have been able freely to draw upon revenues reserved for the crown. Since there was no state budget, the personal wealth and income of the king, including certain revenues reserved for his use, had to serve the needs of the realm. The king had to pay not only his officials but also his army from these private sources. In the first three centuries of the Hungarian kingdom, the king was its largest landholder, and he added to his revenues by a monopoly over the sale of salt, the minting of precious metal coins, customs collected at the borders of the realm, fines collected from lawbreakers, and lands returned to him for the lack of heirs to deceased owners. He also received revenues from the cities, from the Székelys and the Jews and, from the twelfth century on, from the Vlachs and Saxons of Transylvania. In the fourteenth century, these latter royal revenues alone came to 176,000 gold florins a year; in 1453, the total income of the king was only 264,000 florins.[19] During the fourteenth century, the Anjou kings had given away huge chunks of the royal demesne to a newly created aristocracy and the church in exchange for their support. In the early fifteenth century, the royal revenues still included the salt monopoly, customs duties, a levy called *census* that replaced the *lucrum camerae* mentioned above, and the revenues of the mines. But the king now needed the consent of the *regnum* to levy taxes for purposes of rule. Thus, in practice, the king's prerogatives had their limits.

Until recently, Hungarian historians generally accepted the reasoning of Bálint Hóman[20] that the power of the king, which had begun to erode wtih András II in the thirteenth century, reached its nadir during the reign of Sigismund. Hóman showed that he gave away most of the royal fortresses to aristocratic families, thus giving up the major means of control over much of the kingdom. He argued that this contributed to the concentration of wealth in the hands of a few aristocratic families and reduced the king to simply one among equals. Recent research by Elemér Mályusz and Pál Engel has contradicted this view. Mályusz has shown[21] that Sigismund succeeded in emancipating himself from the tutelage of the aristocrats after 1403 and thereafter pursued a policy of promoting lesser-noble families into positions of power. Engel, building on Mályusz' work and unpublished documents that he found in the Hungarian national archive, has suggested that the king's shrewd policies resulted in the creation of a new service-oriented aristocracy whose wealth and power depended upon the will of their patron.[22] With the death of two kings in rapid succession (Sigismund died in December 1437 and Albert I in October, 1439), however, all this was undone. During the interrugnum (which included the short reign of Wladislaw I and the civil war that followed), both aristocratic groups expanded their power and added to their wealth, and when King Mátyás (Corvinus) was elected he had to start rebuilding royal power anew. This only proved, however, that the balance between the king and the upper noble strata in the Kingdom of Hungary depended as much upon the personalities of the actors as upon accidents of history. The trend culminated in the coronation of Albert I; the aristocrats made him promise not to give away properties of any significant size without consulting them first, thus, considerably curtailing his authority. In typical feudal fashion, his authority depended upon the consent of his privileged subjects, exercised most often through the royal council and the sessions of the diet.[23]

The royal council developed during the early centuries of the Kingdom of Hungary and was at first composed mainly of the king's personal retainers. Until the end of the thirteenth century, it probably consisted of mostly the prelates. By the fourteenth century the great lords and by the fifteenth the heads of county administrations, the *comites* or counts, appointed by the king, were also included. This did not meant that all these officials participated in the council's meetings at all times, but that

The Privileged Orders

they were free to participate when they were present at court. It is difficult to ascertain who was not permitted to take part in the council's discussions. There were no rules to determine this.[24] Lesser nobles, the king's retainers, the *milites aulae,* or, occasionally, even non-noble merchants who happened to be passing through attended these meetings and discussed important matters of state. At times, the queen and her personal attendants also took part. The barons participated in the discussion and then acted as executors of the council's decisions in the provinces.[25]

The royal council came into its own when the king was absent from the country or during an interregnum. Although on such occasions the palatine was, by custom, the king's represenative, it was in fact the council that governed the realm and exercised royal prerogatives. Its decisions were, however, considered temporary until confirmed by the king. Its influence was probably greater than its size ad uncertain membership would indicate. Few important decisions were made by the king without consulting it. Its advice was sought on the yearly tax levies, foreign relations, and most important appointments to offices.[26]

The diplomatic transactions conducted at court show that foreign envoys often brought along letters of recommendation not only for the king but also for the more powerful aristocratic members of the royal council. When the king sent his envoys to a foreign court it was not unusual for them to be accompanied by the envoys of certain powerful lords.[27] This did not mean, however, that these aristocrats actually ruled "their" provinces, for the king could dismiss them from office at will. In this respect the system in Hungary differed from that of Western feudal monarchies.

Although the council represented a certain balancing force between the nobles and the king, its existence also served the ruler, and strong kings took advantage of this. It was good to have the great lords and churchmen at hand where they could be easily observed and consulted on short notice and, if necessary, brought around to the king's point of view. That the royal council in Hungary never became a parliament may be to some degree a consequence of its fluctuating membership. The rapid turnover of baronial office holders created opportunities for social mobility for the lower-ranking members of the nobility.[28] Rapid demographic change and the deliberate policies of Kings Sigismund and Mátyás probably also played their part.[29]

The royal administration, if one may use such a term, consisted of the palatine and three groups of barons: the military governor of Transylvania (*voivode*) and the governors of the southern military districts (*bani*), the royal judges, and the attendants of the king's person. But the lines of division among these officers in terms of their tasks were often blurred. For instance, they all participated in one form or another in the work of courts of justice. The palatine was the representative of the king and an important military commander. He also acted as a royal judge. His private army was usually large and his landholdings were extensive. His compensation came to 10,400 florins in Hunyadi's time.

The *voivode* and the *bani* ranked immediately below the palatine. The *voivode*'s salary came to 12,000 florins in cash and salt; the *bani* received somewhat less. They were not only responsible for their region's defense but were also the highest administrators and judges of it. Considerable as their authority was, they were restrained in exercising it by the relative insecurity of their positions (they served at the king's pleasure) and by the privileges and immunities of various corporate entities such as the cities and the church. They did have the authority to grant privileges, but these could not override existing ones granted by the king. Moreover, they were forbidden to interfere in church affairs. When a *banus* revolted against the king, he could cause considerable mischief but could not survive for long. The most important *banus* was that of Croatia and Slavonia. Sometimes his office was combined with that of Dalmatia. Those of Macsó (Mačva) and Szörény were less powerful. In general, a *banus* was appointed from among nobles who possessed estates in the respective territories and had strong influence there to begin with,[30] although this depended entirely upon the king.

The personal attendants of the king and queen, the master of stables, the cupbearer, the steward, and treasurer had clearly defined functions[31] and in addition served as officers of the royal *banderium*. On occasion, they were called on to settle lawsuits in the royal court,[32] but they did not have their own courts of justice.

The king's chancellery issued patents and other documents. It was headed by a confidant of the king, usually a prelate, who was also the keeper of the royal seals without which no document was valid. By the

The Privileged Orders

early fifteenth century there were signs that the chancellery was gradually dividing into two chambers. The smaller of these, called the "secret chancellary," dealt with diplomatic correspondence while the other continued issuing official legal documents.[33] The significance of the royal seal cannot be overestimated. It was the sign of the royal will. However, after the death of Albert I, its importance somewhat diminished since in the turbulent times that followed the *regnum* was run by the royal council and the regent. When László V sought to reestablish some of his prerogatives, the use of the seal was central to the struggle (see n. 27).

The *milites aulae* were more important members of the court and their duties were much more varied than is implied by their title. They were not simply bodyguards but officers responsible for the safety of the king and his family and recruiters of mercenaries for the king's *banderium*. They had their own retainers who fought in the king's army. Their estates were exempt from the jurisdiction of county authorities and their vassals were not counted in the respective counties' contribution to a general mobilization.

By the early fifteenth century, the royal court was permanently established at Buda, although this did not mean that the king always stayed in the capital city. His function as the supreme judge of the realm and his need for amusement dictated extensive travel. He was also frequently abroad at war or for various reasons of the *regnum.* King Sigismund built a magnificent palace at Castle Mountain at Buda[34] and practically all the great lords established separate residences for themselves in the city. They still left their families in the safety of their fortresses, but their presence at court had become a necessity.

The king's court was a busy, often hectic place. Not only were the barons in attendance most of the time together with their bodyguards and myriad servants, not only were the royal attendants crowding in with their own retainers, but there was also a mass of courtiers taking care of the king's and queen's personal needs, including craftsmen, veterinarians, musicians, clowns, barber-surgeons, and others. An army of servants was required, including cooks, butchers, bakers, water and food carriers. The court of the Hungarian king was somewhat cruder, more rustic than that of a Western monarch. Etiquette certainly was not yet established.[35] The highlight of each day was the midday meal. In Hunyadi's time, food was served at long tables. The king sat with the highest dignitaries, while lesser lights were seated separately. The serving of the food was a ritual that demanded a great many servants. Each table received several large pots from which the guests directly helped themselves. They used heavy gold or silver plates and drank wine from silver pitchers. The most important utensil was the knife; each guest brought his own. Forks were not yet used. Since most dishes were stewlike, bread was used to help the food down. The resulting sticky fingers were washed after the meal in silver dishes brought out by the servants. During most meals, enertainment was provided by clowns. Their often crude jokes were good-naturedly tolerated. Musicians were also present, and balladeers were welcome at the royal tables. After meals, dancing was a customary entertainment. The long tables were moved out of the dining hall and everyone danced to exhaustion. The court often amused itself with various sports—hunting, jousting, various ball games, and wrestling. Horse racing was a favorite pasttime for the king's retinue.[36]

In addition to being the focus of political activity, the royal court was the place where disputes involving nobles were settled. Although the king was the highest judge of the realm, he frequently delegated his authority to his officials and the prelates of the church. The first in line for this authority was the palatine, and next came the lord chief justice. Both acted strictly in the name of the king and of the crown. The evolution of Hungary's late medieval judicial system paralleled the political evolution of the *regnum*. By the fifteenth century, personal justice was generally outlawed.[37] Ancient customary property rights were gradually being eliminated. Royal patents were now the basis of most noble landholdings, and disputes over landed properties, along with all other suits involving capital cases committed by noblemen, were conducted at one or another of the royal courts. Since the king's personal presence would have required a great deal of time, many of these were delegated to his officials. Soon various courts such as the *presentia regia*, the *specialis presentia regia*, and the *personalis presentia regia* were set up at the royal court. By the mid-fifteenth century, suits were presented in these courts in writing and decisions were recorded by the scribes of the courts.

The Hungarian judicial system was geared to the defense of the possessors of property, no matter how they gained control of it. There was great advantage of being *in loco* of a disputed estate. If a rightful owner whose estate had been taken over by someone else undertook a suit to regain his property, the process might take a generation to conclude, no matter how valid his claim. The consequence of this was a continuing series of takeover of estates and litigation. As Imre Szentpétery observed,

> A nobleman gathered his household, his retainers, and servants and moved to take over someone else's estate, preferably when the owner was away or at night, but frequently in broad daylight. Sometimes miniature battles followed. This was done, naturally, not only in cases when they wanted to improve their rights. . . . Even the law was impotent, and had to consent to the taking of revenge for coercion suffered.[38]

While the aristocrats were gradually gaining jurisdiction over the suits of lesser nobles where these were their retainers,[39] the king retained his role as the supreme judge, the ultimate court of appeals. If the *familiaris* of a great lord committed a crime, his lord had to answer for it, including providing compensation for the victim. In turn, he was empowered to discipline his vassal, including confiscating his contracted property. In most serious criminal cases concerning nobles, however, the aristocrats had jurisdiction as the king's representatives only, when and if he delegated this authority to them.[40] Away from the royal courts of justice, the regular courts were active in the counties, in the cities, and in the jurisdictions of great lords. There were, however, certain groups of people who did not come under the jurisdiction of any of these bodies. Free men who were neither nobles nor burghers formed autonomous communities separate from the counties and cities and they were judged by their own magistrates according to their own laws. These included the Székelys, Saxons and Vlachs, and the Germans of the Szepesség and Túrmező.[41]

As the number of courts increased, so did their personnel. This gradually resulted in the development of a secular officialdom, the germ of a permanent bureaucracy. The free cities continued to hold judicial proceedings in their own courts, and their first court of appeal was the royal cupbearer. The military governors of the southern districts and Transylvania had extensive judicial prerogatives, and there was no appeal from their decisions. The peasants were gradually brought under the direct jurisdiction of their landlords. The first step in this direction was the appointment by their landlords of village judges. Eventually, the most powerful aristocrats acquired the right to render justice in their manorial courts in cases concerning their peasants, even in capital offenses.[42] The peasants could still appeal their cases to the county courts, but these were run by nobles who had many personal ties to the lords and to their *familiares*.

Judicial developments in general tended to favor the aristocrats vis-a-vis the king. Perhaps no better illustration of this could be found than the development of the office of the lord chief justice, who rendered decisions in all cases in which the king's "personal presence" was required. While in previous centuries this official had been simply a trustee of the king whose judgments usually conformed to royal interests, by the early fifteenth century his role had fundamentally changed. Rather than a judge of the king, he had become a judge of the *regnum*. The king could no longer automatically count on decisions in his favor when his interests were challenged in the court of the lord chief justice. In the process the office had developed a quasi-permanent bureaucracy. While in previous centuries the passing of a king had usually meant the appointment of a new lord chief justice, this was no longer the case. He was now one of the most important politicians after the palatine and at times assumed the rule of the guardian of the interests of the *regnum*. He acquired the title of "chancellor of the Holy Crown of St. István," and his office became more or less independent of the king's person.

The significance of this change lies in the fact that in the absence of a code of laws, it was possible for the lord chief justice to decide important property disputes in favor of the king's opponents.[43] This could only serve to weaken an already shaky royal authority. Moreover, royal justice was reserved for the privileged orders and the free royal cities, and the clergy were the judges in ecclesiastical courts. The lesser nobles who were not retainers of a lord more and more frequently took their cases to the autonomous county courts. An increasing judicial role was assumed by the diets, the congregation of the representatives of the nobility, in which the influence of the aristocracy prevailed.

Hungarian laws in this period still represented only guidelines, not explicit sets of rules and regulations. A plaintiff could chose from among various sets of laws in seeking justice, and the presiding judge was obliged to accept his choice. Except for the *ius* (divine law, the law of the church), however, the validity of particular sets of laws depended upon the power relations between the privileged orders and the king.

The social origins of the nobility of the Kingdom of Hungary are unclear.[44] The leading families of the tribes and clans of the times of the conquest had largely lost their special status in the developing Hungarian realm or had died out by the end of the eleventh century. The new privileged strata had gained their position during the thirteen and fourteenth centuries, largely through appointment to baronial offices. The kings had helped this proces along by often excessive grants of royal lands. By the mid-fourteenth century, a few high nobles had succeeded in making their social status (but not their offices) perpetual in their families. The laws of 1351 further clarified the status of nobleman in the realm.[45] These laws abolished for the nobility the forced exchange of worn-out coins, exempted the *familiares* of the great lords and the servants of the lords from the payment of taxes that were collected after their dwellings. They were also freed of internal customs duties and tolls, and the church was forbidden to excommunicate them for suing clerics. The laws also settled rules for inheritance; they stipulated that a landed estate was to remain the property of a nobleman's family as long as a single male member lived. If there were no legal heirs, all properties reverted to the crown.

The most important privileges of the nobility included personal freedom, freedom from certain levies and taxes, and the right to possess landed estates, and to dispose of their properties as they chose.[46] Nobles had the right to offices. They were immune to arrest except by due process of law, unless caught *in flagrante delicto* in the commission of a capital crime. The king needed the consent of the nobility to collect taxes from the peasants who lived on their properties. Although in theory all nobles shared these privileges, in practice only the aristocrats and the wealthier lesser nobles were ever able to take advantage of them. Only these had the means to support private armies, build castles and fortresses, and hire mercenaries to defend their interests. Thus, the differentiation among the noble strata was based not on law but on wealth. In fact, any nobleman could become a baron, and some lesser nobles, among them the Hunyadis, were indeed elevated to this rank. In turn, the life style of many of the poorer nobles was hardly distinguishable from that of the peasants, since they often owned only a small plot of land which they worked themselves. Consequently, the noble order, ostensibly one, consisted of many layers. The lesser nobility was divided into several substrata including those who contracted with the great lords for personal service. Those who remained independent defended their privileges in the county courts, but they shared unequally in political and economic power in the realm.

The most important nobles, often called *magnifici,* held specific offices at the pleasure of the king. Each of these officials had his own chancellery issuing legally valid documents within his jurisdiction. Barons who were not wealthy at the time of their first appointment to office, soon became so. The great lords and prelates maintained their own courts emulating the king's on a smaller scale. Their courts were usually located in their fortresses where their families resided. These fortresses were strongholds in which comfort was subordinated to the necessities of defense. According to Pál Engel,[47] "in a broad sense any fortified place may be considered a fortress, including a castle that served as a great lord's homestead." However, he further added:

> the function and significance of a fortress and of a castle were fundamentally different.... While a castle (castellum) was part of a large or medium-sized estate, the fortress (castrum) was, first of all, the center of a large clerical or secular estate and an indispensable part of the royal demesne.

Within the walls of fortresses there were several courtyards, one for jousting, one for the stabling of horses, another for general purposes. The main building served as the lord's residence even if he spent most of his time at the royal court. The most important part of this building was a hall in which meals were served. Individual rooms were generally small, badly ventilated, uncomfortable in any season. Separate rooms were provided for the male and female members of the lord's family, and rooms were reserved for visitors, for servants, and for officers of the guards. Furniture was simple: a bed, some boxes serving as benches and wardrobes, perhaps a chair. The beds were filled with straw or hay, only rarely with down and covered with spreads. The rooms were decorated with richly embroidered cloths and rugs, and wall hangings.

Life in these fortresses was often Spartan, but the lords could always count on the presence of young men intent on learning methods of warfare in the lord's castle. There were also jousters, horse racers, and entertainers. Their numbers were augmented by the lord's retainers and servants,

The Privileged Orders

who lived in houses surrounding the fortress and defended it against attacks. Life was not particularly exciting, but there were constant comings and goings. Holidays were few, but celebrations—of weddings, births, deaths—were not rare. Sinkovics mentions visits by

> representatives of notary publics, messengers... captains of distant fortresses, *familiares,* serfs, who were ordered to appear on account of some work to be performed, sometimes famous architects and painters... envoys from Venice, Florence, Rome, or Poland....

and he adds that Sigismund himself liked to visit the great lords.[48]

Eating and drinking were highlights of life; on festive occasions incredible amounts of food and drink were consumed. Eating huge portions was a *virtu,* rejecting food an insult to the lord. There was not as much variety of food as in the castles of some Western lords, but the quantities were enormous. Again, as at the royal court, food and drink were served in silver or gold utensils, entertainment at meals was provided by clowns and balladeers, and the most important entertainment was hunting in which women of the lord's household also took part.

Few great lords knew how to read or write, and their women busied themselves with the kitchen and the servants. The lord's time was often taken up by political discussions even when he was at home. The most learned man of the lord's household was usually the chaplain, and his sermons and conversations were avidly listened to. There was also a notary and sometimes one or more teachers for the children. The international language of culture, Latin, was often unknown in Hungarian fortresses. Dress played an important role in the life of the aristocracy. Rich lords were expected to dress extravagantly, exhibiting their importance in society. It was reported that Miklós Ujlaki's belt alone was worth 60,000 florins. Women preferred heavy silk dresses and men wool suits.[49]

The great lords were surrounded by their servants and retainers when they were at home. Many of them maintained sizable standing armies. For instance, the bishop of Eger had between 3-500 soldiers and his servants numbered close to 200 people. Others were not far behind.[50] The baron's aim in life was to increase his wealth and power. The larger his estates, the greater his revenues, and the larger his income, the larger the private army that determined his political influence. The real source of baronial

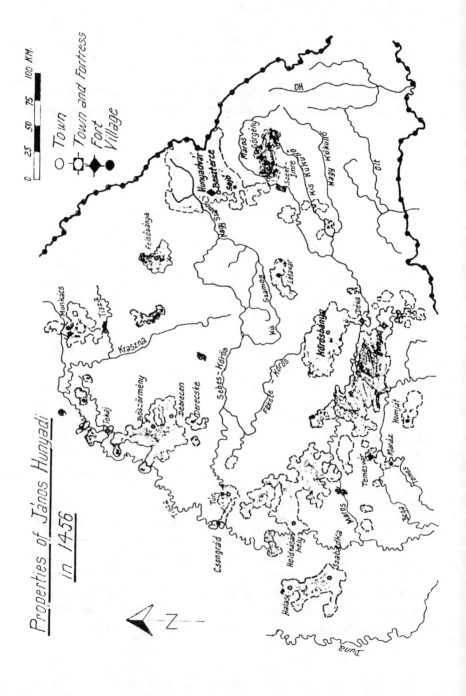

wealth was not so much in the exploitation of the labor of the peasants as the appropriation of revenues belonging to the crown and appointment to important offices. This was evidenced in 1450 when the aristocrats succeeded in convincing the diet that the royal revenues be used mainly to pay the salaries of the barons. Control over the mines and over the wine trade on their estates was also an important revenue source. That the lords were not interested in creating demesnes and producing goods on them themselves is suggested by the fact that the estates of the counts of Szentgyörgyi and Bazini had some 800 serf plots whose occupants tilled more than 20,000 holds (or 28,400 acres) of land in seventy to eighty settlements, but the lords themselves maintained only about 10 percent of their lands under their own tillage.[51] The absence of a rule of primogeniture usually worked against the transmission of wealth to a single descendant of an aristocratic family, especially if there were several children.

By the mid-fifteenth century, many barons were intent on creating small replicas of the government of the realm. They had their own court officials, their chancellors, and, of course, retainers. The next step was to extend their influence over the counties in which they resided and acquire patronage over the local clerical institutions. Finally, they tried to gain control over the cities in their sphere of influence by placing their *familiares* in these cities as captains to "protect" them against external dangers.[52]

Barons were generally appointed from a relatively small number of aristocratic families, although there was no rule restricting the selection to these circles. There were between fifty and sixty of these families, yielding perhaps 350-400 males. As Hunyadi's example has shown, however, lower-ranking members of society could also become barons (usually in the military regions). There were approximately 50,000 lesser nobles in the Kingdom of Hungary in the fifteenth century, and only a handful managed to reach high offices of the realm.[53] About 70-80 lesser noble families possessed considerable wealth but most of them did not directly participate in politics. Most of them, however, had close ties to the barons, usually through marriage, and supported them.

After a baron was relived of his office, he was called a *proceres* or *egregius*, "excellent or outstanding person," a designation also applied to lesser nobles who possessed several villages and played a leading role in the county assemblies. A *proceres* remained an influential member of the *regnum* and was probably welcome at court. Baronial office was seldom inherited; János Hunyadi was among the first to achieve a perpetual baroncy.[54]

By the end of the fifteenth century, descendants of barons were called *barones naturales vel solo nomine,* "natural barons born to the title," a reflection of changes by which baronial titles were gradually becoming a social rank.

It is worth stressing that the basis of baronial wealth and power was appointment by the king and that the king consulted the royal council in most instances before important appointments were made. However, despite their considerable power, the barons were unable to carve out independent or even autonomous prioncipalities from the "body of the Holy Crown." One of the major reasons for this was certainly the fact that few baronial families survived beyond a couple of generations.[55] Furthermore, however circumscribed the king's power in the realm, he always retained enough power to prevent the dismemberment of the *regnum.* Even during times when the royal council or the regent governed the country, this simply did not take place. On the other hand, the aristocrats were powerful enough to insist on and succeed in sharing power with the king on a permanent basis. This was made possible partly by the very nature of their offices and partly by their enormous wealth. According to Erik Molnár, in 1440 some 60 aristocratic families owned a total of 8,600 settlements, another 40-50 families possessed 10-40 villages each; a further 400-450 families owned between 4 and 10 settlements each; 8-10,000 noble families owned a single village each, and 18-20,000 a single plot.[56] All told, there were 268 fortresses of various sizes and strengths. The wealth of some of the individual aristocratic families was truly astounding. The Kanizsai family owned 60 villages in Zala County, 17 in Somogy, and 22 villages, and the fortresses of Borostyánkő, Léka, and Sárvár, and three market towns (oppida) in Vas County. Most of the estates in Pozsony and Moson Counties belonged to the Counts Szentgyörgyi and Bazini. The Garai family possessed the fortress of Csesznek, the estate of Simontornya, and 22 villages in Tolna County, and 45 villages and 3 towns in the county of Bács, along with other extensive holdings in Baranya, Valkó, and Pozsega Counties. The Kanizsai family mentioned above controlled 13,000-25,000 people, living in 187 villages, 8 fortresses, and 8 market towns.⁵⁷ It is worth noting that within a century nothing was left of these huge holdings, the baronial families in question having died out. But the royal holdings were also shrinking; between 1380 and 1440 they were reduced from 3,350 settlements to only 1,100, or about 5 percent of the total.⁵⁸

The barons were the most influential stratum of the privileged orders in the Kingdom of Hungary. By birth and sometimes by ability, but certainly through wealth and family connections, they shared authority with the king over the rest of the population. It must be restated, therefore, that the much vaunted principle of *unam eademque nobilitas* existed in fifteenth century Hungary in theory only. The lesser nobles, however, were carving out a local but increasingly important role for themselves, a process already well under way when János Hunyadi appeared on the scene.

The life of a lesser nobleman centered on his small estate and his *curia* (a term used to depict a house larger than a peasant dwelling) located in a village. Few nobles built houses in the cities; they were usually excluded by the burghers on suspicion of harboring designs on the freedoms of the inhabitants. In some instances the *curiae* were surrounded by walls, mostly as a defense against other nobles. Otherwise many of these dwellings differed from peasant homes only in that they were larger. As Samu Borovszky noted,⁵⁹

> In villages that were not part of lordly estates, there lived the better-to-do and the poor nobility alike. Their *curiae* were simple affairs, seldom built of stone, but mostly of wood, hardly more conspicuous than the hovels of the serfs. They differed from the latter only in that they had servants' shacks and barns standing around them and perhaps also had a mill. If an old tower stood next to the housee, then it was called a "castle."

Their gardens and orchards were part and parcel of the village landscape, and the "estates" were not much different from peasant holdings.

If a lesser nobleman was wealthy, his house contained several rooms, perhaps even a small library, but most noble houses were not so well equipped. Houses were usually built of wood rather than stone. Windows were covered not with glass but with parchment, cloth, or wooden shutters.

Furnishing consisted mostly of tables, beds and wooden boxes in place of cabinets. In the wealthier households, however, even the walls were covered with rugs; this was, according to one historian, an inheritance from the steppes.[60] Beds were still filled mostly with straw and covered with heavy woolen blankets. Food and clothing were somewhat better than those in peasant households. Since inns and hotels were largely unknown, visitors and travellers in general often found lodgings in lesser noble homes, whose hospitality was proverbial. Such occasions provided opportunities for feasts in which enormous quantities of food and drink were consumed. Card games and other games of chance were played on such occasions, but social life was less sparkling and somewhat more rigid than in the castles of the great lords.

The education of the children of the lesser nobility was taken very seriously.[61] Girls were raised at home, but when they grew into their 'teens, they were sometimes sent to the household of a great lord or a wealthier lesser noble relative to learn the ways of good housekeeping. Boys were sent to local schools run by the clergy and then apprenticed as heralds to the court of a baron. Most of the time of the lesser nobleman was spent in managing his property. Beyond this, he often became involved in the administration of the county in which he resided.

The evolution of the counties as autonomus institutions of the lesser nobility took centuries and the process was not complete until the mid-sixteenth century. These institutions, established by the first Hungarian king, seem to have been at first no more than royal estates,[62] each with its administrative center in a fortress and its royal captain. In contrast to the royal counties, the original clans still in existence in the early centuries of the Hungarian kingship held land in common and lived according to their ancient customs under their elders. These clans paid a tithe to the church in a lump sum and fought under the king's flag. With the emergence of the royally supported service aristocracy during the eleventh and twelfth centuries and the gradual distribution of much of the royal demesne through grants to the new aristocracy during the thirteenth and fourteenth, the influence of the clans gradually diminished, and their leadership assumed a secondary role in society. These and the lesser officials of the royal counties probably found common ground for cooperation in their opposition to the growing power of the aristocracy. Thus, they

The Privileged Orders

gradually transformed the counties into institutions of self-defense against both the aristocrats and their ally, the king.

By the mid-thirteenth century, judges were elected in the counties by the lesser nobility and regularly rendered judgments in suits. They held court sessions at regular intervals in which all nobles present were invited to participate. Their offices slowly evolved into those of county administrators in every sense of the term. The vice-count, who presided over these sessions, was usually a retainer of a great lord, the count,[63] but he had the deciding vote only if the elected judges could not agree. Although the count also had an important voice in the affairs of the county, the process gradually led to the emancipation of the elected county authorities from his influence. They still had a long way to go, however, before becoming the protective instiution of the lesser nobility.[64] The court sessions evolved into county assemblies during which all matters relating to county affairs were discussed, royal decrees read, and political decisions made. This process was still incomplete in Hunyadi's time despite the fact that the laws of 1351, mentioned above, had strengthened the lesser nobility and the counties.[65]

Further developments occurred in the first half of the fifteenth century. According to a royal decree issued in 1405,[66] the county courts were empowered to act in cases in which a lord refused to compensate a victim of a crime committed by his retainers. The elected officials of the county in question were authorized to force the offending lord to comply with their judgment by taking over his estate until he did so. The same decree reinforced the counties' responsibility to guarantee the free movement of peasants as long as they complied with the law.[67] Another decree issued six years later gave the counties the right to share in the *census*, and a further ordinance of 1453 empowered them to confiscate the properties of lords whose men damaged the holdings of others during an emergency requiring the general mobilization of the nobility.[68] This was not all; a decree of the same year empowered the counties to restore holdings to their rightful owners if these were usurped, no matter what the offender's rank or social position. Although final decisions in such cases were still being rendered by royal courts, the inclusion of the counties in the enforcement process helped not only in reducing delays, but also strengthening their authority.[69]

It would be still erroneous to maintain, however, that as a consequence of these developments the counties and the lesser nobility had become a third force in the Kingdom of Hungary in the early fifteenth century. That development came only much later. The fact was that the influence of the great lords in society remained quite strong. The count appointed by the king usually came from an aristocratic family, and he headed the county administration, using his retainers to perform his duties when he was away. The counties did, however, elect two or four of their members to act as judges, and they did share power with the count.[70]

The next step in the evolution of the counties was an increase in the number of lesser-noble officials in their administration. Besides their judicial function, they also led the troops in battle if they were called up. Gradually, the lesser noble soldiers of the counties were being withdrawn from under the control of the aristocracy. The county officials also acquired the right to fine those who ignored the call to arms in an emergency.[71] At the same time, the counties created a list of serfs of the nobles living in their jurisdiction on the basis of which noblemen were assessed for general mobilization. The lists were all-inclusive, counting the serfs of all landholders in a particular county. Finally, when the collection of taxes levied for military purposes became the task of county administrators, their autonomy further increased.

Throughout the fifteenth century, the Hungarian kings made deliberate attempts to extricate the lesser nobility from the domination of the aristocracy. Some historians regarded this as a sign that the kings wanted to centralize political power and to break the feudal ties that paralyzed royal authority.[72] However, since the lesser nobility provided much of the fighting forces of the Kingdom of Hungary in previous centuries, the kings' efforts were primarily directed toward bringing these nobles once again into active involvement in military affairs. By the early fifteenth century, very few lesser nobles could afford to go to war. The large majority of them were impoverished and unable to buy the expensive armor and horses necessary. This was the major problem that the kings were trying to remedy. Since I have dealt with this problem elsewhere,[73] suffice it to say that the kings had made several attempts to help the lesser nobles before Hunyadi's time without success; the problem of their poverty went deeper than the kings recognized. Hunyadi, as I have said, was not a social reformer. During his ascendancy, no serious effort was made to strengthen the position of the lesser nobility in the realm. This was only logical; being a great lord himself, Hunyadi could hardly have worked for the weakening of his own authority that this would have entailed. The political gains of the lesser nobles were, however, preserved during his time. The county assemblies continued to meet on a regular basis and to settle suits in their own jurisdictions. As Mályusz remarked, this was a period during which the county assemblies increasingly turned occasional favors into permanent rights.[74] This periodically led to the curbing of the power of the great lords, but not to a permanent restriction of their influence in the realm. In Mályusz' words, "the lesser nobility thus succeeded in deepening its self-consciousness as part of the *regnum*."[75]

In conclusion, the structure of the Hungarian realm in Hunyadi's time was based on a complex system of relations among the various strata of the nobility, on the one hand, and the king, on the other. Alignments fluctuated according to changing political and social conditions and the strength or weakness of the leading personalities. The Roman Catholic church also played an important role in the equation, one that will be explored below. The largest stratum of the population, the peasants, had no say at all in the affairs of the realm, and the inhabitants of the market towns had only begun to stir.

III

HUNYADI'S HUNGARY: THE CHURCH

The historian János Karácsonyi writing in 1915, characterized the relations of church and the *regnum* in medieval Hungary as follows:

> Up to 1241, although (church and the *regnum*) supported each other, each was also trying to preserve its independence. Between 1241 and 1403, the two institutions were practically fused. The high clergy became the first class of the secular state, acting in (both cleical and secular) affairs. The lower clergy enforced the laws of the realm. However, the state also acquired increasing influence over religious affairs, and its suggestions and recommendations were nearly always decisive. After 1403, the *regnum* had the prelates and the rest of the clergy under its control and used them almost exclusively for its own purposes. . . . [1]

The year 1403 is significant for being the year in which most clergymen, with the tacit approval of Pope Boniface IX, supported a challenger to the throne of king Sigismund in the person of Ladislas of Naples. Once the king had succeeded in suppressing the rebellion, he took drastic action against the clergy. He refused to acknowledge the authority or either of the contending popes in the schismatic church, sent the bishops who had opposed him (including the archbishop of Kalocsa and the bishops of Eger and Vác) into exile, and entrusted the governance of their bishoprics to lay overseers. In a decree issued the following year, the king reserved to himself all appointments to clerical offices under royal patronage.[2]

These policies were, however, never accepted by the papacy and king Sigismund therefore took further steps to legalize them. Taking advantage of the confusion created by the continuing schism, he concluded an agreement with the cardinals assembled at the Council of Constance in 1414 (the document of the agreement was issued three years later) legalizing royal patronage rights over all appointments to high church offices, including abbotships, in the Kingdom of Hungary. The cardinals agreed to the primacy of clerical courts in Hungary in all suits in the first instance, and to noble patronage over appointments to lesser church offices when warranted by custom.[3] Subsequent popes continued to contest royal rights of patronage, but their efforts were not successful during the fifteenth century.[4]

Hungarian churchmen resented the often arbitrary actions of the popes in bypassing the recommendations of cathedral chapters to appoint their own candidates to Hungarian bishoprics. As István Barta has pointed out, the decress of 1404 and king Sigismund's subsequent actions were the direct consequences of a long process in which papal excesses gradually created an alliance between the Hungarian clergy and the king.[5] This, of course, did not mean that these relations were always amicable. In fact, there were continuous skirmishes and jockeying for influence between the prelates and their secular counterparts, the great lords. The prelates, however, did not all have the same influence in affairs of the realm—this depended upon such factors as the personality of the man in question, and the income generated by his office—but they could not be ignored.

The assertion of royal rights of patronage over the church also opened the door for secular lords to establish similar authority over parish churches located on their estates. The patron who endowed the parish considered it to be his property and subject to his complete control. He assumed the the right to appoint the parish priest, control (or even expropriate) its income, and bequeath his authority to his heirs.[6] Although this authority eventually had to be shared with the bishops and was often challenged, it was still considerable. Just as the king—or the regent or the royal council—

assumed the right to control the appointment of prelates, the landlords exercised control over that of the lower clergy. In many instances, however, a balance was struck; the landlords were often willing to accept the guidance of the bishop's vicar on appointments of parish priests. The way out of this situation for the church was its growing insistence that a certain level of education be required for all clerical appointments.

At the beginning of the fifteenth century, two archbishops (those of Esztergom and Kalocsa, the former the primate of Hungary), twelve bishops, and twenty-two priors headed the church in Hungary.[7] As was the case elsewhere in Europe, the prelates were mostly statesmen as well as religious authorities. They were members of the royal council and spent some of their time at court.[8] Some of them acted as diplomats or chancellors of the king. All of them maintained private armies (in fact, their position in society demanded this) whose strength sometimes exceeded that of the barons.[9] In most respects, therefore, the prelates were the equals of the highest dignitaries of the realm and led lordly lives.

Nothing illustrates this status more than the fact that the prelates created their own dependent lesser nobility, their own retainers. These were recruited not only from among the regular nobility of the land but also from among the commoners of various church-controlled estates. The origin of this process is unknown,[10] but it probably goes back to the early centuries of the Hungarian Kingdom, to the time when the large holdings of the church were first established.[11] Clerical nobles were called *praediales;* they contracted with the prelate in the same way that the *familiares* arrived at their agreements with the secular lords. They were mostly soldiers in the service of a particular prelate in exchange for a small estate called the *praedium.* The privileges of these nobles often corresponded to those of their secular counterparts. These served a prelate, and their properties were part of the estates of the church. In some instances, these estates were scarcely larger than a serf lot. This was in line with the actual social status of these nobles, many of whom were of peasant stock. Their nobility was the result of their acquisition of landed property, no matter how small; this could then be bequeathed to their heirs—if any—but reverted to the giver if the heirs were unwilling to assume their father's obligations. If such a nobleman proved disloyal to his clerical overlord or neglected the duties prescribed in his contract, he could easily lose his *praedium* and be returned to his previous status.

The Church

During the fifteenth century, certain church properties were permanently set aside for the use of the *praediales*.

The church nobles developed institutions similar and parallel to those of the secular nobility. They had their own counties and judicial courts, whose jurisdiction did not correspond to the territorial limits of their secular counterparts. Their count was a prelate, usually the bishop of the province, who performed functions corresponding to those of the secular one. Their counties and courts had their own elected officials. These nobles were free of taxes and the customs duties and paid the tithe only if their contract to stipulated. They held county meetings several times a year and maintained their own county archives, in which the notes of their meetings and the decisions of their courts were preserved.[12]

There were, however, some important differences in status between the *praediales* nobles and the secular nobility. The former were not entitled to their own coats of arms, nor could they use the designation "de" before their family names as a sign of their nobility. (In this volume the designation was left off from most names for purposes of brevity.) They could not sell or rent out their church-owned properties or even pawn them without the consent of their lord. Their title reflected these differences; they were referred to as *nobiles iobbagiones ecclesiae*, or "ecclesiastical serf-nobles."[13]

A perpetual source of conflict between these conditional noblemen and their clerical lords was their practices in judicial matters. The clerical nobles were imune to the jurisdiction of the royal courts. Their suits were tried in the first instance in clerical county courts; their count was their final court of appeals. The execution of the decisions of these courts was entrusted to their own officials. When a *praedialis* was also a secular nobleman, he often tried to have his case heard at a secular county court. This was naturally resented by his clerical lord and his fellow *praediales*, and disputes over this issue often lasted for decades.[14]

The income of a prelate may best be measured by the sum he paid into the papal treasury upon assuming office. According to fourteenty-century reports, this sum called the *commune servitium* varied between 100 and 4,000 florins.[15] Since this sum represented a third of the prelate's yearly revenue, actual income varied between 300 and 12,000 florins.[16] The report of a sixteenth-century Venetian diplomat shows a tremendous increase in these revenues; bishops' incomes were now between

3,000 and 25,000 florins a year. This increase was probably related to population growth and the expansion of the church's landed properties.[17] The prelates as lords of large estates were collecting all sorts of revenues, including customs duties at tolls, the incomes of mills and fishponds, in addition to the tithe.[18]

The bishops often paid close attention to details of the everyday life of the population of their dioceses. Their vicars visited the local parishes every year—during these visits the parish was required to provide food and accommodations for the vicar and his servants—and issued instructions in both secular and religious matters. For instance, in January, 1440, the vicar of the bishop of Transylvania ordered th parishes of Nyárádtó, Szentkirály, and Vásárhely in Hunyad county to see to it that a dowry promised to a woman in the village of Tuson was paid by her father; if the man refused, he was to be placed under the ban of the church.[19] In another case, the vicar of the bishop of Csanád ordered the transfer of a case from a clerical to a secular court, since "it had nothing to do with matters of religion."[20] Sometimes the bishop himself acted in a minor local matter; Bishop Lépes ordered the lifting of a ban in 1439 in a case when a dowry was paid.[21]

Many bishops were educated men. In the fifteenth century almost half of them had spent time at a foreign university. Many of their immediate assistants, the priors of the cathedral chapters, and the archdeacons who, together with the vicars, were the bishops' personal representatives to the local parishes also received some form of higher education.[22] Together they presided over an institution one of whose primary tasks was the cultural-religious leadership of the people in the Kingdom of Hungary. They were supported by a relatively narrow elite stratum composed of the canons of the cathedral chapters, many of whom carried the title of *magister,* or "master." This title was usually given to those who had received a university education. There were four schools in Hungary during the Middle Ages that were entitled to grant such a degree, at least for brief periods of time, and certainly not in the same time period. These schools were located at Pécs, Buda, Pozsony, and Nagyszeben. In these schools serious learning took place. For instance, the University of Pécs was staffed by some highly competent scholars of Europe-wide reputation.[23]

The Church

The Hungarian canons of the thirteenth century had lived together in a chapter house, celebrated mass in the cathedral, prayed and sang the psalms seven times a day, and assisted their bishop in administering his diocese. The bishop had lived with them in the chapter house in a relationship similar to that between abbot and monks. Over time, they had gradually emancipated themselves from the direct and personal supervision of their bishop. By the mid-fourteenth century they no longer lived in their chapter house but had private residences. They no longer served daily in the celebration of the mass; instead, devoted most of their time to personal affairs, among which intellectual pursuits predominated.[24] By the end of the century, their benefices had become their lifetime personal property; they proceeded to buy books, endow their chapter with money, and sometimes to leave the country altogether in pursuit of studies abroad. In order to ensure the continuation of services at their cathedral, the canons hired assistants whose salaries they paid from their own revenues.[25] They continued to visit the cathedral chapter—at least when they were in the vicinity—to discuss matters of common interest, especially their financial affairs. Two tasks performed by the canons had great cultural-religious significance. One of these was the maintenance of elementary and sometimes secondary schools, and the other was their duty to act as notaries public for their region.

The elementary schools that the canons maintained taught reading, sometimes writing (which was not considered of equal importance), counting, and elements of simple Latin, but their main purpose was to train deeply religious people (including women) in choral singing and prayer. Many of their students became altar boys and assisted in the celebration of the mass. They were also taught the legends of saints and the rules of their cathedral chapter.[26] Some of the cathedral chapters offered secondary education. In most, only the *trivium* was taught. A few schools included the *quadrivium* as well. On the secondary level, the language of instruction was Latin, and successful graduates were entitled to continue their education in a *studium* or a university.

An equally important task of the cathedral chapters was to act as notaries public. This was a Hungarian custom going back to the early thirteenth century, when king András II had entrusted the cathedral chapters and larger monasteries with this task. It meant more than the term would indicate. The priests performing such functions were entrusted with the investigation of complaints, the installation of new owners in their properties, and the preservation of copies of the documents they notarized. In these cathedral chapters the lector, who was responsible for the supervision of the chapter's school, was also the head of the office of notary public. As Béla Miklósy has pointed out, the educational and legal functions of the cathedral chapter came to be closely integrated with the school serving as the training ground for future assistants to the notaries public.[27] It was common in the cathedral schools for students to be used as copiers of documents and manuscripts. The lector sometimes made one student his permanent assistant, and he might go on to become a notary public himself in the service of a secular lord.[28] Nothing shows better the interrelation between education and the role of cathedral chapters in legal affairs that the fact that, of twenty-eight chapters having the right of notary public, twenty-seven maintained some form of school.[29] The cathedral schools of Veszprém, Esztergom, and Kalocsa, maintained *studia,* although we do not know if they were also entitled to grant the title of *magister.*[30] The chapters with notary public duties had their own seals to authenticate the documents issued by them. They preserved the copies of these documents in their archives and also acted as legal representatives of the crown.[31]

The revenues of a chapter derived mainly from the tithe collected in the parishes of their diocese, but it also received extra income from endowments. Up to the early fourteenth century, the chapters received only one-fourth of the tithe. Another share went to the bishop, a third was used for the maintenance of the cathedral, and the fourth share belonged to the parish where it was collected. A chapter's revenue was divided into equal shares; each canon received one share, and the three top officials, the lector, the cantor, and the *custos* or custodian received an extra share each.[32] By the early fifteenth century, however, many chapters had succeeded in acquiring one-half of the fourth share of the tithe originally left for the parish priest.[33] By then, the canons were not only able to secure a comfortable living for themselves, but to emphasize the cultural characteristics of their chapter as well. By hiring substitutes for the performance of most of their religious duties, the canons increasingly provided income for aspiring young men attracted to the clerical life, gradually transforming their chapters into channels of social mobility.[34]

The canons, therefore, succeeded in weaving a complex set of relations among various social groups. They themselves came from various backgrounds, since higher church offices were not reserved for the nobility. The canons, thus, became priests with a special mission, namely, the advancement of learning as a means of upward mobility and the raising of the educational standards of the religious institutions. By these means they also aided the church in asserting itself against securlar control, at least below the level of royal patronage.

According to Elemér Mályusz, there were twenty-two large and twenty-seven smaller cathedral chapters in the Kingdom of Hungary during the fifteenth century. They accommodated approximately 626 canons, a true elite of the Roman Catholic church in Hungary.[35] The income of the average canon was around 70 florins a year. Canons received extra compensation from the chapter for the maintenance of their private residences. Priors earned between 210 and 280 florins. There were some exceptionally high incomes; for instance, that of the prior of the cathedral chapter of Eger came to 480 florins, and that of the prior of Esztergom was 400 florins. The priors of Buda, Pécs, and Székesfehérvár earned about 300 florins. Some of this wealth went to help an ambitious cousin or nephew to acquire higher education and eventually become a canon himself. Most of the time, however, the wealth of these priests did not go to their families. Their last testaments often spoke of donations to a favorite priest friend, to an altar in the cathedral, or to the chapter itself. Sometimes they used their income—even during their lifetime—to improve their cathedral by paying for new decorations or additions to its buildings. More than any other segment of the religious institution, the cathedral chapters were the foci of intellectual and educational life in the Kingdom of Hungary. Together with the bishops, the canons formed an elite, providing intellectual and sometimes even political leadership.[36]

The lower ranks of the clergy included the parish priests and their altarists and chaplains. Parishes differed from one another not only in size but also the privileges and immunities they possessed. There were 144 fully privileged parishes in Hungary proper in the mid-fifteenth century, not counting the Saxon parishes of Transylvania that fell under the direct supervision of the archbishop of Esztergom. The most important privileges of these parishes included their right to a fourth of the tithe and the maintenance of a local church court of justice. Nonprivileged parishes received only one-eighth of the tithe, and their disputes were judged by the vicar of their bishop.

The average parish priest had little chance of keeping up with the canons in lifestyle, but he certainly did not starve. He could not think in terms of acquiring a higher education, his income simply would not support him away from his parish. For instance, the income of the parish priest of Selmec was 52 florins a year; that of the priest of Buda came to 194 florins.[37] Many priests came from peasant families. As children, they had caught the eye of the local clergymen, whom they may have served as altar boys. They had been taught the rudiments of writing and reading primarily to enable them to remember the necessary formulae for the celebration of the mass.[38] The parish priests were in direct touch with the people they served. Sometimes they even lived like peasants themselves. Living in a village, administering the sacraments, and receiving payments and gifts for services rendered brought them into close contact with the people. Even when a parish priest had several assistants he could not fail to be aware of the everyday affairs of the community. Priests often communicated their concerns to their superiors and were, therefore, another important link between the peasants and the prelates. The parish priest was also usually in direct contact with the local landlord(s), or his agents and officials, providing another vital link between the privileged and nonprivileged segments of society.

The most important assistant of the parish priest was the altarist, usually a young priest holding a benefice (prebenda) in the form of a specially endowed altar in the parish church. This was by no means a rarity; during the fifteenth century, a great many donations and endowments were made to churches in Hungary. The usual condition of such a donation was that a priest pray every day for the salvation of the soul of the donor and for his swift passage through purgatory after his death. In the city of Sopron sixteen new altars were endowed in the church of St. Michael during the fifteenth century, as compared with only three during the fourteenth.[39] The situation was similar in other churches, even in small parishes. The church of the village of Kőröshegy in Somogy County, for instance, had six endowed altars, each with its own altarist.[40] The altarists received a fixed income. However, in addition, extra sums came their way from their share of the collection at their altars. They held a secure position, one that could not be terminated by the parish priest as long as they performed their tasks conscientiously and lived according to the rules of the church. As a consequence, the altarists were seldom poor. They did not have as much revenue as the priest, but they were not as poor as most of the chaplains. In some exceptional cases, their revenues enabled them to hire a substitute while they spent time at a foreign university.[41]

The chaplains, on the other hand, were in a vulnerable position. They were hired by the priest to assist him in the performance of this duties, and their number in the parish depended upon his income. They were usually hired for only a year at a time. Their salaries, 4-16 florins a year plus room and board, did not provide them with an easy living. The situation of both altarists and chaplains was, however, more favorable than would appear from this brief description. As the circulation of money increased during the course of the fifteenth century, the parish priests were able to maintain or even increase their revenues even if their share of the tithe was halved. Consequently, they were also able to pay their chaplains better wages. Some chaplains succeeded in becoming altarists; others had a chance to move into the household of the local landlord or even that of a baron. In such cases appointment to a benefice or even to the office of canon became a distinct possibility.

A fourth group was neither strictly part of the lower ranks of the clergy nor exactly part of the elite. These were the substitutes hired by the cannons, who were in a good position eventually to become canons themselves. Living in their own homes, they had their own servants and private incomes. These usually included the gifts they received when hired and took the form of land, including vineyards.

Most members of the lower clergy in fifteenth century Hungary lived comfortable lives. They served as an important channel of mobility and communication among the various social strata. Their educational role, although limited in scope, was important; they were definitely better educated than their predecessors of previous centuries. Many of them had taken their first step out of peasant status, thus offering others inspiration and hope.

The monastic clergy had traditionally played a quite different role, and some orders continued to do so in the fifteenth century while society changed around them. For the Benedictines (with eighty houses), the

Cirtercians (with eighteen) and the Premonstratensians (with thirty-nine), the task of the monk continued to consist of isolating himself from the temptations of the world in his cell and praying for the salvation of his own and mankind's soul. Most houses of these orders were originally built in isolated areas, far from towns and cities, and from busy roads and highways. Only some of their convents were closer to settlements or even to cities, and these did play an important role in the development of urban communities in the Kingdom of Hungary.[42] The monasteries in remote areas that resisted change and continued to prosper did so in part by serving as notary public and receiving the revenues generated by this activity, as did the Premonstratensian house at Lelesz and the Benedictine cloister at Kolozsmonostor. Few houses of these orders, however, were able to avoid a general decline in wealth and membership.[43]

The changes that affected monastic life were gradual and at first difficult to detect. Even the canons continued to pay lip service to the idea of a community of clergy working and praying together long after they had left the confines of their cathedral chapters. But while the old orders continued to believe that they were performing an important service to the church and mankind at large by their isolation and prayers, they failed to recognize their growing need for involvement with lay society.[45]

The general decline among these orders—accompanied by the decline in the monks' devotion to the faith—was hastened by the policies of the kings in fifteenty-century Hungary. As old abbots died and rulers were unwilling to appoint new ones, many of the oldest and richest houses were given into the hands of lay overseers appointed by the crown. More than half of the monasteries of the old orders were ruled by secular overseers during the fifteenth century. This resulted in neglect, the impoverishment of the remaining monks (since the overseers used the revenues for secular purposes), and the depopulation of the monasteries. For instance, the ancient Benedictine abbey of Pannonhalma was in the hands of a lay governor for over seventy years beginning in 1407. The revenues of the monastery which, in 1495, came to 4,000 florins, were used exclusively by the kings. There were times when only four to six monks lived in the monastery as opposed to fourty in the previous century.[46] Discipline was nonexistent in these houses. For example, in the

The Church

Benedictine convent of Vásárhely, the nuns regularly held dances and often wandered around the countryside in civilian clothes looking for adventure.[47]

The fact was that by the early fifteenth century the monk who isolated himself in his cell, renounced the world, repeated his prayers seven times a day, and performed no pratical services for society, had lost his social significance. This was a natural process. The old orders had always been less affected by social changes than the secular clergy, who could and did indeed identify with the realm in crucial matters of politics. On the other hand, the monks were perceived as representatives of a foreign power residing in Rome, an obstacle to the sovereignty of the secular ruler. Their influence had to be removed or severely curtailed. Furthermore, since the Benedictines, Cistercians and Premonstratensians refused to set up schools within their monasteries, they were able to attract only a very few intellectually alert young people into their ranks. Many of these old orders even refused to participate in the life of society in the villages on their estates. Rather, they permitted the appointment of secular priests in the churches on these estates, who were then required to report periodically to the abbot.

By the end of the fifteenth century, the Benedictine order had almost completely disintegrated in Hungary. A commission reporting on seventeen houses in 1508 found that the regulations were simply not being observed. Food was everywhere scarce; buildings were routinely neglected to the point of collapse. The few monks remaining in the houses were either sick or perpetually drunk. At the monastery of Somogyvár, even the roof of the church collapsed.[48] In most monasteries visited by the commission, the mass was no longer being celebrated, and most of the brothers had left for the outside world or for other monastic orders.

In contrast, the mendicant orders showed considerable progress.[49] The Dominicans, Franciscans, and the Augustinians enjoyed great popularity, undoubtedly because of their direct participation in society's everyday life. Most houses of these orders were built near developing towns and cities. For instance, each had a cloister in Szeged, Brassó, Gara, Temesvár, to mention only a few. As these settlements became important commercial centers, the mendicant houses benefited from the flow of wealth into these areas, and the monks had an increasingly active involvement with the entire population. The needs of the inhabitants of these settlements included an educational system that suited the developing division of labor. The mendicants were ready and willing to provide such a system. They were also active in organizing religious societies for laymen and holding regular prayer and singing sessions. As Erik Fügedi had shown, the chapter houses of mendicant orders almost always could be identified with developing cities and towns in Hungary.[50] Although the members of the mendicant orders were not involved in any sort of conspiracy to promote the status quo through "amelioration of the consequences of the emerging class society," as some Marxist historians have recently asserted,[51] they certainly encouraged the evolution of civic consciousness in the towns and cities. These orders were not interested in maintaining notary public offices in their houses, and since their monasteries were generally poor, no secular overseer desired to rule over them.

The best schools were maintained by the Dominicans. Their *studia* at Pécs, Buda, Nagyszeben, and Kassa, were well known.[52] They accepted novices from the age of fourteen on. These were taught at first by the lector of the monastery and then were sent to one of the higher schools of the Dominican province. The Dominicans also taught debate and rhetoric. Exceptional students were sent to one of the universities of the order in Western Europe.[53]

Less is known about the schools of the Franciscans. By the end of the fifteenth century, they had 115 cloisters in the Kingdom of Hungary, and they paid a great deal more attention to education than the old orders. In fact, much of the literature produced in fifteenth-century Hungary was Franciscan-oriented and produced. Moreover, this literature was intended for the improvement of the religious life of the population, and therefore some of it was in Hungarian. The Dominicans and Augustianians also participated in this process. The Franciscans, like the Dominicans, were active in organizing lay religous societies; they were also mindful of the needs of the urban population for entertainment. For instance, their auditorium at Szeged was large enough to seat three thousand people for group singing and prayer on special occasions.[54] The Franciscans were also in the vanguard of the anti-Ottoman campaigns; many friars went along with Hunyadi into the Balkans; they were active in recruiting soldiers when needed and played a crucial role in the defense of Belgrade in 1456.

The Paulist order, established in the Kingdom of Hungary by Hungarian monks, played a role somewhere between that of the older orders and the mendicants. The Paulists were especially active in Croatia and Slavonia, where they maintained schools in their monasteries.[55] In Hungary proper they had ninety houses by the mid-fifteenth century and were very popular in the towns and cities.[56]

If I have created the impression that the Roman Catholic church in fifteenth-century Hungary consisted mainly of educated, intelligent clergy, it is time to correct it. It can hardly be disputed that this clergy was better educated than its counterparts in previous centuries. However, only the bishops and canons, a relatively few parish priests, some members of the mendicant orders, especially the Dominicans, and some of the altarists and substitutes for the canons could afford a higher education. Despite the efforts of the mendicant orders, there was hardly a school during the fifteenth century that was truly comparable to the great universities of Western Europe or the renowned university of Cracow. The fact that Hunyadi did not learn Latin as a child points to the fact that his teachers, the parish priest and his helpers at Hunyadvár, and the Franciscan friars at Hátszeg were badly educated themselves. But there certainly had been progress towards a higher level of culture for the clergy; this was a task that was yet to be pursued in future centuries.

The religious institutions, thus, were providing not only spiritual succor, a channel of communication, and legal help for society in the Kingdom of Hungary during the fifteenth century, but they were also a means of upward social mobility for the lower ranks of the population.

IV

HUNYADI'S HUNGARY: THE PEOPLE

In Hungary, as elsewhere in Europe, most of the people depended upon agriculture for their living. Besides tilling the land, tending animals, and managing flood plains for riverine resources they also engaged in small-scale barter and crafts. Geographic conditions largely determined the methods of food production. The various types of activity were closely related and complementary, and villagers often practiced a combination of them. There were, however, communities that specialized in one or two. Tillage was practiced in every region of the Kingdom; animal husbandry and flood plain management were characteristic of the three low-lying basins—the Little Plain in the west, the Great Plain in the center of the country, and the river valleys of Transylvania in the southeast. In the mountains there were villages that depended upon sheep herding. Transhumance was still being practiced in the high ranges of the north and the southeast.

The river system centering on the Danube, Tisza, Drava, Sava, and the Kőrös-Maros Rivers provided favorable conditions for animal husbandry and flood plain utilization. Tillage, on the other hand, often suffered from the unevenness of rainfall in the low-laying areas of the Kingdom. Average precipitation was probably between 20-30 inches a year in the plains and 40-60 inches in the surrounding mountains, but if the patterns of the last two centuries apply to the fifteenth century—and indications are that they do—most of the rains came during June and October. Thus, during the spring and late summer, drought conditions often prevailed which, coupled with severe winters, made the outcome of tillage uncertain and grain yields very low. No wonder, therefore, that the grain production so important to the peoples of Western Europe, and even to such Eastern European populations as the Poles, was less so in Hungary during the late Middle Ages.[1]

Peasant status in early fifteenth-century Hungary was not strictly defined. Although the laws of 1351 have been considered as creating a unified stratum of serfs, this was true only in the legal sense, and the serfs did not include all peasants. Most rural folk did indeed live under the jurisdiction of lords. Contemporary documents call them "peoples of the lord" (*populi nobilium*) and, as the century progressed, "peoples and serfs of the lord" (*Populi et iobagiones nobilium*). By the mid-fifteenth century, most peasants were simply called serfs.[2] However, there were many exceptions. There continued to be free peasants possessing their own land. Though they provided levies for the state, they owed no obligation to the local secular or clerical lord except the tithe to the church. This category of peasants included the *hospites,* or "guests,"[3] whose status was protected by the fact that the nobles needed hands to work their estates and were, consequently, eager to recruit them. *Hospites* settled in abandoned houses or villages (sometimes taking over an entire settlement that had been deserted by its original settlers) or carved out new settlements from forests or swamplands. Since such work required a tremendous effort, they were granted all sorts of inducements and favors. These consisted of exemptions from various feudal obligations for a specific period of time—5-25 years—and sometimes village autonomy.[4] Even after their privileges had expired, some *hospites* settlements were permitted to remit their obligations to their landlord collectively as a community, providing them with a chance for the equitable distribution of their burdens. It would be reasonable to say, however, that most serfs were restricted in the management of their personal affairs.[5]

Most villages—the only form of organized peasant life in the Kingdom of Hungary—belonged to noble estates, but these estates had not yet developed into compact manors. Sometimes clusters of villages belonged to one estate, sometimes widely scattered settlements were controlled by the same landlord. Small estates owned by lesser nobles or even by free peasants often intruded into territories of great secular or clerical lords.[6]

The demographic conditions of this period are unclear. In his pioneering work on the history of agriclture in the Kingdom of Hungary, Gusztáv Wenzel estimated the number of *portae*—courtyard gateways large enough to permit the passage of a hay-laden wagon which were the units for government censuses—at about 280,000 by the end of the fifteenth century.[7] In a latter study, István Szabó suggested, on the basis of records for 1494-95,[8] that their number was more likely to have been around 250,000. Counting two families per *porta*, Szabó went on to estimate the number of peasant families at around 500,000. Adding an approximate 18,000 village judges, who paid no taxes and were not included in the census, brought the total to 518,000. Suggesting that the average peasant family probably had five members. Szabó concluded that the peasant population of the Kingdom of Hungary was 3.2-3.6 million.[9] Since György Győrffy has estimated the total population of the Kingdom at only about 2 million at the end of the fourteenth century,[10] about 90 percent of whom may be regarded as peasants, Szabó's estimate implies a demographic growth that is remarkable in the light of the severe population decline elsewhere in Europe as a consequence of the Black Death.

A second look at Szabó's numbers, however, immediately raises questions. There are no data on the number of families per *porta*, and the size he suggests for the average family, although perhaps reasonable for recent times, may not be so for the late Middle Ages. Furthermore, his neglect of the possibility of extended families that included several generations under the same roof is hard to explain. It is not surprising, therefore, to find other Hungarian researchers questioning Szabó's estimate.

Erik Fügedi concludes that there was a high mortality rate among the nobility, who were probably better housed, fed, and clothed than the peasants.[11] While he recognizes some demographic growth in the fifteenth century, he argues that, given the life expectancy of twenty-eight years for the population as a whole, it must have been at least partly the result of immigration.[12] Ottoman pressure on the peoples of the Balkan Peninsula in this period brought thousands upon thousands to the Kingdom of Hungary, where they were welcome and relatively safe from Muslim raiders. From Szabó's later studies it appears that apart from years of crop failure, the rural population was generally well-fed, but this alone would not account for the population increase his estimate suggests.

Erik Molnár has suggested that the average family was probably smaller than Szabó's estimate and that peasants probably numbered fewer than

2 million, and the total population of the country about 3.4 million by the end of the fifteenth century.[13] Elemér Mályusz held that in Hungary proper the number of *portae* was only about 215,000, which in his estimation meant 2,150,000 peasants; adding to this the populations of Transylvania, Croatia, and Slovenia, he placed the total number of peasants in the Kingdom of Hungary at about 2,275,000.[14]

Among the many reasons for the disparity of these estimates is the fact that the surviving tax records on which they are based are fragementary. They provide only partial data for only forty-two out of fifty-seven counties in Hungary proper, excluding the lands of the Transylvanian Saxons, Székelys, and Wallachians and of the Croatians and Slavonians, who were part of the population of the Kingdom of Hungary at that time. The census of *portae* listed the heads of households only and did not mention the number of family members. The amounts collected from peasants were not uniform, they depended upon the amount and quality of the land a particular peasant family worked. Those who could not pay or were exempt for one reason or another were excluded from the records, as were those whose landlords had cheated the census takers. Nor do we have much direct evidence on the size of the population of the free royal cities and the very rapidly growing number of market towns.[15] I want to add, however, not as an approval of Szabó's estimate but an explanation for it that he worked with all available data at his disposal.[16]

If population estimates for the period are controversial, so must be surmises about the territorial distribution of the population. Strictly speaking, the territory of Hungary proper comprised (in round numbers) slightly over 300,000 square kilometers. If the total population numbered 3 million in the mid-fifteenth century, then population density was about 10 persons per square kilometer. The early work of Dezső Csánki and Antal Fekete Nagy suggested that the greatest density was probably in the area between the Tisza River and the eastern and southern borders and in the central Great Plain, especially its southern fringes, but this assertion was not supported by later studies of settlement patterns.[17] In fact, it can be safely assumed that, with the exception of the mountainous areas, the Transdanubian counties of what was ancient Roman Pannonia were densely settled indeed.[18] Settlement patterns are, however, weak guides to the density of the population, since we do not know the actual size of these villages. In the final analysis, population densities would have to be determined on the basis of estimates of the average size of the peasant family, and for this we do not have useful data.

It would be tempting to conjecture that, since large tracts of land were covered by primeval forests or swamps and flood plains and the methods of tillage were as inadequate to maintain a growing population as in the rest of Europe, the beginning of peasant unrest in the early fifteenth century was at least partly the result of regional overpopulation. But grain yields, however low, did not provide all or even most of the peasant's diet in fifteenth century Hungary, and further complications are presented by uncertainity about population densities and the direct evidence of decreasing populations in some rural areas. The latter evidence is especially significant; abandoned villages represented 8.5 percent of all settlements, that is, 2,000 villages out of about 21,000, by the end of the fifteenth century. Serf plots showed an abandonment rate of 6-60 percent depending upon the region in question.

Ignácz Acsády, who first examined this issue at the end of the nineteenth century, believed that partial depopulation was not so much the result of a demographic disaster as the reflection of a shift of large numbers of peasants from the villages to the market towns. He maintained that the peasantry as a whole was relatively prosperous in this period of Hungarian history and was therefore able to make such a move.[19] Temporary local overpopulation, to the extent that it was a problem, was therefore relieved by the physical mobility of the peasantry. The fact that abandoned settlements were often resettled suggests that manpower was not in short supply.[20]

The depopulation of some rural areas was not unique to Hungary but paralleled developments in some Western European states. In the second half of the fourteenth century, substantial population losses occurred in European societies because of the plague and feudal wars. Many rural folk fled the countryside for cities and towns. The population of the market towns in Hungary also experienced considerable increases.[21] However, the losses to the plague may have been less severe in Hungary than in Western Europe, since the country had no direct communication with the seaports from which the disease spread. By the time the plague reached Hungary, its ferocity may have been somewhat diminished. The depopulation of some regions, therefore, did not necessarily mean a corresponding reduction in the size of the general population but was most likely the sign of migration to towns and cities.[22]

Molnár argued that the major reason for this shift was the gradual impoverishment of the peasantry because of the increasing demands made on its resources by the king, the nobility, and the church. In support of his argument he cites the undeniable fact that the average size of an individual serf plot was reduced almost by half by the end of the fifteenth century,[23] but the meaning of this is not as obvious as Molnár would have us believe. The reduction in average plot size could have had many other explanations. A possibility advanced by Fernand Braudel is that a general cooling trend in the climate of the European continent had occurred,[24] and this led to the abandonment of marginal lands and the division of tillable acreage into smaller plots.[25] Furthermore, since the wealth of a peasant was in a combination of land use (in which the size of his holding was only one factor), the number and kind of animals he possessed, and the distance of his village from the market town or city in which he traded his surpluses, Molnár's simple explanation therefore will not do. There is ample evidence that many peasant families in fifteenth-century Hungary were rich by contemporary standards.[26]

This was a period in Hungarian history in which economic activities were increasingly acquiring a monetary base. At the same time, many landlords simply refused to produce food and supplies for themselves and relied almost entirely on their peasants for these necessities. Since the landlords also needed money, they either sold the goods they received from their serfs or commuted peasant obligations into cash payments. The king and the church acted in the same way. Therefore, the peasants had to sell some of their produce to satisfy the demands of their lords. Most of this exchange took place in the nearest market town or city. Some peasants became very prosperous in this process, while others became impoverished. Complaints about attacks on peasant travellers coming from or going to market towns abound in this period, and when the documents list the value of articles taken it often comes to a considerable amount of money.[27] The growth of the market towns, therefore, must be taken as a *prima facie* evidence of the physical mobility of the peasantry and their increasing participation in the slowly evolving economy.

There were undoubtedly many poor people, especially in the stratum called the *inquilini*, or landless peasants, but not all members of this stratum were poor. Some of them were laborers and made their living by working for some landowner or other peasants. Others, according to Szabó were village craftsmen such as the blacksmith or carpenter, both respected members of their communities, and those whose lands were excluded from the censuses such as the owners of vineyards or freshly cleared tracts of land.[28] In fact, many of the *inquilini* who worked for wages received a decent income. In some instances, women and children were hired in addition to men, women being paid half and children one-third of the wage of a male laborer, and thus added to the incomes of their families.[29]

We must conclude therefore, that a multitude of causes contributed to the depopulation of certain areas and settlements. For example, the village of Mánya in Tolna County was abandoned because it was periodically subject to flooding.[30] The abandonment of the village of Gyál was simply due to the exhaustion of its land.[31] On occasion, villages were abandoned because lords repeatedly raided them.[32] Peasant mobility continued despite the enactment of laws to slow the process. I suspect that this was at least partly the reflection of the stratification of the peasantry and that it had begun much earlier than the fifteenth century.

The peasantry also had social mobility. The *inquilini* drove themselves to acquire land and often succeeded, since there were many opportunities for this in the abandoned settlements and serf plots. If he were lucky or talented, a serf could become a village judge. Some peasants were called to serve their lord in his castle, becoming *servientes* and actually being ennobled. Others became burghers in the market towns or cities. Yet others became priests. Thus, the peasantry in fifteenth-century Hungary did not constitute a stable, stagnant stratum of society.

A word about the probable ethnic composition of the population of the Kingdom of Hungary is in order here. Although the sources for such an examination are highly uncertain, the recent research of Leslie Domonkos has provided some new data for the task.[33] Domonkos shows that the medieval concept of the *natio Hungarica* included all subjects of the king of Hungary, regardless of their ethnic origin or the language they spoke. The Kingdom of Hungary included Hungarians, Germans, Slovaks, Croats, Saxons, and Wallachians, as well as Magyarized Cumans, Jazigs and even

The People

Ruthenians.[34] According to Elemér Mályusz, the ethnically Hungarian element may have amounted to close to 70 percent of the total population,[35] and was probably concentrated on the lowlands and the river valleys. The forests and mountain ranges wre the homes of Slovaks, Wallachians and Ruthenians. In Transylvania, seven cities were settled by Saxons (hence the German name of Siebenbürgen for the province). Of the 57 counties in Hungary proper, the population of 22 seems to have been almost exclusively Magyar; in 26 others Hungarians probably constituted the majority, and in seven others, they were a minority. Beyond this, the Hungarian element was predominant in counties with larger populations. For instance, Borsod County had 5,000 *portae,* Heves 5,722, Pest 4,500, and Pilis 1,746. In contrast, Árva County had only 301, Zólyom 1,421, and Liptó 791. The largest number of *portae* were located in the southwest; Zala County had 8,979, Tolna 10,031, Somogy 11,085, and Baranya 15,018½. As Mályusz pointed out, although the territory of Trencsén County, where the population was a mixture of Slovaks and Hungarians, consisted of 4,619 square kilometers, most of it mountainous terrain, and Tolna was only 3,600 square kilometers, mostly flat or low hills, the latter had three times as many *portae* as the former.[36]

Transylvania, Slavonia, and Croatia presented a somewhat different picture. In the latter, the number of Hungarians was insignificant. With the exception of a few lesser-noble families, Croatia's population was overwhelmingly Slavic, but its towns also held sizable populations of Germans, Greeks, and Jews. In Transylvania, the majority of the population, or approximately 255,000 people, were ethnically Hungarian. The Székelys, whose origin is uncertain, spoke a Hungarian dialect and lived in compact settlements in southeastern Transylvania, and also scattered throughout the province. Their social organization, even in the fifteenth century, preserved many characteristics of the ancient Hungarian tribes and clans. It seems safe to say that in this period the administration of the province reflected this situation. The Saxon region, in which approximately 70,000 German settlers were concentrated, possessed administrative authority curbed only by their allegiance to the king. The Székelys were considered Hungarian lesser-noblemen, while the Wallachians, numbering about 100,000 in Hunyadi's time, were generally under the rule of their own leaders, the *kniazi.*[37]

Politics in the Kingdom of Hungary was not ethnic-oriented. In the entire fifteenth century, only one "ethnically Hungarian" king ruled the realm, and this was Mátyás Hunyadi (Corvinus), who was of Wallachian descent on his father's side! Many of the leading aristocratic families, such as the Counts Cilli, the Frankopans, the Oláhs, the Drágfis, and others, were of non-Magyar origin. Philippo Scolari was a Florentine, and János Vitéz was part-Croatian or Slovene. All these lords, together with ethnically Hungarian aristocrats and noblemen, served the king of Hungary—or fought against him, as the occasion demanded—and considered themselves members of the *natio Hungarica*. As Jenő Szűcs has summarized this issue;

> The individual was first attached to the person of the king; then, more abstractly, to the kingdom and its symbol, the crown, then to his feudal lord (or his vassal, or his vassal's vassal) or to his landlord. Secondly, his loyalty belonged to the universal Christian Church: . . . One's loyalty to the kingdom was of a different quality than the customs and mores attaching him to the ethnic community. Feudal dependence embraced a narrower, Christianity a wider circle than the circle of ethnicity: . . . One could be *gente Hungarus* while at the same time was also *natione Latinus,* that is, of Rumanian origin and language. . . .[38]

In Hungary, in contrast to Western Europe, the fifteenth century saw a continuation of slow demographic growth. The country lacked large urban centers from which the plague could spread and the mixed diet of the population was probably healthier than the largely cereal-based diet of the peoples of Western Europe. A corollary to this situation was the continuing migration of many ethnic groups, including but not limited to Germans, Slavs, and Wallachians from the Balkans, enticed to Hungary by special privileges and the relative security provided by the realm. In turn, the landlords were compelled to threat the native population well if they were to keep them from running off to the market towns or the cities.

The evolution of villages and other settlements in the Kingdom of Hungary had been interrupted several times during the Middle Ages. For instance, in the thirteenth century, the migration of the Cumans was followed by the devastating impact of the Mongol invasion of 1241, resulting in the nearly total destruction of a well-developed village network.[39] The Black Death of the fourteenth century also caused dislocation, although not as severe as those in Western Europe. After each disaster, the rebuilding of the village network proceeded apace, with special attention to natural defenses.[40] Throughout the fifteenth century, large estate owners and lesser noblemen were always interested in attracting agriculturists to their land. Partly as a result of the population shift to the market towns and partly as a consequence of the landlords' efforts to attract new settlers, a new village network developed. During the reign of Anjou Lajos I the number of villages reached 15,000; by the end of the fifteenth century, there were 26,000 settlements, including several hundred market towns. In the 1490s, between 19,000 and 21,000 settlements were permanently occupied.[41]

The majority of these villages were settled by serfs, but lesser-noble families did reside among them. There were also settlements inhabited exclusively by lesser-noble families, many of whom worked the land with their own hands. The majority of the Székely villages of Transylvania were of this kind, and there were clusters of noble villages in other regions. For instance, in Borsod County, one-fourth of all settlements were popoulated by lesser-noblemen.[42] These villages differed from serf settlements in that they were fully autonomous. Their affairs were decided at meetings in which all nobles took part. Their major obligation consisted of going to war at the call of the king or their lord, and they paid no taxes to the realm. Disputes among their inhabitants that could not be settled locally were adjudicated by the county or royal courts. Their obligation to pay the tithe to the church was much disputed and was finally abolished by king Sigismund.[43]

Most settlements were small, their size being limited by the peasants' preference for defensible sites. For instance, the medieval village of Muhi was surrounded by swamps,[44] and other villages show similar patterns.[45] Many settlements consisted of only a few houses, but some were as large as towns. On the average, villages harbored between 100-115 persons each, and their generally small size was probably a disadvantage for their inhabitants in their struggle for autonomy.[46]

Judging from the settlement patterns of more recent times, the most common village type probably lacked any preconceived plan, dwellings being scattered over the available area without any streets connecting them.

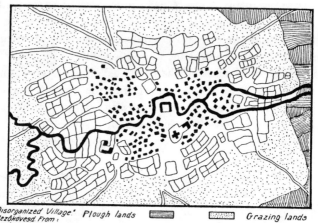

"Disorganized Village." Plough lands ▬ Grazing lands
Mezőkövesd. From:
István Győrffy: *Magyar falu,*
magyar ház, p. 85.

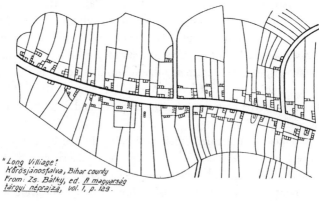

"Long Villiage."
Körösjánosfalva, Bihar county
From: Zs. Bátky, ed. *A magyarság*
tárgyi néprajza, vol. 1, p. 129.

A peasant living in such a "random village" possessed two plots,[47] one of which held his house and garden.[48] One observer remarked of the village of Siklósd, in Udvarhely County in Transylvania, which survived into the twentieth century, that "the plots were not cordoned off from one another; the paths sneaked through the village of yards, gardens, sometimes even through barns. Courteous owners sometimes placed ladders over obstacles in their yards in order to make passing over them easier."[49] Another major village type followed the road, the houses being built parallel with one another. At first glance, this arrangement would argue against defense as a primary consideration. In the medieval village of Móric, the houses were on the average 70 meters apart, the greatest distance between two houses being 140 meters. The defense of such an extended territory by its relatively few inhabitants would have been almost impossible. Yet even here, examination of the medieval topography shows that the village was actually surrounded by a swamp, providing plenty of hiding places in times of trouble.[50]

Each home in such a village fronted on the road and was separated from its neighbors on both sides by fences.[51] In the center of both types of villages there was usually a church, built from readily available materials, with space left around it for a cemetery or a marketplace. There were, however, villages without churches, the population probably gathering on Sundays and major holy days in the church of a nearby settlement. Fairs were seldom held in villages—these were usually held in a market town or a city—since this would have required special charters of privilege. In the lowlands, in central Hungary, and in the river valleys of Translyvania, the long village type predominated, while in the hilly regions the random village was likely to be more common.[52] In each case, the methods used in tilling the soil contributed to the shape the village took. This was most evident in settlements that had been carved out of the forest and were still surrounded by trees. In such places, animal husbandry usually overshadowed the tilling of the soil, and a more orderly settlement pattern prevailed.

The basis of the serf's existence was his plot. This was the land that held his house and its adjoining gardens, the plowlands he used individually, and the forest and grazing lands that belonged collectively to the village. The size of serf plots varied, in general, as I have said above, from about 25 to 284 acres, depending upon the availability of land, the age of the settlement, and local geographic conditions. If land was freely available, peasant families used large plots. If their settlement was old and the available land relatively infertile, then as each subsequent generation subdivided the plots these grew smaller in size. By the mid-fifteenth century, documents often show half or even quarter plots being worked by individual peasant families. Where full serf plots survived, it may be because of the cohesiveness of peasant families harboring several generations of adults and children, or the newness of the settlement. According to István Szabó, the ratio of average plot sizes was 27 percent full-, 42 percent half- and 31 percent quarter-plots.[53] These averages were different in each region, and it was possible for a half- or a quarter-plot in any region to be larger than a full plot in another. It seems that smaller plots were more common west of the Danube, in the southern areas of the Great Plain, in the region of the upper Tisza, and in the northwest, but the pattern was often reversed where new settlers had moved into abandoned villages.

Clearing forest lands and draining swamps were important ways of increasing tillable acreage. Two methods were used, probably introduced by Cistercian and Premonstratensian monks respectively. In Sopron County, for example, the Cistercians cut fire lanes in the forests and burned the designated area inward. After the fires had subsided, the land was cleared of stumps and roots and the ashes were left on the land as fertilizer.[54] The Premonstratensians, on the other hand, dug and maintained trenches from the edge of the swamp to a low lying area or a river or a stream. At first, the land so drained was used only for grazing; when it was completely dry, the plows were set upon it.[55]

A variety of land holding patterns existed in practically every village. In areas where land was freely available or where peasants were clearing new land, they used it as if it were their private property.[56] On the large estates, especially demesne land, baronial or church servants often rented parcels for their own use or received land in compensation for their services. Many large estates rented land to villages or to individual peasants. There were villages that lived entirely by animal husbandry and used all their lands in common. However, "private ownership" of land did not mean that a peasant could dispose of "his" land freely as he wished except in cases where, for instance, he planted a new vineyard. Ultimate ownership rested with the crown, which had granted land to the nobles,

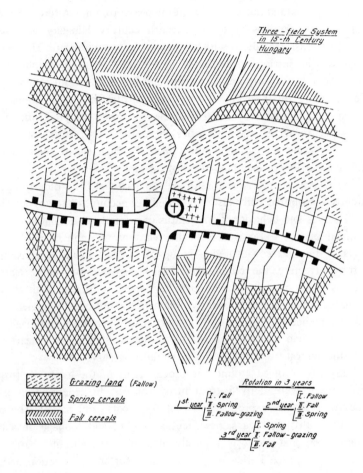

who in turn permitted the peasants to use it for payment in kind, cash, or a combination of the two.[57] By the end of the fifteenth century, individual property rights largely predominated over community rights.[58]

Although data about the daily life of peasant communities and individual peasant families in early fifteenth century Hungary are scarce, those that exist provide us with a glimpse of a strenuous life. The peasant village was an institution dedicated to the welfare of the inhabitants; it existed mainly for purposes of survival and protection against outsiders.[59] The peasantry on the whole lived a peaceful life (though, of course, this does not mean that they never quarreled or raised the pitchfork against each other or against the authorities).[60] As the century progressed, however, they were increasingly drawn into the quarrels of their lords as auxiliary warriors or members of private armies.[61]

The peasant family was traditionally patriarchal. The oldest male apparently distributed daily tasks and owed not accounting to anyone about his decisions and behavior.[62] The status of a family in a village depended as much on the extensiveness of its relations as upon its wealth. The heads of families constituted a group of elders who made decisions in matters affecting the community. Marriages were probably relatively brief as child mortality rates must have been at least as high as those estimated above for the nobility. Elementary notions of hygiene were lacking; medicine consisted of little more than superstition and magic. The seriously ill had to be carted off to the barber-surgeon at a nearby fair or to the nearest town or city and often failed to survive.[63]

Daily life revolved around the procurement of the essentials for survival. These were derived from many sources. In general, four major types of grain were produced—wheat, rye, oats, and barley. The peasants also cultivated beans, peas, lentils, onions, and cabbage on a large scale. Wheat and rye were typically planted in the autumn, barley and oats in the spring. Barley was used mainly for the production of beer, while oats were important to the nobility as the main fodder for horses. There is little evidence on the regional distribution of the types of grain planted, which must have depended on geographic, climatic, and soil conditions. It is likely however, that most of the wheat was produced in the fertile lowlands, while oats were the crop for higher altitudes. István Szabó has argued that wheat and rye were the primary grains, the others being planted mostly as substitutes where the first were difficult to produce.[64]

The lightweight plow was in general use, though hoes and spades were still employed in some areas and the heavy plow had been introduced in others.[65] The blades of the plow were made of iron usually produced by the local blacksmith at the cost of 16-23 denarii. The wooden parts cost the equivalent of a fat ewe, making this the most expensive of farm implements. The heavy plow called for at least four draft animals and sometimes even six or eight, the animals being handled by two or three men. The use of cows or even donkeys as draft animals was common.[66] The Hungarians had a long tradition of breeding excellent horses, and these were also used sporadically to work the soil, but they did not supplement other draft animals during the fifteenth century.[67]

Plowing was inefficient even with the heavy plow. Yields of grain varied between 2.2. and 3 hundredweights per *hold* (1.42 acres). From this, the peasant had to pay the tithe to the church and another tithe to the landlord. Given the widespread use of the three-field system (see illustration, p. 69), the peasant cultivator of the smallest plot, about 25 acreas, of which perhaps one-third was planted in grain, would yearly harvest between 6.6 and 10 hundredweights. After giving 20 percent of this to the church and landlord, and paying other obligations demanded by the king, not much was left for the peasant family's own consumption. However, bread was not the most important element of peasant subsistence in Hungary.[68]

Grain was still harvested with sickles; scythes were not yet in use, and the harvested grain was carried into the barns to be threshed by hand or with horses as the need for it arose. The threshed grain was sometimes stored in pits inside the house. A variety of vegetables enriched the peasant's diet, and fruits of all sorts were raised and dried for the winter. The mills in which grain was ground into flour were as highly regarded as the parish churches. For instance, a criminal could claim asylum if he reached and entered a mill. Drinking, swearing, or fighting on the premises were criminal offenses. Most mills were water-driven, but there were also hand-driven or animal-driven contraptions. Some of them were built on barges Most of the mills were rather inefficient, capable only of turning out rough mixtures of flour from all sorts of produce, including beans, peas, and lentils. In fact, the most commonly used flour was made from a mixture of these products plus oats and barley. "White flour" made from wheat was usually imported from abroad for the royal table and for the barons. Primitive mills were especially numerous on the Great Plain, specifically in the flood plains, and their dams contributed to the spreading of swamps. Mills were also used to grind up fruit, especially apples for juice, to break up pieces of salt, to grind black peppers (an important ingredient of smoked sausage) and even small stones for buildings. There were a few wind mills; when there was no wind, they were driven by animals.[69]

As László Makkai has observed, most of the peoples who have tried to establish themselves in the Danube Basin by cultivation and animal husbandry alone have been swept away in the course of history; it is those who were able to combine these with the skillful management of water resources who have survived.[70]

The Carpathian mountains, averaging about 1,500 meters (4,665 feet) in altitude, block much of the moisture that would otherwise reach the Hungarian plains, collecting immense amounts of snow in winter. Springtime creates flood conditions on the plains, especially since the streams and rivers, once reaching the lowlands, have an average gradient of only 20 centimeters per kilometer. Rivers and small streams meandered slowly through the plains century after century (until the 1880s when they were regulated), developing innumerable channels that became stagnant once the spring floods had subsided, depositing alluvial soil on their banks. Each flood created more channels; these eventually turned more and more of the surrounding lands into swamps and marshes, on whose edges forests of poplar, willow, and alder grew in abundance. As Makkai says,

> the rivers built and destroyed, reshaped their beds in the course of thousands of years, and formed a floodplain area of about 3.5 million hectares, extending over one-third of the plains.... Covered by water for most of the year, ... the flood plains created special conditions for farming, just as did the grass steppes and wooded hillsides, with their closed canopy of beech and pine forests and alpine pastures....[71]

Food production on the flood plains was not simply fishing but fish management. Entire villages worked during the slow seasons connecting stagnant channels with the main flow of the river by digging ditches. These ditches protected the banks from recurring floods and replenished the channels with fresh water—and fish. The peasants then closed the channels and caught the larger fish, leaving the small fry to grow.[72] In areas where there were no flood plains, they dug artificial ponds that, though expensive to maintain, fed entire villages.

Zsigmond Jakó has described how this system worked in Bihar County before the sixteenth century.[73] Bihar, in southeastern Hungary straddling Transylvania, was half mountainous and half relatively flat. The mountains opened into the valleys of the Berettyó, the Sebeskőrös, and the Feketekőrös Rivers, which carried the rainfall of the uplands to the lowlying areas.[74] In the "flatlands," low hills alternated with swamps. Villages —or, rather, groups of houses—were hidden among the reeds, and the life of the population depended upon the utilization of the natural produce of the swamps. The villages were approachable only by hidden paths;

> the village of Mihályfalva was built on low hills amidst the swamps; Székelyhida was surrounded by the reeds of the Ér; Esztár was hidden among the waters of the Berettyó and the Ér; Mindszent was protected by the branches of the Sebeskőrös and the Hévjó; Zsaka lay among the islands of the Sárrét; Komádi was built upon a 200-300 foot piece of dry land surrounded by impenetrable swamps. All these settlements consisted of scattered houses connected to each other by dams and bridges.[75]

The villagers used their environment to good advantage. They raised grain on the hillsides and grazed livestock on pastures that never dried up even in the hottest and driest summers. In winter, the rotting vegetation of the swamp melted whatever snow fell, enabling cattle and other animals to graze at a time when in other regions of Hungary they had to be fed.[76] The reeds of the swamp that grew to the height of 4 meters and were 3 inches thick, were used for many purposes: for house walls and roofs, for fuel, and shelter for livestock in inclement weather, for baskets and other utensils, and even to support vines. The grass of the swamp was used as matting for the floors of houses. The fish caught were sold at Nagyvárad, and the tremendous number of wild birds that nested in the reeds provided eggs by the wagonload in springtime. While the life-style of peasants in Bihar County was not typical for the whole of the Kingdom of Hungary, at least in the extensive flood plain regions peasants probably lived similarly and successfully employed the resources provided by nature in these areas.[77]

Hunting was probably an important source of food for the peasants everywhere in Hungary. They were not yet forbidden to pursue game, although certain types of animals, such as stags, were reserved for the nobility.

Wine production was also important. The Szörénység, the Lake Balaton region, and Tokaj produced excellent wines and Hungarian wines were exported as far as Silesia.[78] Somogy and Baranya Counties produced wine for the internal market.[79] Wine was a much more important beverage than it is today; peasants paid many of their obligations in wine, and it was the beverage everyone drunk.[80] It was also a commodity that turned some market towns into trading centers. Szeged and especially Nagykőrös practically lived by the wine they produced, and their populations tilled the land only as much as it was absolutely necessary. As Makkai remarked: "in some regions wine production became so important that it completely ousted grain as a commodity."[81]

The market towns were not only important centers of the wine trade, but also centers for cattle breeding.[82] The experts on this were the Cumans who had settled the Great Plain during the thirteenth century and brought along with them from the steppes heavy-bodied gray cattle. These cattle, carefully bred, reached average weights of 350 kilograms (770 pounds), about 100 kilograms more than the cattle of Western Europe. They were driven in large numbers to the West by Hungarian traders and also served as the mainstay of the peasants' draft power.[83] Large numbers of horses and sheep were also raised, along with chickens, ducks, geese, and other animals. Brocquiére was surprised at the number of domestic animals possessed by the peasants in the Great Plain, especially the fine horses that he had seen.[84] Most cattle and horses were kept in the pasture year around. In the spring, they were driven to the fallow lands. In bad winters they did receive fodder, but even then they were fed outside in the fields. Horses were mainly used by the nobles for riding, but were also part of the peasant household. The mainstays of animal husbandry were cattle and swine. A great deal of beef, pork, and horsemeat was consumed.[85] Young lambs were considered a delicacy, and fowls were eaten in great numbers. Hogs were especially favored in forested areas, where they were driven into the woods in large herds to fatten on acorns.

In winter, life in the villages slowed down. This was the time for festivals, marriages, and other amusements. The women spent the late autumn

Map of the medieval village of Móric

Explanations:

○ location of excavated houses
⚓ location of the church
→ probable front of houses

From: István Néri "Beszámoló" Archeológiai Értesítö
      81 (1954), 141

days making and mending winter clothing for the family, while the men repaired the barns and made the houses windproof. The building of a house called for the collaboration of neighbors or sometimes entire villages, and it was not an easy task even when many hands were available. Foundations had to be excavated, beams cut, and walls erected. The saw was seldom used; at least, none have been unearthed in excavated medieval villages in Hungary.[86] Beams apparently had to be cut and shaped with axes and adzes, and the result was a relatively large, sturdy building. There were, of course, exceptions. Documents speak of the "abduction" of entire villages "together with their houses,"[87] which must have meant small, movable shacks on wheels, probably drawn by oxen or horses. Houses usually contained three rooms, including the kitchen. The third room was probably used to store tools or as a safe place for the more valuable animals, although signs of stoves indicate that it could also have served as living quarters for members of the household. Rooms were shaped according to the whims of the owner or the requirements of the terrain and were not always rectangular. Excavations of Muhi and other sites have shown that mud or wood, rarely stone, served as building material.[88] The size of peasant houses varied; at Móric they were 17-21 meters long and 4-6 meters wide.[89] A typical peasant house had several fireplaces, some covered, others open. Ovens had their openings in the kitchen and were so constructed that they extended into the sleeping room to keep the inhabitants warm on long winter nights. Few houses had ceilings; a mat of reeds or straw plastered wit mud or clay hung over the open fire to prevent sparks from igniting the roof. In the Great Plain fuel consisted of dry reeds or weeds, straw, or even dried manure. There is no trace of the use of wood in the excavated medieval villages in this region.[90] In the forested areas, of course, wood or charcoal was used. Since it was difficult to cut up an entire tree without a saw, sometimes a trunk was pushed through the door and gradually pulled inside as it burned on the open fireplace.[91]

Beds in our sense of the word did not yet exist in the peasant house. Most peasants slep on hay or straw spread on the dirt floor; as the old saying went, "one of his ears was his pillow, and the other was his blanket."[92] Children and old people probably slept on top of the ovens.[93] Furnishings were sparse and strictly utilitarian. Wooden crates were used to store summer/winter clothing and also served as seats. A few benches

The People

Peasant Implements.

Kitchen plate holder

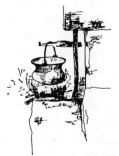

Open fireplace in the yard of peasant house

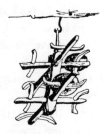

Bread holder and preserver

Salt-cellar for shepherds

From Zs. Bátky, A magyarság tárgyi néprajza vol. I, Nos. 284, 267, 194, 158.

and a low table complemented the furnishings. Chairs were not yet part of the peasant house's furniture.[94] The great variety of pots and pans found in excavated sites suggests a varied peasant menu. Bees were raised for honey and mead, and the wax was used for candles. Salt was purchased from royal vendors, and oil was pressed from the seeds of pumpkins, sunflowers, and poppies.[95] Village craftsmen were able to produce most of the tools needed in their community. Besides staves and hoes, they also manufactured prods for animals, punches, sharpeners for iron tools, axes, adzes, drills, hatchets, and scrapers. The clothing of the peasants were made of flaxen or other coarse materials. The men wore long, skirt-like drawers, and the women many-layered dresses in winter and in summertime alike. Children were dressed like miniature adults. Peasants walked mostly barefooted, only in the coldest winter would they put on some sort of footwear. Both men and women covered their heads.

From birth to death, the life of a peasant in Hunyadi's time was interwoven with beliefs in the teachings of the church as conveyed by the local priests and remnants of magic, witchcraft, and sorcery that certainly go back to preconquest times. The combination formed the basis of popular religion.[97] For instance, the priest Pelbárt of Temesvár, discussing the reasons for the suffering of Christ in an Easter Sunday sermon, told the story of the just and truthful servant who made a bet with his lord that one could not get ahead in life by being unjust and untruthful. Having lost the bet, he paid up by giving his eyes to his lord. As he wandered in his sorrow, he found himself one night under a tree that happened to be the gathering place of evil spirits. Failing to notice the blind man resting under the canopy of the tree, the spirits proceeded to argue over the "merits" they had earned, granting the greatest recognition to the one who had succeeded in convincing mankind that only the unjust and untruthful could get ahead in life. An envious demon then declared that he should be the one so honored, since he had discovered a weed under this very tree that could cure blindness. In the morning, when the spirits had gone, the blind servant groped around and, finding the weed, regained his eyesight. Then he went to the royal court, where the daughter of the king was suffering from eye trouble, restored her to health, and was given her hand and a large estate as a reward. Pelbárt went on to explain that the lord who had blinded his servant heard about his good fortune and, upon learning of the source of his good luck, went to the tree to gather all the weed for himself. The demons came back and caught him at it and had him blinded for trying to steal their secret.[98] Sermons like this were quite common, and it is possible that this mixing of ancient superstitions with Christian beliefs was an attempt on the part of the clergy to make the latter more understandable to the peasants. For instance, peasants often prayed under an old maple tree on Friday evenings during the new moon. After the prayer, they held a feast in which the priest himself participated, sometimes even celebrating the mass after the popular ceremony.[99] Such peasant practices and beliefs were, of course, not uniquely Hungarian; most people living in what Traian Stoianovich has called "permanent culture areas" shared beliefs in various kinds of supernatural forces.[100]

Churches were endowed by landlords, who claimed rights of patronage over them, and some were lavishly decorated, their walls covered with frescoes inside and out. The most frequent figure depicted was St. Christopher.[101] Many churches had walled-in yards, and these provided some protection against raids and at the same time served as a convenient area for festivities. In addition to Sundays, there were many feast and holy days, established by peasant custom during which physical labor was forbidden. In some areas there were as many as fifty such days in the course of a year.[102]

The size of a village church depended upon many factors, of which the number of inhabitants in the settlement was only one. At the medieval village of Ecsér, where the settlement consisted of thirty-eight houses, the church was large and richly decorated, its walls thick and strong. It had been built and supported by an influential local lesser-noble family. On the other hand, the church at Móric, a village of about the same size, was only 12.5 meters long and 6.7 meters wide, providing room only for a few persons at a time.[103] Churches were built of material readily available in the village in question; sometimes they consisted of pilfered stones from ancient Roman ruins, especially along the former *limes* by the Danube River.[104]

There was a certain timelessness about the sleepy villages of Hungary during the late Middle Ages, a stability that survived occasional disturbances, raids, epidemics, or even murderous quarrels among their inhabitants. Even if some of the peasants moved away to a nearby market town or a city, or even if the village was abandoned entirely, peasant life in general continued in its traditional ways.

V

LORD AND COMMANDER

When the Hunyadis became military governors of Szörény, the fortress of Galambóc (Golubac) and that of Szendrő (Smederevo) had already fallen to the Ottomans, and most of Serbia was also in their hands. The despot was a refugee in Hungary. Ottoman pressure on Wallachia and Moldavia was severe, and Transylvania was suffering heavily from intermittent Ottoman raids. Only Belgrade, which had been ceded to Hungary by Stepan Lazarević in 1426 with the agreement of Tata[1] blocked an Ottoman advance into the Carpathian Basin. If the Hunyadis were to keep the raiders away from the Kingdom's southern borders (and they could hardly hope to achieve more) they had to do it with what they had at hand. Similarly, if they were to become successful commanders of large armies, they had to create the necessary conditions themselves. In simple terms, they had to become wealthy enough to raise a private army not only to fight the Ottoman enemy but to protect their own interests within the Kingdom.

As military governors, the Hunyadis saw the defense of the south in a broader perspective than their predecessors. Instead of attempting to defend the frontier districts piecemeal as king Sigismund had done, reacting to raids when the enemy was already within the gates, they devised a comprehensive strategy. First, they created an advance warning system with scouts deep in enemy-held territory. Whether they knew it or not, this was basically the same system used by the Roman defenders of the *limes* in the second to the fourth centuries.[2] Further, they adopted tactics that enabled their troops to coordinate their movements in battle. For instance, the infantry that they increasingly used received close support from both the light and the heavy cavalry, and the maneuvers of the two were also closely coordinated. In time, they increased the mobility of their troops by introducing battle wagons, which also served as a means of transportation.[3]

With the death of Albert I and the uncertainty that surrounded the succession, the Hunyadis needed the support of at least some of the aristocrats. Their principal ally was Miklós Ujlaki but his help was not enough.[4]

During his last days, Albert I had been understandably anxious to secure the succession of his still unborn child to the Hungarian throne. In his last testament, signed on October 23, 1439, he had suggested that if the child were a boy, he should reside in Pozsony, and a nine-member council should govern the state in his name until he came of age.[5] The widowed Queen Erzsébet, in defiance of her husband's last will, was now seeking to be regent herself, and the barons were divided over the succession. Some were willing to accept the queen as regent and, if her child turned out to be a boy, crown him as king of Hungary. Her party included most of those who had been excluded from power during the previous two reigns. She could also count upon the support of Jan Jiškraz of Brandiša, a former Hussite commander whose troops were engaged in a struggle for the control of the northern highlands. This was a formidable "league" indeed.

The opposing camp consisted of barons and prelates who had held office under the previous kings and were at odds with the Cillis and their friends.[6] Its most important members were Simon Rozgonyi, bishop of Eger, Hunyadi's mentor, Miklós Ujlaki, László Kanizsai, Lőrinc Hédervári (the palatine), Frank Thallóczi, the Perényis, the Marcalis and the Pálócis. The still obscure but increasingly noticable Hunyadis naturally joined this group, and their small but disciplined army was to play a decisive role in the ensuing struggle.

The king of Poland, Wladislaw III, appeared to the second group a suitable candidate for the throne of Hungary. A grandson of Hedwig (Jadviga), daughter of the last Anjou king of Hungary and Poland, he spoke fluent Hungarian and was fifteen years old. The royal council, consisting mostly of opponents of Erzsébet, met on January 8, 1440, and appointed a delegation to go to Cracow and invite Wladislaw to the Hungarian throne.[7] On March 8, he accepted their conditions for his election, agreeing to marry the widowed queen and give her a free hand with regard to the properties set aside for her use by her deceased husband. By then the queen had given birth to a son and named him László after the great twelfth-century warrior king of Hungary. Wladislaw promised to protect the infant's inheritance with the exception of his right to the throne. He also promised to respect the rights of the *regnum* and confirm the grants of his predecessors, and to protect the Kingdom of Hungary primarily with his own resources.[8]

Hungarian historians have traditionally given three reasons for the opposition to Erzsébet, but all three are flawed. First, it has been said that many of the great lords feared that the influence of her "foreign" relatives, especially the Cillis, would lead her to act against the interests of the realm. The fact was, however, that she was a woman whose strong will had already been evident during her husband's reign and who had proved that she was not to be controlled by anyone. Ironically, the influence of her relatives was to become stronger after her passing from the scene.[9] Moreover, Wladislaw III was also a "foreigner" and could certainly be expected to listen to his Polish advisers' proposals in the interests of their own kingdom. Secondly, it has been argued that the combination of an infant king and a woman regent was seen as making for a weak government incapable of defending the Kingdom against its external enemies. Here the example cited is the rule of another dowager, also Erzsébet, the widow of Lajos I the Great, during the early 1380s. However, the very selection of Wladislaw III, a brave but often rash fifteen-year-old as king of Hungary, belies this argument. Thirdly, it has been suggested that Wladislaw III was viewed as bringing the resources of two great states to the Kingdom's defense against the Ottoman menace. The barons' demand that he use his own resources for the task, more than any other argument shows that they were really out to advance their own interests. They were simply seeking a free hand in the internal affairs of Hungary by bringing in the young king whom they expected to control as they could not hope to control Queen Erzsébet as regent.

Erszébet was powerless to prevent the election of Wladislaw III as Wladislaw I of Hungary, but on February 22, 1440, while the negotiations were still going on, she gave birth to a son. The previous day her lady-in-waiting, Helene Kottannerin, had succeeded in stealing the Holy Crown from the fortress of Visegrád.[10] In May, six days before the arrival of Wladislaw at Buda, she had the infant crowned king of Hungary. The coronation fulfilled all the legal requirements; it was performed in the ancient coronation city of Székesfehérvár by Dénes Széchi, archbishop of Esztergrom. There was only one problem; it was done against the wishes of the powerful opposition.[11]

Eventually, force was used to decide the issue. A fratricidal civil war was fought among rival baronial factions at a time when the Ottoman sultan Murad II was besieging the fortress of Belgrade and his raiders were looting and enslaving the population of the southern districts. What better proof is needed that most of the great lords cared little for the defense of the realm in their struggle for power? Some historians[12] tried to excuse Hunyadi's participation in this struggle by arguing that he acted in support of the side that had the best chance of establishing internal peace, but there were, in fact, no right and wrong sides in this conflict. Internal peace could just as well have been established if the queen's party had won. It seems better to accept that Hunyadi was not a twentieth-century superpatriot whose every action was designed to serve some imagined "national" interest. He joined the party of Wladislaw I simply because his patron, Ujlaki, was on the Polish king's side and because he saw a better chance of advancing his own career in that direction.

The lines having thus been drawn, the queen proceeded to arrest and imprison the members of the delegation that had invited Wladislaw I to Hungary, despite the fact that she had originally consented to those negotiations. Then she dismissed Wladislaw's supporters from their baronial offices,[13] and her opponent dismissed those of the queen. She also pawned the Holy Crown, the city of Sopron, and her estate of Végles to Frederick III of Habsburg. She entrusted the emperor with the governance of Austria in the name of her son and appointed him guardian of the infant László V. The funds she received from the emperor went for mercenaries under the command of Jiškraz to be used against the opposition.[14] By mid-June, hostilities had begun. In the first skirmishes near the city of Győr, Simon Rozgonyi capatured Ulrich von Cilli and carried him off to Buda in triumph. Now the king had a chance to show his magnanimity and he took advantage of it. He let Cilli go on his promise to abandon his support of the queen, a promise Cilli promptly broke as soon as he was free.[15] In Buda, the palatine Garai was accused of complicity in the theft of the Holy Crown and imprisoned. The king freed him, too, and Garai then acted as dishonestly as the count. On June 29, a diet assembled at Buda and took an oath of loyalty to Wladislaw I. It proclaimed the coronation of László V null and void since it had been performed without the consent of the privileged orders. On July 17, Wladislaw was crowned king of Hungary by the same archbishop who had annointed László V. This time the crown used was taken from the relic of St. István in Székesfehérvár.[16]

The supporters of the queen were not idle in the meantime. During the second half of the year, Garai conquered some fortresses in the southwest, in Vas, Zala and Veszprém Counties. Jiškraz, whom the queen appointed captain of the highlands, launched an offensive against the supporters of Wladislaw and had soon conquered Kassa and the mining towns, cutting off communications between Hungary and Poland. His band leader Axamit conquered most of the area of the Szepesség, including the city of Lőcse, and his captain Talafus took Eperjes, Bártfa and Sáros.[17] Garai allied himself with András Botos, the count of Temes, and the latter led his private army into the field. His first forays were successful, and he was soon joined by Henrik Tamási, who brought along some mercenaries hired with the queen's funds. Then, however, Wladislaw's Polish contingent, having broken through Jiškraz's blockade in the north reached Buda, and joined the troops of Ujlaki and the Hunyadis. They engaged Garai's army near the town of Bátaszék in January 1441. In the ensuing battle, Hunyadi's disciplined troops proved that they had learned their commander's lessons well. Botos was killed, Tamási was captured, and Garai fled. Wladislaw's position was now stronger than before.

Although the queen was not yet ready to give up the struggle, her chances of success diminished. Wladislaw showed his appreciation by appointing Ujlaki and Hunyadi joint military governors of Transylvania and counts of Temes County, and joint captains of the fortress of Belgrade.[18] In addition, the Hunyadi brothers retained their previous office in Szörény. These appointments made the allies the most important military commanders in the state after the king. Hunyadi's income, in spite of the necessity of splitting it with Ujlaki, was now large enough to provide the basis for his future career.

In February 1441, Wladislaw I besieged the fortress of Esztergom, defended by Tamás Széchi (a relative of the archbishop), and the city capitulated after a fierce bombardment. Although in March Cilli's commander Johannes Vitovecz defeated Wladislaw's supporters near Zagreb, there were indications that Wladislaw's side was slowly overcoming the opposition. The Counts Cilli began negotiations with the king in April and in August declared that they were now on the king's side. Dezső Losonci, the queen's military governor of Transylvania, and Djuradj Branković followed their example.[19] Only the highlands were still controlled by the queen's supporters, led by Jiškraz. They besieged the fortress of Pozsony, defended by István Rozgonyi, but failed to take it.

In the meantime, Hunyadi was enlarging his army by using his share of the resources originating in the Transylvanian governorship. His wife's extensive circle of relatives, among them the Gerébis and Vingárts, came to his aid, and he was soon able to force the queen's supporters to give up simply by occupying their estates and denying them their incomes in Transylvania. Ujlaki did not go to Transylvania, and this meant that it was Hunyadi whose reputation and importance was enhanced in that distant province. Beyond consolidating his position in Transylvania, Hunyadi continued to train his men and to increase his private wealth.[20]

Sultan Murad II was well informed about the turbulent conditions prevailing in the Kingdom of Hungary. In April 1440, while the Hungarian lords were preparing for their civil war, he led the imperial army in an assault on Belgrade. The fortress, ably defended by Zovan Thallóczi, military governor of Croatia and Slavonia, withstood the attack and the sultan eventually withdrew. On the way back to Edirne his raiders devastated the Serbian countryside, taking so many prisoners that, as their chronicler triumphantly stated "a beautiful girl sold for the price of a pair of boots."[21] The new threat spurred Hunyadi on to rebuild the long-neglected fortresses of the region. He expected a new Ottoman attack to come soon.

During the late summer of 1441, Hunyadi was often in Belgrade supervising the reconstruction of walls damaged by the Ottoman bombardment the previous year. He also led several small raids on Ottoman-held territory. His rival in this region was Ishak Pasha, the commander of the fortress of Szendrő. A patent of Wladislaw I issued in October 1441 describes one of the skirmishes between Hunyadi and the pasha's troops.[22] It seems that Hunyadi had taken some soldiers from Belgrade on a raid toward Szendrő burning and looting the villages in his line of march. On the way back, Ishak set a trap for him, but Hunyadi avoided it and routed Ishak's troops in the ensuing battle. Hunyadi pursued the fleeign enemy all the way to the walls of Szendrő.[23] This was only a minor engagement, but the fact that a sizable Ottoman host had been beaten on its own territory allowed hope of better things to come.

Murad II's failure to take Belgrade and Ishak's defeat showed that, although Hunyadi was not yet in a position to stand up to the full might of the Ottoman army, he had to be taken seriously. The first real test already was under way. In the late fall of 1441, Hunyadi received news from the city of Ragusa (Dubrovnik) that the Ottomans were preparing a large-scale raid for the early spring of the following year.[24] Mezid Bey, the master of the sultan's stables,[25] had been appointed to lead an expedition with seventeenth thousand sipahis. His task was to sweep through Wallachia into Transylvania, doing as much damage as possible.[26] According to Chalcocondylas, the aim of the campaign was to force the submission of Wallachia to the Ottoman Empire and to undermine whatever support there was for the Hungarians in that province.

The Ottomans, according to plan, moved swiftly through Wallachia in March 1442 and entered Hungary through the Vöröstorony Pass. Despite Hunyadi's network of scouts and the warning from Ragusa, they managed to achieve complete surprise. It is possible that Hunyadi did not take the warning as seriously as he should have—such warnings were regularly received from the endangered lands of the Balkans—or that his picket line was bypassed or overwhelmed by the Ottomans. It is also probable that the attack came sooner than he expected. Mezid's army at first avoided the fortified cities and burst onto the plains of the Maros River valley, spreading panic among the population by its depradations.[27]

Hunyadi had returned to Transylvania only a few days before and had had little time to organize the opposition. He appealed to the bishop György Lépes who had the only available contingent of troops nearby and who was also his friend. The wanton destruction caused by Mezid's troops must have greatly anguished Hunyadi, because for once he acted in haste, rushing to meet the Ottomans without taking any precautions.[28] Mezid had learned of Hunyadi's approach in advance (his system of scouts apparently worked better than Hunyadi's) and set a trap for his opponent. When it was sprung on March 18 near the village of Szentimre,[29] Hunyadi's small contingent was ripped apart and largely destroyed. Bishop Lépes was killed.[30] Hunyadi himself escaped, but Mezid's army was free to continue its depradations.

Hunyadi now sent urgent messages calling upon the people of the countryside to join him. The response was more than adequate; even the peasants, many of whom had been involved in the jacquerie of 1437, responded to his call. Hunyadi had a fresh army within five days of the defeat.[31] This was not a highly disciplined army that Hunyadi preferred, but a "people's army" the more effective because its soldiers were defending their own villages and towns.[32]

Mezid was not worried about the emerging opposition; indeed, he may have even savored the prospect of another battle. He offered a large reward to any of his soldiers who succeeded in killing Hunyadi.[33]

The battle took place near Gyulafahérvár on March 23.[34] Hunyadi had by now reverted to his customary caution. His scouts kept Mezid's troops under constant observation, and his spies even learned of the Ottoman commander's offer of a reward for his head. Hunyadi countered with a ruse. He accepted the offer of one of his retainers, Simon of Kamonya, to dress in Hunyadi's armor and ride his horse. Despite the fact that Hunyadi had him surrounded by some of his best soldiers, Simon was killed but while the Ottomans concentrated on him the real Hunyadi directed his troops in the engagement.[35] At the height of the struggle, the Ottomans' captives revolted, killed their guards, and attacked Mezid's troops from the rear. The Ottoman order of battle was broken, and the troops took to their heels. Hunyadi pursued them, catching and killing many, including Mezid and his son. Most of the other raiders were killed in the mountains by the Wallachians.[36] Hunyadi took the enemy's entire camp as booty and sent some of his prisoners to Buda. According to a chronicler, he also sent along a wagonload of severed Ottoman heads to make a point about his victory.[37]

In the summer of 1442, Murad II decided to send Sehabeddin, commander in chief of his European army, to reestablish Ottoman supremacy in Wallachia and Moldavia, and besiege Transylvania.[38] The sultan attached six Anatolian divisions and four thousand janissaries to Sehabeddin's army. The contemporary Ivanics estimated Sehabeddin's army at close to seventy thousand men,[39] reportedly four times as large as that of Mezid, and it was commanded by several pashas and other beys.[40] The Ottoman campaign was, however, hastily put together, and the carelessness this entailed was to have serious consequences.

This time Hunyadi was ready. He had warned the Wallachians and prepared his own army, calling upon the Székelys and Saxons and recruiting mercenaries. According to Bonfinini, he had about fifteen thousand soldiers at the time of Sehabeddin's arrival. This spectacular increase resulted partly from Hunyadi's vigorous recruitment and partly from his increasing fame as a successful commander.[41] The Ottoman army moved once again through Wallachia, but it found few inhabitants in the villages. Forewarned, they had fled into the forests and swamps. The prince of the province, Vlad Dracul, had his soldiers stationed on the mountaintops, waiting for the opportunity to pounce upon Sehabeddin's army. The absence of resistance gave the Ottomans a false sense of security. According to the chronicler, he told his soldiers, "when the infidels catch sight of my peaked turban, they will start running to many a day's distance out of fear and discouragement. My sword is like a pregnant cloud, raining blood instead of water. I am not Mezid; do not be afraid of the infidel while you are under my protection."[42] One would, of course, have to wonder—if Sehabeddin indeed uttered these words—why it was necessary for the brave Ottoman soldiers to hear such encouragement. Were they, perhaps, apprehensive about the new force that had arisen in Hungary?

Sehabeddin's scouts reported that Hunyadi's army was small compared to his. Nevertheless, the sultan's general took few chances. Although he did permit some of his troops to disperse for looting, he kept the main body together and his camp was well guarded at night.

The two armies faced each other near the village of Vaskapu. The Ottoman army was in its traditional formation; the janissaries formed a solid block around the commanders, with the sipahis and akinjis on the wings. (Our sources do not mention Ottoman artillery.) Hunyadi matched his opponent's order of battle.[43] He also placed his infantry, with some of his armored horsemen, in the center and his light and heavy cavarly on the wings. Behind the footsoldiers he placed a squadron of bowmen and two more squadrons of heavy cavalry. In addition, he may have had some battlewagons behind both wings to provide shelter in the event of a retreat.[44]

Hunyadi realized that the Ottomans' advantage in numbers could be neutralized only by a bold, direct attack. He ordered his heavy cavalry to form a wedge and drive at the center of the janissaries. These veterans were accustomed to such tactics, however, and their line held. Then the Ottoman cavalry began moving on the wings, intending to encircle Hunyadi's army. It did not succeed. Sehabeddin ordered his reserves to enter the fighting; Hunyadi countered with his own and won. The Ottoman wings collapsed and the janissaries fell under the attack of Hunyadi's heavy cavalry. The battle was soon over. Hunyadi made a halfhearted effort to follow the fleeing enemy but prudently gave up the pursuit. Even in defeat, Sehabeddin's army was several times larger than his own, and he did not want to risk another battle.[45]

Since the battle took place in a narrow valley that offered little room for escape, Chalcocondilas' assertion that half the Ottoman troops fell in the fighting seems plausible. Over two hundred flags and five thousand Ottoman soldiers were captured.[46] This was the first occasion in Hungarian-Ottoman encounters on which an imperial army that included janissaries, sipahis, and akinjis suffered such a devastating defeat. As a consequence, Hunyadi's name became a household word in Western courts, and the Ottoman chronicler Nesri stated that "the Osmanli army ran away after suffering a decisive defeat whose magnitude was difficult to describe."[47] Hunyadi sent part of the booty to Wladislaw I and distributed the rest among his soldiers.[48] While Hunyadi was not yet the popular hero "calling the people to arms in the defense of the homeland" as a nationalist Hungarian historian has recently envisioned[49] he was nevertheless acquiring attributes of fame few others had before him.

The importance of the victory over Sehabeddin would be hard to exaggerate. It put an abrupt halt, at least for the time being, to Ottoman plans for large-scale expansion into East Central Europe and opened a new phase of offensive operations against the Ottoman Empire in the Balkans.[50] It also consolidated Wladislaw I's position in Hungary and may have helped to persuade Queen Erzsébet to come to terms with the Polish-Hungarian king.[51] While Hunyadi was fighting the Ottomans in the south, the king led several campaigns against the queen's supporters. In February 1442, he besieged the city of Pozsony which had fallen into their hands, but failed to take it. To counter the resulting loss of prestige, he called the diet into session in June and induced it to offer amnesty to anyone who abandoned the queen's cause. The diet repeated this offer at another of its sessions, held at Hatvan, but it was only in September that Erzsébet finally offered to negotiate with the king. On December 13, the negotiations were completed. According to the agreement, Erzsébet recognized Wladislaw as king of Hungary for his lifetime, reserving the right of her son to succeed him. Wladislaw was to wed Erzsébet's older daughter, Anna, cementing the accord with domestic arrangements. Both sides were to retain control of the fortresses in their possession. No disposition was made concerning Erzsébet's debts to Frederick III.[52]

While Hunyadi's victories undoubtedly contributed to Wladislaw's progress in securing his rule in Hungary, the victory in Wallachia was not sufficiently overwhelming in terms of the relative sizes of the contending forces to represent a turning point in the struggle between the Ottomans and the Hungarians. It would certainly be unwarranted to regard it as a first step in the expulsion of the Ottomans from Europe. Nevertheless, the victories of 1441 and 1442 served notice on the Ottoman Empire that the risks of attacking the sphere of influence claimed by the Kingdom of Hungary had increased and that it would have to face battles in territories it already controlled. This undoubtedly encouraged some of the rulers of Balkan states to resist Ottoman expansion. An Ottoman embassy that arrived at Buda just as Hunyadi's victory over Sehabeddin became known at the Hungarian court, haughtily demanding that the fortress of Belgrade be turned over to the sultan, was sent away in shame. A new force had emerged that promised to change the pattern of dismal defeats suffered by Christian forces confronting the Ottoman armies.

VI

FROM VICTORY TO DEFEAT

As a side effect of Hunyadi's victories over his Ottoman opponents and the victories scored by Wladislaw against the supporters of the widowed queen, the king's position became more secure.[1] Erzsébet drew the lessons of her failure and decided to accept the situation. (Too few historians have so far been willing to give her credit for this; her biography has yet to be written.) Her reconciliation with Wladislaw, however, was made meaningless a few days after its ratification by her sudden death. While a reconciled Erzsébet could have restrained her supporters and insisted on the observation of the agreement, her death freed them to resume the struggle. Frederick III, the guardian of László V, became their champion and proceeded to threaten the kingdom with war.

Wladislaw I was not entirely sure he wanted to pursue a war with the Ottomans. The easiest way out of this dilemma was to consult with the diet and sound out his supporters as to their intentions. Two men had a decisive influence at this diet; Julian Cardinal Caesarini, the legate of Pope Eugene IV to Hungary, Poland, Germany and Austria, and the Serbian despot, Branković.

The cardinal's tasks were twofold; to strengthen the pope's authority in the region and to organize a crusade against the Ottoman Empire. In an effort to accomplish the first, he hoped to persuade Wladislaw I and his supporters, on the one hand, and Frederick III, on the other, to submit their dispute to the pope or the college of cardinals. For either of these two institutions to act as judge in such an important matter would increase the authority of the papacy, and the resulting peace would enable the king to raise an army against the Ottomans. This was, however, a difficult thing to achieve. The emperor had not been consulted during the negotiations between Wladislaw and Erzsébet, and with the death of the queen, he had lost not only a valuable debtor but also his key to a possible control of Hungary.[2] Failing to make any headway, Caesarini turned for help to Aeneas Sylvius Piccolomini, whom he had befriended at the council of Basel (which the latter had attended as a clerical secretary). During the summer of 1442, Piccolomini was employed at the emperor's court and soon became an influential member of Frederick's entourage. The cardinal also appealed to Casper Schlick, the emperor's chancellor, for support. Accompanied by Nicholas Lasocki, a canon from Cracow who was a member of Wladislaw's inner circle, he visited Frederick III in Hainburg and advanced the idea of a compromise. Frederick said that he was interested in an agreement but thought that the best way to achieve it was through a personal meeting with his adversary. Wladislaw, however, did not want to go to Hainburg, since this would have given the impression that he was a supplicant before the emperor,[3] and Frederick would not come to Buda.

Branković, for his part, was continuously urging the king and his supporters to turn their attention to the south. The Ottoman danger, he reasoned, was real and if neglected would lead to the same result for Hungary as it had for him.[4] Branković, of course, had very good reasons for urging the Hungarians to go to war. Most of his kingdom was in Ottoman hands, including the strategically important fortresses of Galambóc (Golubac) and Szendrő (Smederevo). Only Belgrade continued to withstand the Ottoman pressure. Branković's two sons were the captives of the sultan; he himself was a refugee in the Kingdom of Hungary. The interests of Serbians and Hungarians now coincided; unless the Ottoman advance was checked and pushed back deep into the Balkans or even Asia Minor, Hungary's turn would be next. It was obvious to all that the king could not pursue war on two fronts simultaneously. With Branković arguing that priority should be assigned to the Ottoman war, the cardinal could succeed in at least one of his tasks by helping the Hungarians to organize a successful anti-Ottoman campaign.

From Victory to Defeat 93

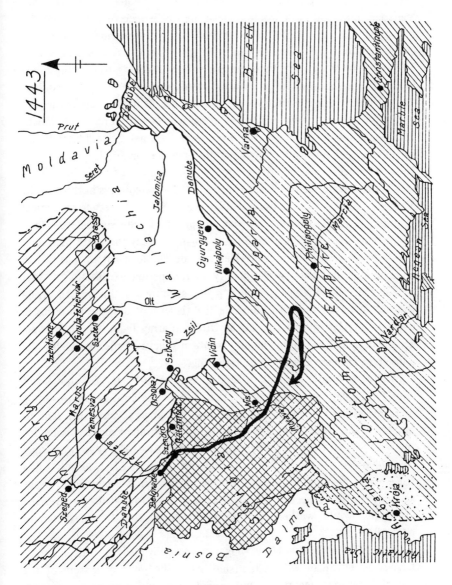

Hunyadi's and Wladislaw I's route during the Long Campaign.

In April 1443, Pope Eugene IV approached Venice about the possibility of providing galleys for an Ottoman war. Leonardo Venerio, the Venetian ambassador to Rome, agreed on a plan according to which the papacy would levy a tithe on the revenues of the Florentine and Venetian clergy and use the funds to equip the galleys and pay the sailors who were to man them. The Venetian Signoria was willing to cooperate but believed that the revenues in question would not amount to the required 20,000 gold florins. Furthermore, it made one of its conditions for providing the galleys the establishment of peace between Florence and Milan. The pope appointed his cousin Francesco Cardinal Condolmieri legate to Venice and entrusted him with the organization of the naval force. He also named Condolmieri the commanding admiral of the galleys when and if these were ready to sail. However, there were delays in the project. Venice's worries were fully justified; the funds collected from clerical revenues proved sufficient for the equipping of only six galleys. When no further funds were forthcoming, the plan for using the warships against the Ottomans was abandoned. This episode would merit no more than an extended footnote in the history of this period except for the fact that in the following year a similar plan was proposed, this time involving the use of naval forces to blockade the Hellespont and the Bosporus in order to prevent the passage of the Ottoman army from Asia to Europe. This plan ended in sending about seventeen galleys to the Straits, but the consequences were anything but gratifying.

Wladislaw I now decided to send emissaries to Poland for troops and considering half a victory better than none, Caesarini began recruiting mercenaries in Germany and Bohemia. Messengers were also sent to Moldavia and Wallachia and even to the Teutonic Knights asking for their support in the coming campaign.[5] But most of the envoys returned empty-handed. Frederick III, although he declared his readiness for a truce with the king, was still reluctant to enter into a permanent peace agreement. He suspected that a decisive victory for Wladislaw over the Ottomans would weaken his own position and therefore hesitated to contribute to such a victory.

The military forces of the Kingdom were obviously insufficient for a large-scale Ottoman war and, in any case, the military system of the feudal Hungarian realm was not geared to offensive operations, especially beyond its borders. Such a campaign would have required extensive cooperation from the major European monarchies, and this was largely out of the question. The emerging national monarchies of the West were busy organizing their own states and challenging the authority of the universal institutions of the Roman Catholic church and the Holy Roman Empire. Under these circumstances no common action against the Ottomans could be expected. The time for crusades was over. Although propaganda about "common Christian interests" continued to flow from the courts and the papacy in Western Europe, it was but lip service paid to outdated ideals.

Nevertheless, Branković and the cardinal continued to press for war at the royal council, and the Hungarian king and the lords finally gave in. They had received news from Ragusa that the sultan had left for Asia Minor to settle scores with the emir of Karaman and that he might already have suffered a serious setback at the hands of his enemy.[6] The lords felt that, if necessary, they could restrain Frederick III while the king was in Ottoman-held lands. Simon Rozgonyi arranged a truce with Jiškraz, the most dangerous of László V's supporters, thus freeing some troops but not extra funds for the Ottoman campaign.[7] Hunyadi was entrusted with the organization of the army. Branković offered to finance part of the costs and bring his own troops along. Hunyadi and Ujlaki were to contribute their own armies.[8]

Matters progressed slowly, however, and Wladislaw became impatient. Finally, on June 22, 1443, he left Buda in the company of Caesarini, Branković and several Polish and Hungarian lords, taking such troops as were available. When the rest of the army was finally collected, the number of soldiers turned out to be quite respectable, and no wonder; Hunyadi had spent 32,000 gold florins of his own funds to hire thousands of battle-hardened mercenaries, including former Czech Hussites and Serbian refugees. He had a sizable cavalry and a host of battlewagons.[9] Caesarini brought along Czech and Austrian mercenaries. The armies of Ujlaki and Hunyadi rounded out the forces, although Ujlaki himself was ill and did not initially accompany his troops. As they marched along the lower Danube, Moldavian and Wallachian soldiers joined their ranks. After crossing the great river at Belgrade and bypassing the fortresses that were in Ottoman hands, they were joined by the troops of Branković, nearly eight thousand strong, accompanied by Vlad Dracul of Wallachia.[10] Altogether, about thirty-eight thousand soldiers marched under the flag of the King of Hungary and Poland.¹¹ Hussite-type battle-wagons are reported to have numbered some six hundred.

The campaign lasted from early September 1443 to early February 1444. Thus, it began when the season for war was almost over and was of unusually long duration. Hunyadi's calculations (he was undoubtedly the mastermind) included the assumption that the European contingents of the Ottoman army had already been dispersed for the winter. He knew that the sultan had not yet returned from Asia Minor and would need time to assemble his European troops. At the same time, his army carried along sufficient provisions, and counted on the help in food and fodder from the Serbian population that Branković's presence guaranteed.¹² Just in case, the army also carried along spare arms on its battle-wagons, whose draft animals could be (and, as it happened, were) used for food.

Historians generally disagree on the number of engagements fought during this, the Long Campaign. The discrepancies probably originated in the confusion of the several smaller battles that preceded it with the events of 1443.¹³ All accounts agree, however, that king Wladislaw I's and Hunyadi's army won all its engagements. Skirmishes began almost immediately after the crossing of the Danube near Belgrade. Hunyadi sent small detachments ahead of the main army, large enough to defend themselves but highly mobile. The main army moved south in the Morava Valley in preparation for the crossing of that river. A raiding party consisting of 500 light cavalrymen riding toward the town of Aleksinac on the opposite bank of the river, surprised a small Ottoman detachment camping nearby and annihilated it, but the appearance of a larger contingent forced the scouts to turn back. Hunyadi now crossed the river with his *banderium,* leaving all his baggage behind with the main army. He approached the unsuspecting enemy with such stealth that he managed to surround them under cover of darkness without being noticed. At daybreak, Hunyadi attacked and dispersed the group, which consisted of about two thousand Ottoman soldiers, killing and capturing many including some high ranking officers.¹⁴ The main army now crossed the Morava and established its camp near Aleksinac.

Hunyadi, however, did not wait for the main army, now led by the king himself, to catch up with him. Still without the encumbrance of baggage, he swiftly moved on to take the city of Niš by surprise, burning it to the ground and pillaging its neighborhood. Just before he reached Sofia, his scouts reported three Ottoman army groups slowing converging nearby.[15] One of them was led by Ishak, the pasha of Szendrő; the other two were moving from the directions of Knjazevac and Pirot-Sofia respectively. According to a letter from Wladislaw, Hunyadi swiftly engaged the three forces separately and destroyed them on the same day, but this is not likely to have been the case. More probably, Hunyadi first attacked and defeated the pasha of Szendrő around the village of Malca, then crossed to the left bank of the Nišava attacked and dispersed the column advancing on the road from Sofia. It was probably on the following day that he confronted the third Ottoman detachment, led by Turkhan Pasha, on the road to Leškovac and defeated it. He probably then returned to his camp near the Morava where, on receiving the news that a new concentration of Ottoman troops was moving toward the main army, he doubled back, surprised the enemy, and annihilated it.[16]

It seems that Ragusa's report about the unpreparedness of the Ottomans had not been entirely correct. At least there were plenty of Ottoman soldiers ready and willing to resist the invasion, even if in a disorganized fashion. Hunyadi now moved on to Sofia, always a day's march ahead of the main army. He crossed the Kunovica Pass, destroyed Pirot, and reached and burned Sofia. Here he rested.[17]

At this point, Ujlaki arrived from Hungary with some fresh troops and joined the king,[18] and the united army proceeded into the foothills of the Balkan Mountains on its way to Edirne. Here it encountered the first serious obstacle to its further progress. Three passes led from Sofia to Philippopolis and Edirne. The one by way of the Khitman and Traian's Gate had the best road. A second, through the upper valley of the Maritsa River, and a third, through the valleys of the Zlatitsa and Topolnitsa, were more difficult to traverse. By the time the invading army reached the mountains, Murad II was ready for it, although his forces were strong enough only for the defense of the passes.[19] In addition, circumstances began to favor the defenders. Before reaching the mountains, the Hungarian army had enjoyed mild, good weather, and its food and fodder supplies were still holding out. Now, however, the weather was turning colder; food shipments became rarer, and the fodder supply was soon exhausted. In mid-December, the united army tried to cross the Khitman Pass and was repulsed. Hunyadi was forced to turn toward the Zlatnitsa

Pass but once again he failed to cross it. The Ottomans barricaded the road, felled trees, and rolled boulders on top of the attackers and succeeded in stopping them.[20]

As the Hungarian army, showing sings of exhaustion began slowly winding its way back to the north, Murad sent the commander in chief of the army of Rumeli, Kasim Pasha, in pursuit. Hunyadi, not to be surprised, set a trap near Slivnitsa for the pursuing enemy. The rear guard of the main army, led by Branković, joined the battle; then Branković, according to plan, retreated, drawing the Ottomans across the Cervenka in great haste. Here Hunyadi's troops were waiting and surprised the enemy from the rear. The Ottomans were soon in disarray, fleeing back toward the mountains. Hunyadi pursued them all afternoon, killing and capturing a great many, but by now the Hungarian army was no longer capable of sustained efforts. It is likely that the king himself was slightly wounded in this last engagement, in which he also participated.[21] The Hungarians carried many prisoners along with them; among other dignitaries, they captured Kasim Pasha and Mahmud Celebi, the latter a brother-in-law of the sultan and brother of the grand vizier.[22]

Having learned their lesson, the Ottomans followed the Hungarian army at a respectful distance, but they continued to harass the stragglers. To speed up the retreat, unnecessary equipment was destroyed and some of the booty burned. The bodies of fallen soldiers, which the army had continued to carry along, were now buried. Its load considerably lightened, the army reached Belgrade in late January and, after a few days' rest, moved on to Buda by February 2.[23]

The results of the Long Campaign at first seemed nothing short of electrifying. Thousands of Ottoman prisoners had been taken, among them thirteen high ranking officers. The myth of Ottoman invincibility seemed to have been broken for good and the Ottoman threat to Hungary removed. Perhaps the time was right for an all-out effort at expelling the Ottomans from Europe once and for all? A closer look at the situation reveals, however, that the Long Campaign was something less than the overwhelming success it was believed by contemporaries. Serbia was not freed; the major fortresses remained in Ottoman hands—except, of course, Belgrade, which they had been unable to conquer. No matter how much Europe rejoiced over the victory, it was no more than a tactical success.[24] Branković was correct in urging the king and Hunyadi to plan for the renewal of the campaign. It is an entirely different matter whether the Hungarians could have continued the war, exhausted as their army was, by December, 1443. In retrospect it seems clear that only a concerted European effort could have had the desired effect, and this was clearly outside the realm of contemporary possibility. Ottoman power in the Balkans had been merely dented. The Hungarian and Polish lords understood this and were hesitant to follow up the Long Campaign with another war unless they had substantial help from the West.

When Wladislaw I and his troops arrived at Buda, the victory celebration began in earnest. A whole flock of Western envoys were waiting to greet them. They came from the kingdoms of Spain, France, Aragon, even England; there were representatives from Milan, Florence, Venice, and even Genoa. The pope's envoys were also there, as well as those of Burgundy. Excited about the Long Campaign, they urged the king to follow it up with another war. Even the Byzantine emperor John Paleologue sent his ambassador to Buda, offering his cooperation against the Ottomans.[25] Most importantly, as it turned out, the pope's envoys stated that the joint navies of the Italian states and Burgundy would be ready to sail to the Hellespont by mid-year, when Wladislaw was expected to renew the attack on the Ottoman Empire.

All this was so much wind. The Western European states were not directly threatened by the Ottomans and were not really interested in a joint enterprise. They were quite willing to urge the Hungarians to go on with "their war," promising support that they never seriously considered providing. Venice and Genoa had lucrative trade with the Eastern power and had no intention of destroying the source of their income. Milan's duke sent a letter comparing Caesarini to Moses and ordered a three-day thanksgiving holiday in his city for the success of the Long Campaign, but he sent no money or troops for the renewal of the struggle.

The members of the Hungarian royal council were understandably divided over the issue of the continuation of the war. Their hesitation was underscored by the fact that the king was approached by the sultan's envoys while still on the march back from the Long Campaign, offering a long-term truce on favorable terms.[26] Although there was some suspicion that this was an Ottoman ruse, some of the lords were interested in exploring the offer. The Polish nobles in the king's entourage were especially worried about the long absenceof their king from

Poland. Rumors about a Mongol raid allegedly conducted against Halich and news of unrest in Oppeln had reached the royal court. Hunyadi himself was now having second thoughts about the renewal of the war. Probably at the urging of Branković, who was impressed by the sultan's offer, he took an interest in a truce with the Ottomans.

The most outspoken supporters of the war were Caesarini and the foreign envoys. The cardinal argued for a new campaign on a much larger scale than the last one, ideally culminating in the expulsion of the Ottomans from Europe. His motives certainly included the prospect of the unification (by force, if necessary) of the Orthodox and Roman Catholic churches, based on the agreement reached between the two institutions at the Council of Florence in 1439. In anticipation of this, the pope had already extended Caesarini's jurisdiction as his legate to Greece and Asia Minor. The cardinal spoke eloquently of the need for a new war. The Byzantine envoy stated that the time was right for a new effort, since according to information he had received from Constantinople, the sultan had once against crossed into Anatolia, and a coordinated campaign was sure to succeed in ending the Ottoman threat once and for all.[27] The Venetians declared that the fleet that was being prepared in their city would block the Hellespont and the Bosporus, not only stopping the sultan's recrossing to Europe, but also preventing the Ottomans fleeing from the Balkans from reaching Asia Minor. Furthermore, news was received that the pope had renewed his order for the use of the clerical tithe in Venice and Florence to equip galleys and recruit mercenaries. The cardinal went so far as to offer the city of Gallipoli to Venice for its help in conquering the Ottomans.

Wladislaw still hesitated to commit himself. Despite loud proclamations that he would go to war no matter what happened, he kept his options open. Unknown to Caesarini and the foreign envoys—and even to the royal council—he secretly sent a delegation, accompanied by the representatives of Branković and Hunyadi to Edirne, to explore the sultan's offer.[28] The royal council seems to have been halfheartedly inclined toward the continuation of the war, but the king decided to consult the diet before making his decision. In the meantime, negotiations with Frederick III had been continuing, eventually producing a two-year truce that included neither Jiškraz nor the other supporters of László V. In order to iron out the problems, Wladislaw invited the Cillis, Garai and Jiškraz to be present at the diet in early April 1444.

When the diet met, the nobles were more interested in the internal conditions of the realm than in the Ottoman war. First of all, they proposed the introduction of measures to strengthen royal authority. They ordered the restoration of all royal revenues "usurped by barons and others," no matter how they had been acquired. Then they offered amnesty to all opponents of the king, threatening recalcitrants with the confiscation of their property. They also regulated the currency and issued recommendations for the reorganization of the judicial system.[29] When they at last turned to foreign policy matters, the nobles eventually let themselves be convinced by the war party. This was not a difficult matter to achieve. After all, the lesser nobles could not be compelled to participate in a war outside the borders of the realm. Wladislaw swore that he would lead another army against the Ottomans that summer. That the nobility's support for the war was mainly rhetorical is evident in their stipulation that the king was to use his own resources and their refusal to order the mobilization of the lesser nobility.[30]

The king was inclined to accept the advice of his Polish ministers and return to Cracow before embarking on another expedition. This worried his Hungarian supporters, since his absence from the realm could easily lead to the renewal of the fratricidal struggle. Skillfully supported by Caesarini, they finally convinced him to follow the war party's suggestion. Hunyadi was ordered to begin assembling his troops for a renewal of the Ottoman war.

The barons, however, remained true to their colors. Most of them were scarcely willing to risk their lives in battle against the Ottomans. Only three offered to accompany the king to the Balkans: these were, besides Hunyadi, Bishop Simon Rozgonyi of Eger, Bishop János Dominis of Nagyvárad, and Bishop Raphael Herceg of Székcső. Not surprisingly, they were all friends of Hunyadi. Although the nobles voted for a "donation" to be collected from their peasants for the campaign, that was as far as they were willing to go. In the end, the army that entered the Balkans in September 1444 consisted of the king's *banderium* and Hunyadi's, the armies of the three bishops, and the king's Polish contingent, supplemented by about a thousand mercenaries recruited by Caesarini (who had fewer resources than in the previous year).[31]

Once again the dreary business of sending envoys to Western monarchs was undertaken. The pope sent Condolmieri to command the united navies, and the Byzantine emperor promised to mobilize his forces and coordinate his attack on the Ottomans with that of the Polish and Hungarian king. Skanderbeg (George Kastriota) of Albania was notified and he promised to join the expedition with thirty thousand soldiers. Help from the West, except for a small fleet of galleys, was not forthcoming.[32]

At time passed, Branković was becoming more and more dubious about the campaign's chances of success. He observed that, this time around, the army would be even smaller than in the previous year. He also noted that the plan of the campaign, as proposed by Caesarini, would once again bypass the Serbian fortresses. It was he who had received the sultan's message, and it is possible that he had concluded a very favorable separate truce with the Ottomans.[33] Hunyadi himself was concerned about the lack of Western support, but he did go to Transylvania to put his *banderium* on a war footing.[34]

Sultan Murad II did not expect a renewal of the war with the Hungarains. He was convinced that his offer was too good to be rejected. Confident of the conclusion of the truce, a copy of which he had signed before leaving for Asia Minor, he entrusted his son Mehemed with the European regency and left for Anatolia.[35] At the same time, he sent his ambassador to Branković, offering him ransom for Mahmud Celebi and requesting once again that the Serbian urge the king to accept his offer of a long-term truce. Before the matter could be settled, however, one obstacle had to be removed. Hunyadi had spent 32,000 florins for the Long Campaign and had already committed twice as much for the new war. Since Branković was to benefit most from the truce, he gave Hunyadi the estate of Világosvár, consisting of 110 villages and a fortress in Zaránd and Arad Counties in Transylvania, adjacent to other Hunyadi properties.[36] It is also possible that he pawned other properties to Hunyadi, including the city of Debrecen. With this the sultan considered the truce assured, since without Hunyadi's support no war could be conducted in the Balkans by the Hungarians.

The royal council must have learned about the king's negotiations with the sultan at about this time. The Ottoman terms were so favorable that the council was seriously tempted by them. The terms included the return of all the Serbian fortresses to Branković's control and the freeing of all Serbian lands from Ottoman domination. Since Branković was a vassal of the king of Hungary, this would have meant the strengthening of the king's position in the Balkans as well. At the same time, the truce would have freed Wladislaw's hand to settle accounts with the opponents of his rule in Hungary, including Frederick III. Besides, as we have seen, there was little enthusiasm for the renewal of the war among the Hungarian and Polish lords. The pope's offer of help meant little in view of his lack of funds, and the Italian city-states showed no great enthusiasm for changing the status quo in the Balkans. Finally, Hunyadi himself now favored the truce.[37]

The events of the following months are not entirely clear.[38] We know that the king went to Szeged with a large retinue and there he met with the sultan's envoy. In the royal council Caesarini continued to argue against the sultan's offer on the grounds that its acceptance would be a betrayal of promises previously made and that the combined navy was nearly ready to sail. On the "other front," Frederick III was not showing much enthusiasm for an agreement, and there was news confirming the rumors about the Mongol attack on Halich.[39] Both Hunyadi and Branković favored the truce, as did the Polish and Hungarian lords. Caesarini finally gave up, although it was in his power to impose ecclesiastical penalties on the king and Hunyadi if they did not honor their previous oaths. Thus, the council advised the king to accept truce with the Ottomans, and the indications are that he did so. Contemporary chroniclers such as Dlugosz reported that he did and attributed the subsequent disaster to his having broken his oath.[40] Later historians, however, came to believe that he had never signed the truce agreement.[41] No copy of such an agreement has ever been found, and a formal peace treaty was in any case impossible according to Ottoman law. However, one of the conditions of the truce—the return of the fortresses to Branković's control— was gradually undertaken, although there were delays and even some fighting in the process.[42] Despite all this, on August 4 Wladislaw I issued a ringing declaration of war. That the campaign did not start immediately suggests, however, that he was still hesitant to make an irrevocable committment.[43] It must have been about this time that news of the departure of the galleys from Venice reached the court. What effect this may have had on the irresolute young king we cannot really tell, but it may have provided the push he needed. Although war was now clearly in the offing, preparations for it went forward at a snail's pace.

In a further declaration issued at Futak on September 20, Wladislaw gave his reason for the renewal of the war as being the slowness of the sultan's forces in returning the Serbian fortresses, *as agreed upon in the treaty*.[44] Here he could have been referring either to an agreement that Branković had concluded with the sultan on his own behalf or the truce that he had himself may have signed at Szeged. Teleki's report that despite Branković's generous compensation for his expenses, Hunyadi had taken over the fortresses of Kučevo and Braničevo may indicate Hunyadi's eventual rejection of Branković's separate truce with the sultan.[45] Hunyadi, now in full support of the war, may have suggested that the king postpone the formal declaration of war until at least September in order to give Branković time to recover his fortresses and provide more time for preparations for the campaign.[46]

Pál Engel has advanced an ingenious and imaginative explanation for the apparent confusion surrounding the so-called "peace of Szeged." He suggests that the negotiations with the sultan and the seeming vacillation of Wladislaw were simply a ruse designed to gain time and keep the Ottomans guessing. He maintains that the declaration of the king, issued in August and September respectively, show that he was determined to return to the Balkans and that all subsequent discussions were overshadowed by this determination. In the August declaration, the king stated that "all other oaths about peace were to be invalid," suggesting that he knew beforehand that the truce would not be observed. Thus, Engel argues, "the peace of Szeged (really of Nagyvárad) was a well-acted out charade... (for which) Hunyadi accepted responsibility, while the more timorous king simply acquiesced in his oath." Engel further argues that the motive for Hunyadi's action was his previous agreement with Branković. I have mentioned the transfer of the estate of Világosvár; according to Engel, it is possible that about half of Branković's properties in Hungary were pawned to Hunyadi as his price for supporting the separate truce. There may even have been a secret pact between these two to arrange the treaty, Hunyadi having then changed his mind after the king's August 4 declaration. Since Caesarini probably considered Hunyadi's position a defection from the "Christian cause," he may have designed a formula for the agreement in such a way that it could be easily annulled. Engel further states that the plan was a complex one and the full details were probably known only to the cardinal.[47]

One must admit the plausability of Engel's argument. It explains the king's seeming vacillation, the changing of sides by Hunyadi, Branković's subsequent hostility to the war, the sultan's outrage at the broken truce, and his having left for Anatolia while the Hungarians were apparently preparing for war. A less complicated explanation suggested by Oscar Halecki, however, explains the events equally well; if Branković had concluded a separate truce with the sultan and promised to persuade the Hungarians to do the same and then proceeded to "buy" Hunyadi's support, all the major actors would have behaved in the same way. Halecki is wrong, however, in insisting that the king never signed any agreement at all. What eventually mattered was the dream of expelling the Ottomans from Europe, and this notion was fostered by the success of the Long Campaign and the news of the sultan's Anatolian troubles.[48] Neither Hunyadi nor the king could have easily overlooked the opportunities these circumstances seemed to present. Obviously, the undertaking of such an enterprise involved some hesitation, but going to war in 1444 was the logical outcome of recent events that no one in Hungary could ignore.

The king had by now received news that Murad II had freed the sons of Branković and that the transfer of the fortresses was proceeding. Branković was now vigorously opposed to the war but the king received new encouragement from the Byzantine emperor's renewed pledge of help and Skanderbeg's announcement of his readiness to join the king's army.

Thus, when the army began moving into the Balkans in mid-September,[49] it was much smaller than that of the previous year, but this did not unduly worry the king and Hunyadi. They crossed the Danube at Orsova on September 21, numbering only about ten thousand soldiers in the army. Hunyadi expected to lead his own *banderium,* and therefore lingered at the crossing until October 3. Thereafter, he moved on slowly, gathering additional soldiers, and reached the vicinity of Vidin only on October 9.[50]

The army avoided the straight road to Edirne that led across the mountain passes. Instead, it followed the one to Nicopolis, winding between the sea and the Balkan Mountains. It shunned all battles, although it is true that no serious opposition was mounted by the Ottomans. Shortly before reaching Nicopolis, Hunyadi caught up with the army. This campaign was in no way similar to the one the year before; Hunyadi's troops crossed Wallachia "looting all the way,"[51] and they did the same in the vicinity of Nicopolis. In spite of the Wallachian "episode," Vlad Dracul came along with his men, but he was justifiably angry with Hunyadi, and this did not augur well for the future.[52]

The leaders—the king, Caesarini, Hunyadi, the three bishops, Vlad Dracul and Frank Thallóczi (military governor of Croatia and Slavonia)—held a council of war at Nicopolis. Dracul noted that the king's army was smaller than the sultan's hunting entourage and counseled retreat.[53] He also observed that the thousand or so battlewagons that the army had brought along did not carry provisions and ammunition as on the previous occasion but were loaded with booty.[54] He urged the king to abandon "this foolishness" and turn back. Many of the lords in the king's entourage thought that he was right, but Caesarini and Hunyadi would not hear of retreating. Hunyadi even voiced his suspicion that Dracul had notified the sultan of the planned moves of the army.[55] At this accusation Dracul left in anger. His son stayed behind with four thousand soldiers, however, and before leaving, Dracul offered to leave a bodyguard for the king to protect him in case of trouble. The king would not accept the sober advice of the Wallachian prince. Influenced by Hunyadi and the cardinal, he continued the campaign despite the fact that his army now consisted of barely twenty thousand men.

The original plan for the campaign called for the army to take the short route through the Balkan Mountains and march through Sofia, Philippopolis and Edirne to Gallipoli. Because of the lateness of the season and the experiences of the previous year at the Zlatitsa Pass, it was decided to proceed to Varna, moving along the coast toward Constantinople. Wladislaw's and Hunyadi's confidence was maintained by two factors: the memory of the ease with which their army had won its victories the previous year and the conviction that Condolmieri's galleys would prevent the sultan's recrossing to Europe. They also expected the arrival of Skanderbeg and the troops of the Byzantine emperor. Their hopes seemed justified by the swiftness with which the army had conquered and looted Nicopolis. However, by then a small Ottoman detachment was shadowing the army's march.[56]

As usual, Hunyadi secured the passage of the main army in the vanguard, his troops consisting of the Wallachians and his own *banderium*. Behind him came the battlewagons and at the end of the line rode the king amongst five hundred selected knights. The army took Jenibazar; it reached Sumla on October 25 and swiftly conquered it. A small Ottoman

From Victory to Defeat

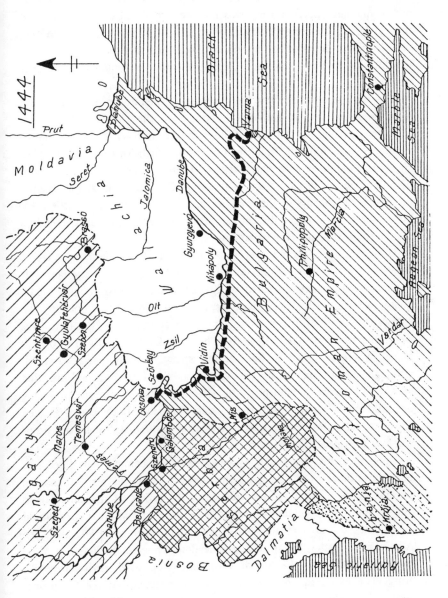

Hunyadi's route to Varna.

naval force that was stationed at the Jantra River near Sumla was surprised and burned. This army was not the disciplined one that had won the battles of the Long Campaign. Emboldened by the successful looting of Nicopolis, the soldiers continued their depradations. Villages were left burning in their wake and Orthodox churches denuded of all their treasures.[57]

The army stopped for five days at Sumla. Then it went on to loot and burn Provadia. On November 6 it conquered the town of Petrec and took two smaller forts by the following day. It reached Varna on November 9 and Hunyadi established his camp northeast of the abandoned city, surrounding it with battlewagons. Then the news came like a thunderbolt: Condolmieri's messenger reported that the sultan had succeeded in crossing the Straits to Europe with his entire Asian army. By the evening of the same day, the distant campfires of the Ottoman army could be seen in the rear of the Hungarian troops.

Historians have argued ever since about Murad II's crossing, placing the blame variously on Condolmieri, the Genoans, or the Venetians, but the number of galleys assigned to guard the Straits was probably inadequate to begin with. The Byzantines, for their part, failed to occupy the European shores of the narrows, and as a consequence, the Ottomans were able to harass the galleys from both banks, forcing them into midstream where they had to fight against strong currents. It was rumored, although never conclusively proven, that the Genoans had provided barges and crews to transport the Ottoman army to Europe, receiving one gold florin per soldier in the bargain. As is usually the case with such controversial issues, accusations of treachery abounded, but no real proof was ever provided.[58]

Upon receiving this startling news, the king's council considered two possible courses of action. Caesarini suggested that the army remain in the enclosure of the wagon-fortress until the arrival of the united fleet, but no one had any idea where the galleys were or whether they would ever come to Varna at all.[59] Still expecting the eventual arrival of the Albanians and the Byzantines, the leaders, Hunyadi included, advised the king to stay near the city of Varna and accept battle with the sultan's army. The expected help, however, never materialized; the Byzantines were now afraid of the sultan and Skanderbeg was prevented from joining the Hungarians by Branković's troops.

The Serbian despot had, of course, every reason to resent the renewal of the war. Not only had he compensated Hunyadi for his expenses, but he had regained the Serbian fortresses without encountering serious problems. To lose all this for an uncertain campaign that he knew to have been carelessly prepared, appeared to him nothing short of madness. Now was the time for the king and Hunyadi to heed Dracul's advice and turn back, but it was not to be. As Thuróczi said, they would have been ashamed to turn back without even attempting battle with the enemy. Besides, Murad II, after the crossing, went directly to Edirne, where he gathered all his forces. Then, having received information about the line of march of the Hungarians from captured cavalrymen, he marched directly to Varna. Arriving there, his troops came between the Hungarians and their possible line of retreat, leaving them no choice but to fight.[60]

Hunyadi did not even know the size of the opposing army and suggested that before anything else they should try to find out. Since no one could offer a better suggestion, Hunyadi's advice prevailed. Thus, battle was accepted on November 10.[61] The two armies were of vastly unequal strength. Murad II's troops were reported to have numbered between sixty and a hundred thousand men, as opposed to the approximately nineteen or twenty thousand on the Hungarian side. The sultan's janissaries alone were a match in numbers for the entire cavalry force of the Hungarian army.[62] According to Zotikos, who was a much better observer than Palatio (the latter of whom provided much of the fantasies of Dlugosz and Callimachus and, not the least, Prochaska) the battle began by the Ottoman's irregular cavalry. The Anatolian akinjis and asabs, stationed on a hill near Varna, suddenly swarmed over the side of the hill and fell upon the right wing of the Hungarians. When their attack was repulsed, the Anatolian commander Karadsa moved to the attack. He was opposed by Hunyadi's own forces which beat back the sipahis and killed their leader. Then Daud Pasha, the commander of Rumeli, led his troops against the Hungarian left wing. Hunyadi turned against him and sent his troops fleeing. It seemed that the battle was won Only the janissaries still stood their ground unperturbed. The sultan himself was said to have been ready to run away from the battlefield but was restrained by some of his commanders. Zotikos says that an old, grizzled janissary grabbed hold of Murad's horse preventing the sultan's escape:

>...one of the janissaries, brave, satanic, stopped Murad's horse ...and talked to the sultan angrily and bravely; sultan, admirable lord, Ottoman Murad, get off your horse this minute to die with us and we with you. Because if you turn back now, I say on your gold-adorned head... that I will kill you with my own hands![63]

Naturally, this colorful description cannot be taken literally, but it does appear that Murad was ready to give up. The events that followed are just as controversial.

Up to this point Wladislaw I seems to have stayed out of the battle. Now with victory apparently at hand, some of the lords in his entourage urged him to take part in the fighting. Some may even have suggested that if he did not fight personally, all the glory would go to Hunyadi.[64] As the chronicler put it, Wladislaw decided that "it was fitting for a king to fight a king." Thus, he led his troop of five hundred cavalrymen against the center of the line of the janissaries. His attack carried him through the first opponents, but his horse was cut from behind. He himself fell to the ground, where his head was cut off by a veteran soldier and at once raised on the tip of a lance for all to see.[65] Hunyadi, just returning from the pursuit of the fleeing sipahis, desperately tried to stop the quickly spreading panic,[66] but he did not succeed. By the time dusk settled on Varna, the battle was over. The Hungarian army was thoroughly beaten, and its remnants were trying to get as far away from the battlefield as possible.

The sultan's victorious army, also exhausted, was unsure that it had won. Murad ordered his troops to retire to camp for the night. Only the following morning did their victory become obvious, and by then the Hungarians and their allies were gone. The Ottoman army entered the abandoned wagon-fortress and butchered the sick and the wounded left behind, but it was too late to follow the fleeing enemy. Nevertheless, few Hungarians escaped from Varna. Many of those who survived the battle died of disease or were killed by the aroused peasants of the region, whom they had previously despoiled.

The losses were, therefore, staggering. Not only was the king killed, but Caesarini was among the missing. It was later reported that he had escaped from the battle but had been killed either by robbers or, possibly, by enraged Hungarians who attributed their defeat to him. The bishops of Nagyvárad and Eger and the lords István Báthori, Miklós Perényi, Henrik Tamási, and Gregory of Sztropka were all dead.[67] The losses of the Ottomans were equally serious and the sultan later added to them by ordering the execution of the officers whose troops had deserted during the battle.

The political consequences of the defeat of Varna were even greater than these losses would indicate; it virtually ensured Ottoman domination of the Balkan Peninsula and the eventual fall of Constantinople. If there had ever been a chance to save the Byzantine capital from the Ottoman conquest, it was at Varna. After the defeat, it was only a matter of time before Constantinople fell to the Ottomans. Hunyadi himself escaped, but for some time afterwards he was content with defending the frontiers of the Kingdom of Hungary only. Few would believe from that time onward that the Ottomans could ever be expelled from Europe.

Bickering over the responsibility for the defeat was to continue for centuries afterward. Some would say that it was God's punishment for the king's breaking his solemn oath. Others were to accuse Hunyadi of cowardice, a charge for which there was no evidence whatsoever. The causes of the defeat were, however, obvious. They included the vacillation of the great lords about going to war in the first place and the almost lighthearted, casual, careless preparations for the campaign; the promises of the pope, the Western monarchs, and the Byzantine emperor; the inadequacy of the naval force guarding the Straits; the failures of the Byzantines to occupy the European shores of the narrows; the inability of Skanderbeg to join the Hungarians; and the unreliability of Branković, whose troops interfered with the efforts of the Albanians and who himself refused to join the campaign. Above all, the leaders of the campaign, especially Hunyadi, must bear a major responsibility for the defeat. Hunyadi and the young king were overconfident. The propaganda they generated about the overwhelming success of the Long Campaign and its promise of breaking the Ottoman's hold on the Balkans once and for all was all too successful: it fooled them as well. Only Sultan Murad II emerged from this sordid episode as a true statesman, and if there is any historical justice his victory was fully deserved.

Historians of the Hunyadi-era usually treat the Long Campaign and the Crusade of Varna as two isolated events. In fact, they were part of a single strategy, namely, the effort to take the initiative away from the

Ottomans and engage them in warfare in the occupied territories of the Balkans. When the Long Campaign brought a measure of success, the leaders of the Hungarians were emboldened to follow it up. The defeat at Varna was, therefore, the direct result of the efforts of the previous year, whose ultimate purpose was the elimination of the Ottoman threat from Hungary's borders and the eventual expulsion of the Ottoman Turks from Europe.[68] The Long Campaign was a glorious enterprise, even if not so successful as many contemporaries wished to believe, and gave the aggregate of *nationes* whose soldiers participated in it a whole set of new heroes. Varna was a disaster by any measure, one in which a valiant king was killed and which all but ended efforts by the Hungarians against the Ottoman Empire. While the Long Campaign forged a Polish-Hungarian military alliance that might have become a permanent basis for East Central European security, Varna ended in mutual recriminations. Treating the two events separately gave historians of the various nations involved a chance to balance success with failure and place the blame for Varna "on the other side." This closer look at the two events, however, should make it clear that the defeat was rooted in the earlier success.

VII

THE REGENT

The loss of the vigorous young king at Varna created a tremendous impression, greatly increasing Europeans' fear of the Ottomans. It also raised the spectre of civil war in Hungary. Now that the symbol of central authority had been removed, the great lords could be expected to make a concerted effort to divide the Kingdom among themselves. In the north and the northeast, Jiškraz's Czech mercenaries were creating a situation that was near chaotic; in the Vág River Valley, Pongrác Szentmiklósi was leading raids against his neighbors. Frederick III was preparing war against Hungary in the west, and the Ottomans were expected to renew their attacks in the south. Only the royal council, headed by the palatine Lőrinc Hédervári (which, ironically, included many of the contending barons), stood between internal chaos and a semblance of order. The council took the logical step; it spread the rumor that Wladislaw escaped from Varna and was alive and well in Poland, raising a new army for the renewal of the struggle against the Ottomans.[1] In this way it gained time to stave off immediate disaster. Its ultimate success, however, depended upon the speedy return of Hunyadi, and Hunyadi was delayed. On his way back to Hungary with some of his remaining soldiers, Hunyadi was arrested and imprisoned by Vlad Dracul.[2] Upon learning of his, Hédervári threatened the Wallachian prince with war if Hunyadi were not immediately freed. Dracul responded by not only setting Hunyadi free but loading him with presents and personally escorting him to the Hungarian border.³

It was no accident that Hédervári acted so quickly. By then, Hunyadi was among the richest, most powerful lords in Hungary, the actual head of state in fact if not in name. His estates extended over large areas of the east and Transylvania. Within this region, his friends and retainers, including the Csákis, the Perényis, the Rozgonyis, and many others, provided him with unconditional support. In the Great Plain his friends included the Pálócis, the Hérderváris, the Marótis, and others, and he could count on the help of the retainers of these powerful lords in the event of need.⁴ By then, Hunyadi's wealth was almost half that of all the other lords combined. If, at this point, he had decided to reach for the crown, he could have easily become king, but he declined to do so. We do not know his reasoning, but it is possible that he considered the kingship a burden he did not need. Assuming it would certainly have pitted him against the Garais, the Cillis, and the Holy Roman emperor. At this time, he was more concerned with the defense of internal order.

It could be argued with some justification that his preoccupation with the defense of the south was the consequence of the location of his family's properties, which lay in the path of most Ottoman raids. This was, however, a measure of Hunyadi's greatness. He was a powerful lord in an age in which self-interest, rightly or wrongly perceived, drove some of the great lords of Hungary to overreach themselves. Hunyadi recognized that without great wealth he would be at the mercy of the other lords. Therefore, he drove hard to amass then hold onto his fortune. At the same time, he was aware that using his wealth only for the aggrandizement of his family would not be enough; it had to be used for the defense of the realm. He strongly believed that a struggle against the Ottoman Empire was unavoidable. His personal interests, therefore, coincided with those of the Kingdom.

On returning to Hungary, Hunyadi faced several important tasks. One of these was the steadying of the shaky government, which, for all intents and purposes, consisted of the royal council. In order to do this, he had to rebuild his army, and for this new resources would have to be found. He may have had an idea of organizing the lesser nobility of the counties as a possible counterweight to the various baronial alliances that opposed him. In addition, he had to try to balance these alliances against each other, not only in order to prevent the outbreak of open conflict among them but to ensure that they did not combine forces against him. The emperor supported both the Garai-Cilli-Branković leage and the Jiškraz-led alliance of the north, and Ujlaki openly flirted with the former.

The royal council met at Székesfehérvár in early February 1445. Hédervári obviously knew about the death of the king, but he was careful to conceal this knowledge from the rest of the nobles. Many of the barons present at the meeting, especially Hédervári and Ujlaki, disliked the idea of accepting the infant László V as king of Hungary. They were concerned that, at least during the guardianship of the child, the emperor would meddle in the affairs of Hungary. Thus, as an interim measure, the council approved the appointment of several "vicars" and entrusted them with the temporary supervision of various regions. Hunyadi's responsibility was to be eastern Hungary and Transylvania, Ujllaki's the Great Plain and most of the area on the right bank of the Danube, and Jiškraz's much of the highlands. The council felt the need to consult with the lesser nobility concerning the organization of the new government and called for a meeting of the diet at Pest on the eighth day after Easter.[5] Hunyadi quickly restored order in the area entrusted to him. He called the lesser nobles of the counties together, and, obviously at his insistence, they declared their intention to punish wrongdoers. He also began maneuvering for the appointment of his friend, János Vitéz, as bishop of Várad in Bihar County.[6]

After several delays, the diet gathered in late April or early May 1445. It was unusually well attended. Besides the barons and prelates, there were representatives of the county assemblies and even some royal cities, including Pozsony. Although we do not know about all the diet's decisions, it is likely—as Piccolomini reported—that Hédervári would have liked to see Hunyadi elected king.[7] When Hunyadi declined the suggestion, the lords discussed the possibility of establishing a "republic" controlled by the barons, but they decided that this was not a viable solution for the Hungarians. Facing the possible renewal of Ottoman attacks, they did not want to risk the civil war that such a decision would have entailed. It is most likely, as Teleki maintained,[8] that the diet wanted to gain more time. One way of doing this was to maintain the myth of the survival of Wladislaw I. The nobles, becoming impatient with waiting for him to show up, decided that if he did not return soon, they would accept László

V as king of Hungary, but only for his lifetime; his issue, if any, would have to face a new election. They further stipulated that László V would be king only if the emperor delivered him to Hungary along with the Holy Crown.[9] The diet refined the idea of the royal council that led originally to the appointment of "vicars;" it appointed seven "captains" to maintain peace and order in the various regions of the country. Hunyadi and Ujlaki were made captains of eastern Hungary and Transylvania; György Rozgonyi, Imre Pelsőci, and Jiškraz were made responsble for the north and northeast, including the royal city of Kassa; the northwest and the Vág River area were entrusted to Mihály Ország and Pongrác Szakolcai. The captains were also charged with the dismantling of all fortifications built since the death of Albert I, except those constructed against the Ottoman threat, and the restoration of the tithe to the church whereever it had been expropriated. They were also instructed to abolish all illegally established tolls and insure the free travel of merchants.[10]

The diet also instructed the royal council to make sure that clerical appointments were given only to members of the *regnum* and stipulated that abbots for monasteries were to be chosen from the same order that controlled the abbey in question.[11] It also reconfirmed the freedom of peasants to move once they had fulfilled their contracts with their lords and ordered the return of serfs who had been forcibly removed from one lord's estate by another. The royal revenues were designated first of all for the salaries of the military governors (for the maintenance of border defenses) with anything left over to be saved for the future king. The lords were warned that squandering royal revenues intended for the defense of the military districts would be considered as a criminal offense. In the event of a new Ottoman attack, the diet was to call for the general mobilization of the nobility and no exceptions were to be granted for anyone.[12]

Internal peace remained fragile, however. Ujlaki refused to return some properties to their rightful owners, and Jiškraz was unwilling to destroy fortresses in the north that served his interests.[13] Frederick III sent his troops to conquer the fortress of Kőszeg in western Hungary and raided parts of the region.[14] Hunyadi's nephew, János Székely, added to the instability by illegally taking over some villages owned by Nicholas Lodomerici in Zagreb County.

A delegation was sent to the emperor in the early summer of 1445. Many dignitaries were scheduled to go, including Ujlaki, but the latter feared the emperor's wrath because of his role in bringing Wladislaw into Hungary, and he stayed behind to await a promised safe-conduct. This eventually arrived. Jiškraz was also present when the delegation reached the emperor, but he was not admitted as a member; the lords considered him an upstart and not a member of the *regnum* in whose name they were speaking. As instructed, the envoys demanded the release of László V into their custody and the return of the Holy Crown. They also demanded that the emperor relinquish the estates and castles that had been either illegally given him by the former Queen Erzsébet or were conquered by his troops. The emperor was quite naturally unwilling to comply with these demands. His tactic was to attempt to persuade the envoys to disregard their instructions and come over to his side, but it was unsuccessful. Too much was at stake even for the proponents of László V's kingship, for Garai and Széchi, and no one was particularly anxious to have the emperor's influence prevail in Hungary.

After many days of fruitless negotiations—and a visit with the infant László V—it was obvious that the emperor would not change his mind unless he was forced to do so. He declared that the Hungarians would not need to crown the child again, since this had already occurred, but if they were so anxious to do so he would not object provided there was no new annointment. He insisted, however, that in that event the Hungarians issue a patent declaring that the second coronation did not negate the validity of the first. After the coronation, however, the infant would have to be returned to him, since he was his guardian. He would agree to let the infant king reside in Pozsony, but in that case the fortress would have to be guarded by his own soldiers. On the other hand, if the child died, he would return Pozsony and the crown to the jurisdiction of the royal council. He also suggested that the council meet him in Pozsony in order "to discuss matters related to the governance of the Kingdom of Hungary," making it clear that his aim was to gain control of the affairs of the realm.

The Hungarian envoys were understandably disappointed at the outcome of these discussions. Not so Jiškraz, who could only benefit from the turn of events; it would make it more difficult for the Hungarians to dislodge him from the north. The situation was also welcomed by the alliance led by the Counts Cilli; as the envoys were about to take their leave from the emperor, a delegation arrived from Branković to acknowledge László V as king of Hungary and ask that the new king confirm his holdings in the country.[15]

While the diet was in session in Hungary, the anticipated renewal of Ottoman raids had begun in the south. Hunyadi had hurriedly left for Belgrade but the danger had apparently passed before he arrived there. The Cillis had taken advantage of the situation; Johannes Vitovecz, their general, had raided Slavonia to demonstrate the power of the supporters of László V.[16] The raid had done considerable damage, especially in the bishopric of Zagreb in Croatia which the raiders reached, where a dispute over the possession of the see kept the region in turmoil in any case. The bishopric of Zagreb had been without its prelate since 1433. Neither Sigismund nor Albert had ever filled it, and when Erzsébet and Wladislaw became rivals, each had been intent on having his/her supporters occupy it. Erzsébet, on the advice of Ulrich von Cilli, had appointed Benedict of Zólyom and obtained papal approval for this appointment. Wladislaw, for his part, had placed Demeter Csupor, a friend of Hunyadi, previously the bishop of Knin, in charge of the bishopric. The rivalry enabled the Counts Cilli to take over the estates of the bishopric. Eventually Benedict who was the choice also of the cathedral chapter of Zagreb, had agreed to pay the Cillis 20,000 florins for the return of the estates. Unable to raise that much money, however, he had ended up as a prisoner of the Cillis, who had kept him in confinement for sixteen months. When he was finally freed, Benedict had approached Cardinal Caesarini, offering to transfer the bishopric to Csupor if he were given the see of Knin in exchange, but the battle of Varna had interrrupted the negotiations. When Hunyadi's defeat and Wladislaw's death became known, Benedict had made peace with the Cillis and given up on the idea of the transfer.[17] Csupor was a friend of Vitéz and took refuge with him when he was forced, by the approaching troops of Vitovecz, to flee Zagreb. Hunyadi supported Csupor against Benedict, but the backing of the cathedral chapter for Benedict was enough to make the pope hesitate in making a choice.[18]

In the meantime, Hunyadi, anxious to prove that he was not discouraged by the defeat at Varna, made plans for another campaign. In late March, Waleran de Wavrin, the commander whose ships had been part of the naval force before the battle of Varna, sent messengers to Hunyadi

The Regent

offering his support for a renewal of the war. They reached Buda in early May, and it was agreed that Wavrin would come to Nicopolis in August with eight galleys. Hunyadi would be there waiting for him with eight or ten thousand soldiers. The envoys were to carry a message to Vlad Dracul in Wallachia on their way back from Buda, uring him also to prepare for the new campaign.[19]

At first glance, Hunyadi's plan for a new campaign appears absurd, but he was certainly aware that he could not expect to achieve decisive victories with so small an army. That he sent envoys to Pope Eugene IV and Charles VII of France for help suggests that he had some hope of receiving aid from these powers, but he was once again disappointed. The pope, for his part, was satisfied with sending letters to the Western monarchs urging them to support Hunyadi's plans, but the French king explained that his war with England had priority over everything else.[20]

The Burgundian galleys, Dracul's six thousand men, and Hunyadi's *banderium* did in fact meet at Nicopolis. Hunyadi visited Wavrin in his galley and found the commander seriously ill. Before his arrival, Dracul's troops, in cooperation with the gallyes, had besieged Little Nicopolis, on the left bank of the Danube, but failed to take it. Hunyadi now suggested that the united army cross the river to do battle with the Ottomans massing on the other side. The crossing was accomplished without mishap, but Hunyadi was unable to force the battle. The Ottomans withdrew in good order, destroying their supplies rather than leave them behind. Since Hunyadi had only enough food left for two days, he declined to pursue the Ottomans and recrossed the river. By the beginning of October, the campaign was over without having achieved anything.

Once again, the diet was called into session by the royal council to deal with the Cillis. Few, however, attended and the meeting had to be postponed until February 1446. Hunyadi himself failed to appear, although it was obvious that the diet would have had to rely on him for the execution of its decisions.

The maneuverings among the baronial factions continued. Ujlaki and Hédervári were both strongly opposed to the kingship of László V. Hédervári suggested that the Hungarians follow the example set by the Czechs, who had elected George of Podiebrad regent. Although Ujlaki himself aspired to the Hungarian regency, Hédervári wanted Hunyadi. Therefore, Ujlaki entered into a mutual-aid alliance with the Cillis; he knew that

Hunyadi's word would be decisive at the next session of the diet and wanted to be ready for any eventuality. Hédervári warned Hunyadi of Ujlaki's plans, however, and in order to show his good will, Ujlaki traveled alone to meet Hunyadi before the opening of the diet at Székesfehérvár. Hunyadi's main task now was to achieve a modicum of peace and order in the realm. He knew that there was little chance of that unless the emperor was pacified and the Cillis were forced to submit to the decisions of the royal council. Ujlaki and he therefore agreed to share power to achieve these aims. They sent a joint message to the emperor declaring that they were loyal to the cause of László V, but in order to keep the other lords in line they needed more influence in Hungary. If the emperor would cooperate with them, they would see to it that all future actions of the royal council favored László V's side. Frederick III seems to have accepted this proposal.[21]

By the time Hunyadi arrived at Székesfehérvár in March 1446, the diet was already in session. Its members were deeply disappointed by the failure of the Hungarian envoys to the emperor and determined to settle the issue of governance themselves. They lost no time in sending Hunyadi to punish the Cillis for their action in Slavonia and Croatia. In April, Hunyadi led fifteen thousand men to Styria and proceeded to devastate the Cilli's estates. He moved with such speed and efficiency that his opponents were thrown off balance and were soon suing for peace. In agreeing, Hunyadi stipulated that they must respect the sovereignty of the royal council over their estates in the Kingdom of Hungary.

At the June session of the diet, Hunyadi was the obvious choice of the assembled nobles for the regency. The election took place on June 5, 1446, but it is likely that it had been arranged beforehand.[22] Although the election was unanimous, the diet insisted on certain conditions. One of these was that when Hunyadi was away from the country, Ujlaki was to be his substitute.[23] This condition may have been agreed upon before the diet by Hunyadi and Ujlaki. Other conditions limited Hunyadi's power. First of all, the diet insisted upon naming a commission of two barons, two prelates, and six lesser nobles to assist the regent in his judicial functions. His power to grant estates was limited to the equivalent of 32 serf plots. He had to use some of the royal revenues to redeem properties given away by previous kings. Furthermore, royal revenues were to be collected by the royal council, and only their disbursement was left to Hunyadi.[24] A special oath was also designed for Hunyadi in Hungarian, since he did not understand Latin.[25] Gaining the regency therefore provided Hunyadi with only limited control over the realm. Nevertheless, his election was still a remarkable achievement for the son of a lesser noble, and it was only the first step.

After the election, the diet proceeded to distribute the available offices. Hédervári remained palatine and in control of the fortress of Buda. Hunyadi and Ujlaki continued as joint military governors of Transylvania. László Garai was reappointed governor of Macsó (Mačva), and László Pálóci was named lord chief justice. Treasurer was Mihály Guti-Ország, Hunyadi's nephew, Tamás Székely, was named prior of the abbey of Vrana.

Characteristically, Hunyadi assumed his responsibilities in a spirit of reconciliation. Garai had been left in an important position, and his allies could hope for an accommodation with the regent. Civil war was, therefore, averted, and Hunyadi was free to embark upon the tasks that he had set for himself. If he wanted to be effective, he had to increase the revenues of the crown and strengthen the forces opposed to baronial anarchy. His dilemma was that he was himself a baron and had to thread carefully if his powers as regent were not to be diminished. During the last years of King Sigismund's reign, royal revenues had amounted to 200-250,000 gold florins a year. By the mid-1440s, large amounts of this revenue were being usurped by competing barons and prelates.[26] Hunyadi approached the task of restoring royal revenues to the crown in a roundabout way.

The largest part of royal revenues consisted of income derived from the salt monopoly and mining rights. The mines, however, had been neglected during the confusion surrounding the death of Albert and Wladislaw I. The Italian middlemen who controlled most of the sale of salt were not closely supervised and cheated the treasury out of its rightful share. Many of the greater and lesser nobles simply pilfered shipments of salt as these passed through their estates. In order to stop cheating by the merchants, Hunyadi installed his own retainers as traveling compansions, and this in itself resulted in substantial increases in the income from the salt monopoly. He then increased the wages of miners, which stimulated production. Toward the end of Hunyadi's regency, the salt revenues were once again near 100,000 florins a year.[27]

Hunyadi was less successful in regaining other royal revenues. Some of the most important mints remianed out of his reach,[28] in areas controlled by Jiškraz, and the Czech would not let such prizes slip out of his hands. He simply declined to accept Hunyadi as the representative of the Hungarian crown, and it was obvious that Hunyadi would have to use force against him if he wanted to change his mind.

In his effort to establish control over the nobility, Hunyadi sought to follow the example set by Western monarchs, who had enlisted the cooperation of the cities in achieving this aim. Since urban development in Hungary was much slower than in the West, he had to begin by strengthening the cities. He encouraged the establishment of an alliance of free royal cities; he spurred them on to build and repair roads and he tried hard to eliminate brigandage. He also attempted to establish a unified system of coinage in order to further the interests of commerce.[29] He made sure that the cities had their appeals judged only by the royal cupbearer and insisted that jurors be chosen from among the burghers. He also provided help for the developing market towns against the depradations of the nobles, encouraging them to look to the regent in their struggle against baronial usurpation.[30] Most of the cities of the north, however, continued to support Jiškraz, even providing military help for Hunyadi's opponents.

Hunyadi also ran into problems in attempting to organize the lesser nobility as a counterweight to the barons. He called the diet into session at least once a year during his regency, and in these sessions he tried (without success) to educate the nobles to assume greater responsibility for affairs of the realm. He also made strenuous efforts to maintain a standing army capable of opposing not only his internal enemies, but also the enemies of the Kingdom.

One of Hunyadi's priorities as regent was a move against Vlad Dracul. An opportunity was provided for him by a revolt led by Dan in Wallachia that succeeded in driving Dracul out of the country. That the prince fled to the court of Murad II at Edirne convinced Hunyadi that Dracul had treasonous relations with the sultan, especially since the Ottoman ruler proceeded to provide the Wallachian with troops to regain his princedom, and go on to raid Transylvania. Dan fled to Hunyadi and in August 1446 Hunyadi led his troops to Wallachia. These surprised Dracul at the Jalomitsa River, annihilated his Ottoman raiders, and captured the prince and his two sons. Dracul was then taken to Turgivişte, where he and his elder son were beheaded and the younger son was blinded.[31] Thus, Hunyadi took terrible revenge for what he considered the humilitation he had suffered at Vlad Dracul's hand when he was imprisoned briefly by the Wallachian prince after the battle of Varna.

The situation with Frederick III did not improve with Hunyadi's regency. In light of the emperor's refusal to free László V and the Holy Crown, and his continuing occupation of Hungarian territory, would have fully justified the use of force against him. However, Hunyadi did not want to do that. Pope Eugene IV had finally obtained Frederick III's agreement to support the papacy against the Council of Basel. The diet of the empire had met at Frankfurt in late 1444 and recognized Eugene IV as the legitimate pope. In return, the pope had become a supporter of the emperor in his dispute with the Hungarians. Hunyadi therefore had to move carefully if he did not want to turn the pope against him, especially since he still hoped for financial support from the pope for his military plans against the Ottoman Empire. With this in mind, he wrote to Frederick on June 11, 1446, stating that his aim was to arrive at an understanding with the emperor.[32] However, when it became clear that only force would compel the emperor even to negotiate with the Hungarians, Hunyadi set out to do something about the situation. He was determined to force the issue, but he had to make it clear that he wanted to tangle with the emperor only, and had no intention of hurting the Austrian nobles or the city of Vienna. If they took the side of the emperor, Hunyadi could easily find himself facing superior forces. Thus, he persuaded the royal council to send letters to Vienna and the Austrian nobles and, just in case, to Venice, notifying them in advance that his actions were strictly directed against Frederick III.

The diplomatic ground having been prepared, Hunyadi moved swiftly against the emperor in November 1446. He hit Steyrmark, Karynthia, and Krain, encountering little opposition. His troops freely looted and burned the countryside. Cities such as Baden and Mödling were forced to pay ransom for being left alone.[33] Frederick tried to get help from Vienna, but the good patricians were hesitant to face so formidable a commander as Hunyadi. Hunyadi set up his camp at Neukirchen, where a delegation trying to mediate peace reached him from Vienna. From here he moved to Wienerneustadt and was visited by another delegation, this time on behalf of the emperor.

Hunyadi did not hesitate to set out his conditions. He demanded the immediate transfer of the fortress of Győr, which the emperor had acquired through bribery, to the jurisdiction of the royal council. Other matters could, he said, be discussed at a more appropriate time. He gave the envoys four days to return with the emperor's reply.

When the emperor procrastinated, Hunyadi marched on to Laubersdorf. From here, he sent several detachments as far as Hainburg and the Viennese mountains. Although the emperor was powerless to stop him, he still refused to accept Hunyadi's terms. The regent nevertheless felt that he had taught the emperor a lesson and at the end of December returned to Buda with a great quantity of booty.[34]

The emperor now offered a truce, but it was soon apparent that he intended to use the time so gained to incite opposition to Hunyadi. When he sent letters to the free royal cities urging them to refuse obedience to the regent, the royal council decided to approach Poland with the suggestion that the two countries establish an alliance against him[35]

For two long years Hunyadi had labored to stabilize the government and his own authority in the Kingdom of Hungary. It is not at all certain that his underlying purpose was an eventual reckoning with the Ottoman Empire on his own terms, as some historians would have us believe.[36] Be that as it may, he was not yet ready to resume the offensive in the Balkans. His priority at this point was to urge the continuation of negotiations with the emperor. The royal council agreed with Hunyadi and sent several delegations to Frederick III during 1447 and 1448. The pope's legate, Juan Cardinal de Carvajal, also worked on a solution to the dispute without much success. The emperor finally did agree to return Győr to Hungarian control, but he extracted 3,000 gold florins for his expenses —the amout of the bribe that he had to pay to acquire the fortress.[37]

At this point the royal council, concerned about Hunyadi's increasing power, called the diet into session. When it met on March 12, 1447, it attempted to balance the power of the regent with that of the rest of the barons. It stipulated that, at an annual session held on the day of Epiphany, every official, including the regent, would have to face reelection. On the other hand, the diet freed Hunyadi from the tutelage of the commission entrusted with the collection of the royal revenues, making him free to collect as well as spend these revenues as he saw fit. The diet also declared that, since it had elected László V king, there was to be no further discussion about the succession. Those who were disturbing the internal peace with such talk, were to be judged guilty of treason without the possibility of pardon. If the young king were to die, the royal council and the representatives of the counties were to meet and choose another ruler. Furthermore, it was stated that the royal revenues over which the regent had control until the coming of age of the sovereign consisted only of the *lucrum camerae;* this was to be collected in cash only, and all noblemen were exempted from paying it. It was from these revenues, along with the private income of the regent, that the defense of the realm would have to be financed. The diet also insisted that, although the regent appointed the counts, he had to seek the advice of the royal council on each appointment. Appointments to clerical offices were to follow the same procedure.[38]

The internal balance of forces thus settled, the diet disbanded, but it left behind many unresolved problems for Hunyadi to tackle. The most important of these was the struggle with the emperor. A new delegation including the palatine and Cardinal Széchi went to see the emperor to take up the negotiations where they had left off. Their efforts were reinforced by the pope, who sent strongly worded letters to both the emperor and Hunyadi urging them to come to terms. The emperor himself was now anxious to establish some sort of peace with the Hungarians, since he planned to travel to Rome to be crowned Holy Roman emperor by the pope. However, he continued to haggle with the delegation, and the negotiations dragged on and on.

Hunyadi had begun to plan for his next move in the south. He sent one of his retainers, Károly Csupor, to Moldavia with an army to secure the province for his candidate, Peter. The army destroyed Peter's opponents and installed him as prince of Moldavia. In return, the new prince gave Hunyadi the fortress of Chilia. Located at the delta of the Danube River, this fortress was an important strategic base for any continued effort against the Ottoman Empire.

Meanwhile, the Hungarian delegation to Frederick III had achieved a minor breakthrough. They agreed on a two-year armistice, beginning on June 8, 1447, which confirmed the transfer of Győr to Hungarian jurisdiction and the compensation previously promised the emperor. This freed Hunyadi from the threat of war in the west, removed the constraints that the control of that important fortress by the emperor placed on trade with Austria, and enabled Hunyadi to start looking for ways to arrange another Ottoman campaign. But Hunyadi was still being delayed, partly by the ticklish problem of the archbishopric of Kalocsa. The holder of this see, Joannes Buondelmonte, had died in early 1448. Hunyadi's first candidate for the bishopric was his personal friend Nicholas Lasocki, a Polish prelate who had come to Hungary with Wladislaw I and stayed on after the death of the king. He had acted as Hunyadi's envoy to Rome during the struggle for the appointment of János Vitéz to the bishopric of Nagyvárad. It was important for Hunyadi to have another one of his friends occupy the second most prestigious see in the realm, since the archbishop of Esztergom, Dénes Cardinal Széchi, was a member of the Cilli-Garai-Branković league. Lasocki first accepted, then declined Hunyadi's offer. According to Vilmos Fraknói,[39] he was unwilling to take up the bishop's miter because it would have involved him in considerable difficulties with some of the nobles who had usurped properties belonging to the bishopric. Instead, he recommended that the bishop of Transylvania be transferred to Kalocsa and that he himself be appointed bishop of that ecclesiastical province. Lasocki himself carried this proposal to Rome in 1448, but while there, he changed his mind once again and now wanted no bishopric of his own at all. Thus, Hunyadi made another recommendation to the pope; he wanted Mátyás, the bishop of Transylvania to be appointed archbishop of Kalocsa and chose Vince, a canon of Nagyvárad, obviously a protege of Vitéz, for the bishopric of Vác. Pope Nicholas V approved all these recommedations.[40]

However, this did not solve all the problems. The Bishop of Transylvania did not want the transfer. Hunyadi turned to the pope once again, asking that the Holy See require that Mátyás accept the new appointment, but the pope had had enough; he simply declined to make yet another appointment. Thus, while Ágmándi become archbishop of Kalocsa and the canon Vince bishop of Vác, Mátyás was left bishop of Transylvania. However, fate once again intervened. Ágmándi died before his appointment was confirmed, and Hunyadi recommended the appointment of another of his supporters, Raphael Herceg, the former bishop of Bosnia (whose see was now largely in Ottoman hands). This was confirmed by the pope in September 1450.

Another complication was presented by the death of Lőrinc Hédervári. A session of the diet originally called to deal with the agreement reached with Frederick III instead faced the task of choosing a new palatine. The diet proceeded to elect László Garai, one of Hunyadi's major opponents, in his place. Hunyadi was removed from the governorship of Transylvania, and Ujlaki and Imre Pelsőci were jointly appointed to that position. However, the diet transferred control of the fortress of Buda from the jurisdiction of the palatine to that of Hunyadi, a step that may have been prompted by Garai's previous role in the theft of the Holy Crown from the fortress of Visegrád. At the same time, a new delegation, headed by Cardinal Széchi, was charged with resuming negotiations with the emperor. Hunyadi had no choice but to go along with these changes. The conclusion that one must draw from the resolutions of the diets of 1447 and 1448 is that his authority had shaky foundations. His plan for a peaceful solution to the internal rivalries and his efforts at securing the southern and western borders were checked by a coalition of barons in the royal council and the hesitation of the lesser nobility to support him in the diet. It seems that a consensus had emerged that the regent was becoming too powerful. It also seems that the emperor accurately gauged the true state of affairs in the Kingdom of Hungary. Thus, when he refused even to discuss giving up control over László V and the Holy Crown, he was in fact practicing *Realpolitik.*

It was under these circumstances that it must have dawned on Hunyadi that Frederick III's game might be turned to his own advantage. If the emperor was so anxious to keep the young king of Hungary under his control and out of the Kingdom, so much the better. This would at least deprive Hunyadi's enemies of a new focus of power around which they could rally. From then on, Hunyadi was no longer anxious to reclaim the king from the emperor, although he was to go through the motions for the benefit of his opponents. He was determined to use the regency to make his family's position so strong in the realm that no coalition of barons, not even one led by the king (if he were ever freed), would be able to harm it. In this he nearly succeeded. He seems to have recognized, at the same time, that a corollary of this policy was the need for a great victory on the Ottoman front. If, as regent, he could repeat his earlier successes, he would once again be hailed as the savior of the realm, and all opposition to his regency would be silenced. This was surely at the bottom of his insistence on a new Ottoman campaign in 1448.

The diet did authorize a new campaign, but Hunyadi had to rely on his own resources if he wanted to bring it about. He still hoped for support from the West. Although the papacy remained locked in a struggle with the Council of Basel and participated in the power-struggle over control of the Italian peninsula, the pope could still offer a great deal to the Hungarians, but he had neither money nor soldiers to spare for an Ottoman campaign. Instead, he made Hunyadi a prince. Hunyadi never used this title, showing how much he cared for it.[41] Although Pope Nicholas V made some vague promises about paying the salaries of four thousand mercenaries, they remained only promises.[42] The other Western powers were preoccupied with their own problems. Genoa and Venice continued to show lack of interest in tangling with their trading partner in a war. Alfonso I, king of Naples, promised 100,000 florins as part of a scheme that included the prospect of having his son elected King of Hungary. There is no evidence that this promise was ever kept, although Alfanso did send three beautiful horses for Hunyadi.[43]

Hunyadi himself spoke of recruiting forty thousand soldiers for the planned campaign, but he did not have the resources. Besides, he had to depend upon the royal council for funds for a campaign outside the borders of the Kingdom, and the council was in no mood to make large sacrifices. According to Marino Sanuto the available military forces for a campaign outside Hungary were around forty thousand men. In comparison, Sanuto estimated that the Ottoman Empire could muster ten times as many soldiers in an emergency and half as many for an offensive outside its own territories.[44] These numbers are, of course, only the estimates of a frightened contemporary, and it is certain that it was not always possible for either side to muster as many soldiers and Sanuto thought. Thus, Hunyadi's chance for success lay in the possibility of coordinating his campaign with that of the Albanians, the new princes of Wallachia and Moldavia, and possibily even Branković. Although the diet met in April 1448 and it did authorize the use of the *lucrum camerae* against the Ottomans, this was not nearly enough to hire and equip the necessary number of mercenaries. In any case, Hunyadi spent most of the month of September at the ford of Kevi, with János Vitéz, waiting for his army to gather for its thrust into the Balkans. The new Wallachian prince, Dan, appeared there with eight thousand men. Branković, in contrast, not only refused his support but he actively sided with the sultan. The Serbian despot harbored many resentments against Hunyadi. He was an important member of the Cilli league, and in addition, was more afraid of the sultan than he was of Hunyadi. He was also appalled by the small size of Hunyadi's army. To complicate matters, the regent, upon learning of Branković's reluctance, threatened the despot that, after his return from the Balkans, he would have him deposed.[45]

The army crossed the Danube into Serbia on 28 September. While on the march, Hunyadi received a letter from the pope suggesting the postponement of the campaign until the next year, "when he could offer more help." He answered with a bitter note, an important document of his motives for the anti-Ottoman campaign of 1448:

> ...the enemy attacks our neighbors, incites (them) to war against us. We have decided to attack him instead of waiting for him to attack us: We have had enough of our men enslaved, our women raped, wagons loaded with the severed heads of our people, the sale of chained captives, the mockery of our religion: ...I am worried that our struggle with the Turk will bring into the war the entire territory of Asia: ...But we shall not stop until we succeeded in expelling the enemy from Europe....[46]

More than any of his contemporaries, Hunyadi understood the nature of the Ottoman threat to Hungary, and he had the right ideas about dealing with it. This letter simply showed his determination. The problem was that not all the lords shared his views, and he himself simply could not accept that his forces alone were no longer sufficient to deal with the situation.

Hunyadi's army eventually numbered twenty-four thousand, including eight thousand Wallachians, under the command of Dan and several thousand mercenaries, most of them armed with muskets.[47] Many of the great lords accompanied him to the Balkans; besides the Wallachian prince, these included Imre Pelsőci, his brother, László, the Count of Gömör County, Frank Thallóczi, military governor of Croatia and Dalmatia, János Székely, military governor of Slavonia and Hunyadi's nephew, Imre Marcali, the royal steward, Rajnald Rozgonyi, Tamás Széchi, Bebek Losonci, and

István Lendvai-Bánfi.[48] The armament of the troops was excellent; according to Chalcocondylas, there were about two thousand battlewagons, manned by two infantrymen each, one to handle the canon and the other to protect him.[49] This time around, Hunyadi's preparations were painstaking and detailed. According to some historians, this was probably the best-armed and prepared army that he had ever commanded against the Ottomans.[50]

Sultan Murad II was spending the summer of 1448 on a campaign of his own in Albania. His army had destroyed much of the countryside and besieged Skanderbeg's main fortress at Kroja. On receiving a message from Branković about Hunyadi's plans, Murad broke off the siege and hurried to Sofia, where he summoned his troops to join him from all over the empire.[51] He had about a month and a half for preparations before Hunyadi crossed the Danube. He declared a jihad and collected a large number of troops from Europe and Asia. His army was certainly larger than that of Hunyadi, but its exact size is unknown. He must have had more than the sixty thousand soldiers that were reported.[52] Some of the janissaries were now armed with muskets, and there was also a small artillery contingent. Larger did not necessarily mean better; the Ottoman chronicler remarked that all the horse thieves from Karaman had come to join the army.[53]

Hunyadi's plans were far-reaching. His ultimate goal was, as before, the expulsion of the Ottomans from Europe. As he wrote to the pope in the letter quoted above, "it is necessary for us to go into the lands held by the enemy, not just to stop him on the banks of the Danube. Our purpose is not simply to wage war, but to finish it once and for all." He was, of course, much too realistic a commander not to know that he could not accomplish this with the small army under his command. At the same time, he knew that a decisive victory over the sultan would help him both personally and as the regent of Hungary. Thus, his initial aim may have been to secure Macedonia and through this, free Skanderbeg to join him in the campaign against the Ottoman Empire.[54] The liberation of Macedonia would also have cut the Ottoman Empire in Europe in two, making it easier for the Venetians and Genoans to gain control of the western Balkans and the endangered islands in the Aegean and Mediterranean Seas. Consequently, Hunyadi did not follow the previous route to Edirne. He turned toward Kosovo-Polje, the battlefield on which

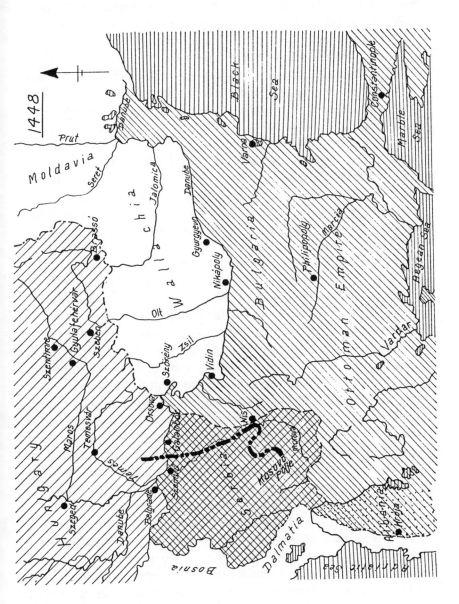

Hunyadi's route to Kosovo Polje.

Murad I's army had destroyed the united armies of Serbia and Bosnia in 1389. The Kačaniki Pass, separating Macedonia from Kosovo, was only forty kilometers away, and thus a united Albanian-Hungarian army could easily reach Macedonia in less than two days' march.[55]

Kosovo-Polje (Rigómező in Hungarian or the Field of Blackbirds) lies in the center of an imaginary square whose corners are Ragusa, Sofia, Belgrade, and Salonika. It is a plain about 40 kilometers long, and 15-17 kilometers wide, surrounded on all sides by the Balkan Mountains. The plain is a watershed; it is also watered by several streams and the Sitnitsa River. In Hunyadi's time, there were several villages in this area, the largest of which was called Priština and lay about 11 kilometers east from the river. The southeastern end of the plain is dominated by a hill about 10 kilometers long and some 25-30 meters high. There was a memorial on this hill commemorating the death of Sultan Murad I at the hand of a Serbian soldier, Milos Obilić, in the first battle of Kosovo. The strategic value of the hill was obvious in Hunyadi's time.

Hunyadi did not plan to fight a battle on the Kosovo-Polje. When he arrived he did not know that the sultan's army was on its way to meet him there. He ordered a rest for his tired troops and waited for the arrival of the Albanians. On October 17 the advance guard of Murad II's army appeared on the northern edge of the plain. Its line of march led it toward Pristina, about three and a half kilometers from Murad I's hill. If Hunyadi did not stop it, it would soon control the strategically dominant position and would be able to block the valley of the Sitnitsa. Thus, Hunyadi decided to defend the hill and, though his light cavalry was equal to the task, this meant that he could not delay an engagement with the main army. Consequently, he ordered his battlewagons to form a fortress on top of the hill to serve as a basis for both attack and defense. He set up all his heavy cavalry in two lines in front of this fortress, having the advantage of being able to sweep down the hill if necessary.[56]

The Ottoman lines extended from one end of the plain to another. The left wing included all the European cavalry and some infantry and was probably commanded by Halil Pasha.[57] The second line comprised the center, while the third included the baggage train. Murad had learned from his previous experience at Varna, when most of his cavalry had run away; this time he had surrounded his camp with a rampart and armed the porters.

The battle began on October 18 with Hunyadi's light cavalry attacking the Ottoman left wing, and the struggle seesawed all day long. Although the Ottoman sipahis did run away as they had in 1444, they were prevented from escaping to the rear by the fortified baggage camp. This forced them to turn toward the mountains, but here they were confronted by the aroused local peasantry, who killed some of them, and the survivors eventually returned to the sultan's camp. Thus, when Hunyadi thought that much of the Ottoman cavalry had been dispersed by the end of the day, he was mistaken. During the evening lull, Hunyadi called a council of war. Daud Celebi, a grandson of Murad I,[58] recommended that the sultan's camp be attacked at night, and Hunyadi agreed.[59] He led the surprise attack himself and made some headway during the initial confusion, but the sultan's army recovered and the engagement ended in a draw. Hunyadi's troops returned to their camp after fighting most of the night, but they were exhausted.

The next morning the battle was renewed, but now the sultan threw his rested Asian cavalry into the fight. Hunyadi was still able to hold his own, but the Ottomans were slowly gaining the upper hand. Finally, Hunyadi's heavy cavalry made a concerted attack on the center of the janissaries' line. The charge carried them through, but when they reached the baggage camp with its armed defenders they were surrounded by Ottoman troops and destroyed. As this point the Wallachians, who were on the left wing of Hunyadi's army, were surprised from behind by the troops of Turkhan Bey, and most of them were massacred. The confusion generated by the double disaster was compounded by the death of János Székely. The battle was soon over; the Ottomans were victorious. More than seventeen thousand of Hunyadi's men were killed or captured, including most of the barons who had accompanied him, and the entire Wallachian contingent.[60]

The sultan's army had also suffered heavy casualties, and consequently he did not order the pursuit of the fleeing enemy. Those who fled toward Albania were the luckiest; within 30 kilometers of Kosovo-Polje they met the troops of Skanderbeg, who were on their way to join Hunyadi. The Albanians protected them and helped them to get back to Hungary.[61] Hunyadi himself was not so lucky. He escaped toward Serbia, but his horse gave out and he had to walk. He was captured for a time by Ottoman booty-seekers, but they did not recognize him and he eventually escaped.

As he traveled through Branković's realm, he ran into the despot's men, who took him to Szendrő and here he was imprisoned by his old enemy.[62]

The news of Hunyadi's survival and escape soon reached Hungary. The royal council moved to Szeged and began bargaining with Branković for his freedom. This was a far cry from the prompt action taken by Hédervári after the battle of Varna. The council was apparently no longer as enthusiastic about the regent as before. Its baronial members considered his predicament a golden opportunity to trim his power even further. The regent was freed at the end of December 1448 and arrived at Szeged on Christmas Day. Here he found his powers severely restricted. First of all, he was compelled to return to Branković all of the properties that he had acquired or took away from him. He had to consent to the betrothal of his younger son, Mátyás, to Elisabeth Cilli, the granddaughter of Branković, and send his older son, László, as a hostage to Szendrő.

After the defeat of Kosovo, Hunyadi was no longer able to enforce his policies in the realm. His party was permanently weakened by the death of many of his supporters at Kosovo-Polje. He was never again able to muster the support of the lesser nobility for his schemes of defense of the Kingdom of Hungary and was forced into all sorts of compromises with his baronial opponents.

VIII

STRUGGLE FOR SURVIVAL

The defeat of Kosovo-Polje had grave and lasting consequences. Hunyadi's earlier attempts at strengthening centeral authority—that is, his own—in the Kingdom of Hungary had to be abandoned. He was now barely able to hold on to the regency. Although at least one historian had suggested that even after Kosovo-Polje, his basic aims remained the same,[1] this was not really the case. He had to give up his post as military governor of Transylvania and abandon his efforts to create a strong affinity of interests with the lesser nobility. His attempt to come to an understanding with the free cities had come to nothing, and he was never again able to muster the necessary forces for an invasion of the Balkans. His later forays were little more than holding actions, until his last great campaign in defense of Belgrade in 1456.

Hungary's chaotic internal situation paralleled the decline of Hunyadi's prestige. It was during this time—now that it was too late—that his earlier role as the keeper of internal peace was fully revealed, at least for later historians. The great lords had now lost all fear of him, and their depradations increased. Paradoxically, the same lords were anxious to establish peaceful relations with the Ottoman Empire in order to have an even freer hand inside the Kingdom of Hungary. It should not be surprising, therefore, that they did everything they could at Szeged in December 1448 to discourage Hunyadi from breaking the agreement that freed him from

Branković's capitivity. They were afraid that, if Hunyadi regained possession of Branković's estates in Hungary, he would soon recover his balance and once again become too powerful for their liking. Arguing that the Hussites of Peter Komorowski and the mercenaries of Jan Jiškraz were causing a great deal of damage in the north, they insisted that the suppression of these bandits whould have priority. Thus, the royal council forced Hunyadi to give up for the time being any such plans.

Perhaps, from the pont of view of the interest of the *regnum,* the royal council was right. The regent had hardly arrived at Szeged when he ordered his envoy to the papal curia to report that the defeat had not broken his spirit and that he would soon be ready to resume the offensive against the Ottomans. However, although this talk contributed to the fears of the royal council, the fact was that the resources of the Kingdom were exhausted and Hunyadi could not possibly organize another large scale campaign. It was not only the defeat of Kosovo-Polje, but the internal dissentions and the depradations of the Hussites in the north that had sapped the strength of the Kingdom of Hungary. For Hunyadi to focus his activities on the south once again—and especially for him to regain his supremacy over Branković—would not have benefitted the *regnum,* at least not immediately, because if nothing else Kosovo-Polje had proved that it was no longer possible to defeat the forces of the Ottoman Empire in open battle with numerically inferior armies. The massed troops of the sultan, armed with cannon and muskets, could now prevail in a protracted fight simply by their overwhelming numbers. The Kingdom of Hungary alone could not match the sultan's army without outside help, and this was not forthcoming. Thus, the royal council's insistence that Hunyadi abandon any plans for a Balkan campaign were realistic. The trouble for Hunyadi was that this decision left him hostage to an agreement with Branković that had been extorted from him under duress.

Having no choice, then, he turned the disputed estates over to their original owner, sent his elder son to Szendrő, and engaged his younger son to Elisabeth Cilli. He sacrificed Demeter Csupor, accepted Benedict Zólyomi as bishop of Zagreb, and consented that the Cillis be confirmed as joint military governors of Croatia and Slavonia.[2] In turn, the royal council instructed Branković to seek immediate peace with the sultan.[3] In vain did Hunyadi call the diet into session in June 1449 to put pressure on the council to change its views; his former allies among the lesser nobility refused to support him at the session. Finally, he had to agree to the approach to the sultan for peace, but his agreement ultimately did not matter; it seems that the offer that the royal council transmitted to Branković was so one-sided that the Serbian despot did not dare to present it to the sultan.[4] Branković may have had other motives as well. He was undoubtedly suspicious that if the Ottoman threat were removed from Hungary so soon after Kosovo-Polje, the regent would have more time and room to maneouver and would eventually be able to turn against him.[5]

Hunyadi did make an effort to rebuild the shattered alliance system with some of the rulers of small Balkan states that he had so painstakingly constructed before Kosovo-Polje. In this he had some success; for instance, the prince of Bosnia, Twatrko, renewed their alliance in November 1449, and Peter, the prince of Moldavia, followed suit in February 1450. The most important aspect of these agreements was reviving the early warning system of Ottoman troop movements that had played such an important role in Hunyadi's previous plans.[6]

After the Szeged meeting of the royal council was over, Hunyadi sent a letter to the pope describing the new situation as it had developed since his return to Hungary. The pontif's answer was delivered by a Pauline monk, Bálint Kapusi, a minor confessor at the curia sent to Hungary to take possession of the abbey of Dömös. When he received the papal letter, Hunyadi called the diet into session, ostensibly to discuss the message but most likely as part of his continuing campaign against the policies of the royal council. The tone of the papal letter, urging restraints on the Hungarians and suggesting that they postpone any further attack on the Ottoman Empire until they had established domestic peace, only strengthened the lesser nobility's reluctance to support Hunyadi's plans.[7] The diet was, however, at least disposed to comment on the papal letter; it noted with surprise the pope's suggestion of caution in dealing with the Ottomans, failing to mention that there was already an effort under way to arrange a truce with the sultan. The prince of Wallachia, instead of Branković, was now acting as a middleman, and actually succeeded in arranging a truce that lasted through 1450. Both parties benefited from the pause in the hostilities; the sultan continued to receive tribute from the Balkan principalities, and the Hungarians had a chance to put their own house in order.⁸ Hunyadi, in accordance with the wishes of the royal council, turned his attention to the north.

Since Hunyadi's power had diminished so drastically that it could not threaten theirs, the Counts Cilli had made an honest effort to cooperate with him. This was evident in a case in Croatia involving the Blagays. Members of this family were feuding with each other in Zagreb County and one of them had called on the Cillis for armed support. Ulrich von Cilli notified Hunyadi of the problem and asked for his advice in dealing with it. Hunyadi recommended restraint and neutrality, and Cilli acted accordingly.⁹ But the spirit of reconciliation between these two great lords did not last. They harbored deep suspicion of each other's motives, and long lasting cooperation between them could not really be expected. Hunyadi was now determined to settle the problem of northern Hungary, hoping that once this was accomplished, he would be able to move against Branković. However, he did not take into account all the factors that favored Jiškraz. The Czech was so well entrenched in northern Hungary that only a major campaign, using the united forces of the crown and the nobility, could dislodge him. Jiškraz was not only an astute military commander but a good politician. He was successful in gaining the voluntary cooperation of the northern cities, something that had always eluded Hunyadi. The cities, whose burghers were more attracted to the side of László V, were also sympathetic to Jiškraz, who was allegedly acting in the name of the young king. They paid taxes to Jiškraz in exchange for his protection against aristocratic encroachments. His alliance with the cities provided Jiškraz with sufficient funds to become virtually independent. Like Hunyadi in the rest of the realm, he acted as regent in the north. He used force judiciously where persuasion did not work. His main problem was that he was unable to discipline the freebooters who joined him in the highlands, such as the troops of Peter Komorowski and the highwayman Axamit.

Hunyadi's aim was not simply the destruction of the freebooters. He wanted to bring Jiškraz to his knees. He sent Tamás Székely with a small army to accomplish this in the mistaken belief that this would suffice. However, Székely's troops were surprised in their camp and dispersed without serious resistance. Now Hunyadi decided to move against Jiškraz. He took the small fortress of Moldva, near Kassa, inflicting terribly cruel punishment on the captured defenders; he had each of them blinded in one eye and their ears and hands cut off. Still, Jiškraz did not offer peace. Hunyadi turned west and marched through Gömör County toward the city of Körmöc, loyal to the Czech general. Jiškraz had already supplied the city, famous for its mint, with plenty of arms and provisions, and Hunyadi failed to take it. In the meantime, envoys had reached him including the Polish cleric and historian Joannis Dlugosz (Longini), offering to mediate the dispute with Jiškraz.[10] Hunyadi made an attempt during the negotiations to attract Jiškras to come over to his side and offered mutually advantageous terms but these terms were not fulfilled and fighting resumed. The skirmishes were indecisive small engagements, hit-and-run affairs, and faints. Finally, negotiations were resumed in March 1450 and an agreement was reached, but Hunyadi apparently considered it only a means to gain time. As a sign of his real intentions, he offered protection to Pongrác Szentmiklósi against the forces of Cilli, who were besieging this robber baron in his fortress of Szakolca.[11] Hunyadi was obviously worried that, if Szakolca fell, Cilli and Jiškraz would be able to establish a united front against him. His condition was, therefore, that Szentmiklósi transfer the fortress to his forces in exchange for the protection that he would extend to the baron. Thus, a stalemate was created, each side keeping a wary eye on the other.

In June 1450, Hunyadi took a step to strengthen his position: he concluded an agreement with László Garai to consider each other "brothers" and coordinate their actions in cases were their interests coincided. If one or the other would die, the surviving partner would support his heirs to the best of his ability. Miklós Ujlaki was invited to join this new alliance and accepted, giving it extra weight and importance.[12] The pretext for the agreement was the liberation of László V from the hands of the emperor, but it was obvious that its real aim was to keep the partners in control of their respective spheres of influence.

Hunyadi proceeded in late October to occupy the fortress of Pozsony, over the protest of its citizens.[13] It commanded one of the most important trade routes to Austria and its occupation also helped Hunyadi to isolate Jiškraz from his allies. Moreover, it was likely that, if László V were freed, he would want to reside in Pozsony, as suggested by his father's last testament, and possession of the fortress would give Hunyadi added influence at the royal court.

He also succeeded in persuading the royal council to finally permit him to move against Branković for his behavior in 1448. The council was by now dissatisfied with the despot because he had failed to arrange the desired truce with the Ottoman Empire. Hunyadi was therefore permitted to occupy the despot's estates in Hungary and to begin military preparations for the freeing of his older son from Szendrő. To acquire the money to accomplish all this, he persuaded the council to accept a brilliant scheme. A joint letter was sent to Rome requesting that the Hungarians be permitted to celebrate the holy year of 1450 not only by going on pilgrimages to Rome, but also by visiting the schrines of the Holy Kings, St. István and St. László in Székesfehervár and Nagyvárad respectively. They suggested that the pilgrims to these shrines receive the same indulgences and blessings as those who went to Rome. The donations they would make at the shrines would then be used for the planned Ottoman wars.[14] This was, of course, a ruse; Hunyadi wanted to use the funds so collected against Branković. The pope agreed to this suggestion on the condition that only high lords and prelates should receive such benefits, lesser nobles, peasants and women being excluded. However, when the royal council and Hunyadi protested, the pope eventually agreed to permit everyone to participate in the pilgrimages and receive appropriate benefits. Thus, funds were gained for the replenishment of the treasury.[15]

When Branković learned of the preparations against him, he immediately freed László Hunyadi and canceled the agreement of Szendrő. He also proposed that his and Hunyadi's representatives get together to settle all their differences.[16] He was influenced not only by Hunyadi's obvious determination to get even with him, but also by the alliance the regent had formed with Garai and Ujlaki. Hunyadi was amenable to such discussions, but this did not mean that he would entirely forget the past. There was at least, however, a chance and willingness on both sides to come to terms, and this could only benefit the Kingdom.

In reviewing Hunyadi's actions following the defeat at Kosovo-Polje, one must say that these were at least consistent. For two years he strove to nullify the agreement with Branković forced on him by the despot, and in this he had finally succeeded. He was unable to change the emperor's mind about restoring the forts and other properties that he held in western Hungary to the control of the regent or to expell Jiškraz from the north. His alliance with the lesser nobility and the cities, such as it was, crumbled, and his next step grew out of this uncertain situation.

In October 1450, Hunyadi concluded an agreement with Frederick III in which Garai took part. This agreement left the emperor legally in possession of the disputed properties and confirmed his guardianship of László V, but it also stipulated that, before the emperor freed the young king from his supervision, he was to notify Hunyadi of his intention and arrange to turn the king over to him. The stated purpose of this agreement was that it would provide the regent with the opportunity to give the young man the advice he would undoubtedly need when he became the ruler of the Kingdom of Hungary.[17] The real purpose was, however, clear: it gave Hunyadi imperial assurance that he would be able to retain his influence in the realm even after his regency came to an end. Hunyadi in turn recognized the emperor as "his lord" and accepted László V's right to the throne by inheritance.

Hunyadi actually gained little by this agreement. It is true that the emperor implicitly recognized his influence even after the freeing of the king, but there was nothing in the agreement that compelled him to keep his word. As it happened, both he and Hunyadi broke their promises. The fact was that Hunyadi no longer had the resources to fight the emperor, but he was still anxious to safeguard the prerogatives of the Hungarian crown, and an opportunity was soon provided him. When the papal curia interfered with an appointment to a church office, Hunyadi seized the opportunity to manouver the royal council and the diet to take his side.

The conflict emerged around the abbey of Dömös. About twenty-five kilometers south of the archbishop's see at Esztergom, at the insignificantly small village of Dömös, King Béla I had had a small summer residence built during the 1060s. Later in that decade, however, the house had collapsed, burying and killing the king under the rubble. Half a century after that tragic event, Prince Álmos, brother of King Kálmán, had had an abbey built upon the site, probably in order to commemorate the tragedy, and had had it richly endowed. However, the prince had soon found himself in trouble with his royal brother, and the king had him and his son, Béla, blinded. The two had taken up residence in the abbey of Dömös, where the monks cared for them. When Béla II (the Blind) succeeded his uncle on the throne, he had the buildings of the abbey expanded and rebuilt the church. He had further rewarded the monks for their hospitality by new endowments. According to Vilmos Fraknói, the income of the abbey was soon serving the interests of high ranking clerics at the royal court or members of the aristocratic families.[18] In time, this had led to the dissolution of the abbey and its abandonment by the monks.

King Sigismund, intent on reviving the abbey, had invited monks from the Italian order of the Holy Virgin of Mount Olive in 1433. He had visited some of the abbeys of this order while traveling in Italy and had been deeply impressed by the piety and devotion exhibited by the monks. However, the Italian order had sent only a few monks, with their abbot, Bernardin Philipponi, to Dömös. The abbot had died in 1441, and his successors had proved unable to defend the properties of their abbey against lordly encroachments. They had also complained about the harshness of the climate in Hungary for which they had not been prepared. Thus, in 1445, the monks had left the abbey and returned to Italy. In the chaos that followed the death of Wladislaw I, they lost all hope for prosperity and tranquility, and their abbot turned jurisdiction over the abbey to the pope.

The trouble started when Bálint Kapusi, the Pauline monk from the curia mentioned above, asked the pope and received the abandoned abbey on behalf of his order. As it turned out, the Paulines had not asked Kapusi to do this. Another cleric by the name of Benedek Fábián also asked the pope for the abbotship of Dömös, and he was also granted the appointment. When Kapusi learned of this, he turned to Pope Eugene IV once more and had his rival's claim annulled.[19] The patent of donation for him was never issued, however; Pope Eugene IV died on February 23, 1447, before he could sign it. Bálint appealed to the new pope, Nicholas V, who finally issued the appropriate document, turning the abbey into a Pauline monastery. He also removed the abbey from all other clerical jurisdication but his own and charged the archbishop of Esztergom with carrying out this decision.

However, Kapusi's troubles were not yet over. The abbey, having been established by a Hungarian prince, had its patronage vested in the king, the royal council, and ultimately the regent.[20] The pope's gift of the abbey to the Pauline monks was considered injurious to the rights of the Hungarian crown. It is possible that Hunyadi had known nothing of the goings-on in Rome concerning Dömös until he saw Kapusi's patent of papal donation. In any case, he and the royal council had other plans for the abbey. Since there was no cathedral chapter at Buda by which state documents issued by the crown's representatives could be notarized, they had decided to use the revenues of the abbey of Dömös for the establishment of such a chapter. Hunyadi as regent, relying on his power of royal patronage, appointed István Bothos as abbot.[21] Bothos was a friend of Bishop Vitéz; they had served together in the chancellery of King Sigismund during the 1430s. After the death of Albert I in 1439, Bothos had sided with the Queen Erzsébet, but on her death he had gone over to the side of Wladislaw I. As a result of this—and some good political sense—he had acquired three ecclesiastical benefices at the same time. He was canon of Vác and Nagyvárad, and provost of the cathedral chapter of St. István at Esztergom. He also held the post of chief notary public of the Kingdom of Hungary, an office previously held by Vitéz.

The conflict between the papacy, on the one hand, and Hunyadi and the royal council on the other, came into the open during the spring of 1449, when Kapusi arrived in Hungary with his breve. By then, the pope had learned about Hunyadi's choice for the post and disregarded it in siding with Brother Bálint. He charged the monk with establishing peaceful relations among the rival baronial factions in the Kingdom and promising papal support for another anti-Ottoman war. At the same time, Kapusi was to warn the Hungarians to postpone any hostile action in the Balkans until the appropriate number of soldiers could be recruited. Kapusi did a credible job of trying to promote reconciliation among the lords, but in an inadvertant direction; they all agreed to oppose papal interference in Hungarian affairs. The diet met in June 1450 and sent a strong letter of protest to Rome. The letter stated that the Hungarians would not accept interference with their rights of patronage, adding that, if the pope wanted to retain Hungary's loyalty, he had better not meddle in its affairs.

Eventually, a compromise was worked out. Kapusi returned to Rome and resigned from the abbotship. The pope established a new deanship at Buda and unified it with the abbey of Dömös; then he appointed Bothos as its first dean. Thus, both papal dignity and royal prerogatives were preserved; Hunyadi had his way and the authority of the pope was left intact.[22] But Hunyadi did not leave it at that; he proceeded to restrict the power of local churchmen in secular affairs.[23]

The struggle for political power in the kingdom did not stop while these matters were being concluded. Jiškraz was building new fortifications in the north, and Hunyadi's relations with Branković did not improve even though new negotiations to straighten out the situation were undertaken. In these talks Ujlaki and Pálóci represented the royal council while János Vitéz, László Orbovai, and János Berendi-Bak argued Hunyadi's case. According to the agreement that was finally reached, Hunyadi's younger son, Mátyás, was to marry Elisabeth Cilli on December 6, 1453. Most of Branković's estates were to be returned to him except the ones located in Bihar County. If the marriage did not take place for whatever reasons (including the refusal of the would-be bride to accept Mátyás as her husband, a remarkable concession to a woman in that age), Hunyadi was to take possession of all of Branković's estates. The only exception was if Elisabeth died before the marriage could take place. Cilli retained his governorship of Slavonia and Croatia, but Demeter Csupor became the bishop of Zagreb. Garai received the revenues of the convent of Vrana. In addition, his troops occupied the fortress of Ujdombró in the Mura-Sava Rivers region. The agreement stipulated that future conflicts among the parties would be submitted to a court of "honorable inhabitants of the realm" for adjudication.[24]

This was a propituous time for consolidating peace in the Kingdom of Hungary. Sultan Murad II had died on February 9, 1451, and his son, under the name of Mehemed II, had assumed the throne. He needed time to consolidate his authority in the Ottoman Empire and did not want any trouble with the Hungarians while doing so. The settlement with Branković and the prospect of peaceful relations with the Ottoman Empire freed Hunyadi for another attempt at eliminating Jiškraz from the highlands. This time he was determined to force the issue to its conclusion. Nothing showed his determination more than his insistence that as many of the barons as possible accompany him to the north. The barons who went along included László Hédervári, now bishop of Eger, László Pálóci, the lord chief justice, Simon Pálóci, the master of the royal stables, and Dénes Cardinal Széchi of Esztergom. It is, of course, difficult to know if it was Hunyadi who wanted to keep on eye on the lords or the other way around. In any case, Hunyadi's preparations were not adequate. One of the most important problems, the loyalty of the northern cities, was left unresolved, and Hunyadi had left most of his seasoned troops behind in the Great Plain.

On August 10, 1451, Hunyadi's army surrounded Szentkirály, Jiškraz's main fortress[25] near the city of Losonc. But the fortress withstood the siege until, on September 7, Jiškraz himself arrived with a small army. Hunyadi turned his troops around to face the new threat, but while he engaged Jiškraz his army was attacked from the rear. It seems that the contingent that he left behind to contain the besieged fortress had been surprised by the defenders and dispersed. It was later alleged that some of the barons had prearranged Hunyadi's defeat. In any case, Jiškraz triumphed and pushed the retreating Hunyadi as far south as Eger.[26]

The regent, however, was never discouraged by defeat in battle, and he collected his troops he had left on the Great Plain resuming the struggle. Now he forced Jiškraz to retreat and seek refuge among his northernmost strongholds. However, by this time the royal council had had enough of civil war. It initiated negotiations which resulted in a new treaty. Hunyadi was allowed to retain his gains, while Jiškraz's status was left to be decided by the future king.[27] Hunyadi never fought Jiškraz again.

This episode underscored the fundamental weakness of the regent's position. It was at this point that he took a step that was to have important consequences. He saw no alternative but to provide support for the liberation of László V from the emperor. This was a breach of the agreement with Frederick III. He must have known that if the effort were successful, some of his baronial rivals would gain great influence at the court of the young king at his expense, but he was obviously willing to take the risk. He probably hoped to be able to play off the two sides against each other. If the emperor held to their agreement, the king would be delivered into Hunyadi's hands, and he would undoubtedly be able to continue directing the affairs of the realm as before. If, on the other hand, the king were freed but not given into his hands, then his alliance with Garai, Ujlaki, and Branković would enable him to maintain his influence. He may also have hoped that more resources would be available in either case for the defense of the south, especially if Austria, Bohemia, and the Kingdom of Hungary were ruled by the same king. Since he expected to remain the real power in Hungary, he could then use these resources as he saw fit. In any case, the gains promised by the new situation seemed to outweigh the possible losses; but, in a situation like this nothing ever turns out as expected.

During the autumn of 1451, Frederick III went to Rome finally to have himself crowned emperor by the pope and to be married to Eleanor of

Portugal by the pontiff. He took László V with him, but he left behind an alienated Austrian nobility, deeply resentful of his expropriation of László V's Austrian revenues—in which the lords had hoped to share. The Austrian nobles were led by Ulrich von Eizinger, a former Bavarian lesser nobleman—now an Austrian lord—who induced them to form a government of their own. Eizinger contacted Hunyadi and George of Podiebrad, urging joint action against the emperor.

The Czechs and Hungarians were more cautious than the Austrians. They were quite willing to have László V liberated if someone else would do it. The Austrians, however, were determined to break the emperor's hold on their young king, and Hunyadi decided to lend his support to their efforts. He called the diet into session in Pozsony in late February 1452. On March 4, the Hungarian privileged orders decided to move to Vienna to join the Austrian nobles and there they agreed upon the need to liberate their young king. Count Cilli lent his support to this alliance.[28]

Frederick III, having been crowned in Rome, left for home in April, bringing his new bride and László V with him. When he reached Florence, a joint Austrian-Hungarian delegation visited him, requesting the release of László V into their hands, but he refused even to receive it. The nobles therefore saw no other alternative but to resort to force. When it came to action, however, only the Austrians were willing. Jiškraz, the self-proclaimed "captain of László V," would not lift a finger in his king's behalf. In June 1452, the troops of the Austrian nobles besieged Wiener-neustadt, where the emperor was staying, and forced him to give up László V. But Frederick III had the last laugh; instead of handing the boy over to Hunyadi or Eizinger, he gave him to Ulrich von Cilli, repaying both by strengthening the hand of their greatest opponent.

Cilli thus acquired an overwhelming influence over László V. He took his charge to Vienna, where they were received with great jubilation. The Austrian nobles, especially the Eizinger brothers, contested his influence in vain, at least for the time being. For the moment, the young king could be approached only through Cilli.[29] At the same time, Cilli insinuated that the Hungarian regent wanted to be king himself. In order to refute the charge, Hunyadi traveled to Vienna, arriving in early December, and on the 17th resigned the regency into the hands of the king. His sovereign rewarded him lavishly, appointing him chief captain of all the armed forces of the Kingdom of Hungary and perpetual count of

Beszterce, a label especially created for his fiefdom in Transylvania.[30] He was also entrusted with the handling of all royal revenues in the realm. His possessions were reconfirmed by a special royal patent, his older son was appointed military governor of Dalmatia, Croatia, and Slavonia together with Ulrich von Cilli. His close friend and confidant Bishop János Vitéz, was made head of the king's small (secret) chancellery. All these arrangements were ratified by a diet at Pozsony in February 1453. At this diet, the king took his coronation oath, confirming the traditions of Hungary.[32]

At first glance, Hunyadi's plans seemed to have been accomplished, and his position appeared to be as strong as ever.[31] Now he possessed authority granted him by the lawful king, and his possessions were secured. Although he was no longer regent, he was still in control of Hungary's armed forces. Furthermore, he no longer had to contend with Jiškraz, who had been relieved of his position by the king, a decision approved by the diet. He also seemed to be getting along with his chief rival, Ulrich von Cilli. This seems to have been the opinion of contemporaries; consequently, the rulers of Moldavia and Wallachia renewed their alliance with Hunyadi. Even such a veteran observer of international affairs as Piccolomini considered Hunyadi's position unshakable.[34]

However, this was only a surface appearance. The influence of Cilli over the young king was unchallengeable. His allies in Hungary, including Garai and Széchi, were given large estates as rewards for their earlier support of the king.[35] Cilli soon succeeded in exiling the Eizingers from court and inducing the young king to interfere directly with the authority that he had granted to Hunyadi.[36] This was especially obvious when the king ordered the chief captain to move against the Hussite troops of Axamit in northern Hungary in May 1453, at a time when news of the sultan's preparations for a large-scale campaign in the Balkans had been received at Buda. The king ordered László Hunyadi to accompany his father, suggesting that they use the troops of the barons—the same ones who had run away from Jiškraz during the previous campaign.[37]

While the court plotted to remove the only man capable of defending the Kingdom of Hungary against the Ottomans, events began to move quickly into the Balkans. On May 29, 1453, the sultan succeeded in capturing Constantinople, putting an end to the more than a thousand-year old Byzantine Empire. The shock waves of this event were felt all over Europe; its consequences for Hungary were severe indeed. At one stroke, Hunyadi's carefully cultivated system of early warning and defense collapsed. The peoples of the Balkans finally realized that no one was going to defend them against the Ottomans and began to move toward some sort of accommodation with the Muslim power. Moldavia's prince perceived the weakness of the Kingdom of Hungary and swore feudal loyalty to the king of Poland; Wallachia's friendship with Hunyadi became uncertain, to say the least.[38]

The Ottoman success forced the royal court to pause in its intrigues against Hunyadi. Cilli was temporarily removed, and the Eizingers were recalled to royal favor. Hunyadi was once again confirmed as chief captain and he accompanied the king to Prague in October for the latter's coronation as king of Bohemia. While they were in Prague, the papal envoy reached the king with the usual message: the following year there would be another large-scale campaign against the Ottomans to which the pope would contribute large sums of money. But the Hungarians had heard many such promises before. Hunyadi was more interested in concluding an alliance with George of Podiebrad and some Austrian and Czech lords including the Eizingers, the Sternbergs, and the Plankensteins. Although the alliance was approved by the king, it was obvious that its main aim was to provide as free a hand for these barons in their respective countries as possible. Hunyadi may also have hoped that the alliance would help him obtain resources for the defense of the south.[39] If this was his expectation, it was certainly not fulfilled. Since neither the Austrian nor the Bohemian nobles were directly threatened by the Ottomans, they were mostly interested in consolidating their own positions. László V cared the least of all about the Ottoman threat; he remained in Prague for over a year, amusing himself with the organization of all sorts of spectacles. The only advantage for Hunyadi was that he was relatively free to conduct the affairs of the realm while the king was away.

Hunyadi, thus, called the diet into session in late January 1454. As King Sigismund had before him, he tried to convince the nobles of the necessity of modernizing and expanding the armed forces with approximately the same result. In a surge of temporary enthusiasm the diet decided to set up an unusally large army, for the duration of one year. A committee of six lords, six prelates, and six lesser nobles was to supervise the organization of the troops, and these were to include the *banderia* of all the notables. The lesser noblemen were all to be required to join the troops in person. The size of the army was to be increased by contingents of armed peasants, equipped at the expense of the cities and market towns, and the troops of the Wallachians of Transylvania. Four peasant horsemen equipped with bows and arrows and two infantry swordsmen were to be sent for every hundred *portae* owned by the nobles. The committee was to keep an eye on the royal revenues, part of which were to be used for the maintenance of the army. No exception was to be granted to anyone, and huge fines were to be levied on those who disobeyed the command of the diet.[40]

However, not all the army would be required to fight the Ottomans outside the borders of the Kingdom of Hungary. Custom dictated that the lesser nobility could not be forced to do so. They were to supervise internal peace while the rest of the troops were fighting the enemy. An innovation concerned the introduction of virtual martial law while the army was in action. The regular courts were to cease operations during the time of war, and violent acts committed against persons or property were to be judged without delay by the officials of the counties.[41] But the enthusiasm of the nobility did not last long. Although some lesser noblemen did join Hunyadi's troops, there was no general mobilization, and no serious attempt was made to fulfill the decrees of the diet. Hunyadi had to rely on his own troops in the renewed skirmishes with the Ottoman raiders who were appearing in increasing numbers in the south.

The king himself did not fully understand the situation. His major concern seems to have been to get as much money out of the Kingdom as possible. For instance, he notified Hunyadi that, since Ulrich von Cilli declared his willingness to return to him the fortress of Trencsén and other fortresses along the Vág River (which King Albert had pawned to Cilli for 15,000 gold florins), for less than the original sum (13,000 florins) Hunyadi should advance him the money forthwith from the royal revenues.[42] It is, of course, likely that this was simply an excuse to get money. László V also called a diet into session immediately after the one of January and instructed it to form two committees, one consisting of eighteen members (six from each privileged order), to advise him on the collection and spending of royal revenues, the other to be stationed in Vienna for consultation by the king in all matters of governance.[43] This was clearly an attempt to reduce Hunyadi's influence in the realm, and it would have made him one of the advisers of the king—if he could manage to get himself elected to one of the committees.

It seems that the king had acted in this with the tacit approval of János Vitéz.[44] Vitéz was not being inconsistent in giving him such advice. As long as Hunyadi was the symbol of undivided royal authority, Vitéz was his strongest supporter. When he perceived that the chief captain was gradually becoming a rival of the king, dividing the realm and creating a shadow authority, he began to oppose him. When Hunyadi joined the Garai-Ujlaki-Branković alliance, Vitéz's fears seem to have been confirmed. Hunyadi's treaty with the Czech and Austrian lords could only reinforce his opinion. Thus, the relations between the two cooled at a time when their friendship was more necessary than ever for the good of the Kingdom.

When Hunyadi inquired about the meaning of the king's action, he could not get a straight reply. In fact the king denied that he intended to reduce Hunyadi's authority and claimed that the diet had acted without his approval,[45] but this was untrue. In any case, he did not think it improper to ask Hunyadi in the same letter for 3,000 florins for his travel expenses and 5,000 florins to pay the salary of his troops in the Szepesség, among whom the highwaymen of Axamit were now enrolled.[46] At the same time, he ordered the northern fortresses previously controlled by Jiškraz to be returned to the Czech soldier whom he had reappointed royal captain in the highlands. This was another move toward reducing Hunyadi's power.[47]

In April 1454, news reached Hunyadi that Sultan Mehemed II was preparing for another campaign. It was not clear at first which state he intended to attack, but the answer was not long in coming. In the early summer, large Ottoman formations appeared in Serbia. This was not a raid, but an all-out effort to conquer the country and attach it to the Ottoman Empire. The silver mines of Novobrdo were soon in Ottoman hands. In July the sultan's army reached Szendrő, Branković's capital, and laid siege to it.[48]

Hunyadi responded to the crisis with his customary speed, reaching Belgrade with his troops on August 7. His army was not large enough to engage the sultan in open battle, but he trusted in speed and harassing attacks. He marched swiftly to reach the hinterland of the sultan's army. In a few days he reached Trnava, having burned everything in his way.

This brought immediate results; the sultan retreated in haste to Sofia. Mehemed II was not yet sure of himself in the face of Hunyadi's determined opposition. He certainly did not want to become involved in chasing Hunyadi all over the Balkans. But he left a large detachment near Kruševac under the command of Firuz Bey with instructions to cause as much damage and terror as possible.[49]

While Hunyadi was on the move, he received important news. The Cillis had taken advantage of his preoccupation with the Ottomans and moved their troops to Croatia. However, Hunyadi's nephew, Tamás Székely, the abbot of Vrana, had beaten them back. Hunyadi also learned that on the same day the battle was fought, Friedrich von Cilli, Ulrich's father, had died in Saneck. Thus, fate had freed Hunyadi of one of his most ardent enemies.

The chief captain of Hungary now moved on to challenge Firuz Bey at Kruševac. During the last days of his approach, he moved his troops under cover of darkness. At dawn he attacked, completely surpising his opponent, and annihilated his contingent. His light cavalry pursued the fleeing Ottomans, capturing many including Firuz himself. His troops recpatured the silver mines of Novobrdo. Hunyadi then turned his captives over to Branković to be exchanged for Serbian captives in Ottoman hands.[50]

Although this battle did not involve the main Ottoman army, it had shown once again that Hunyadi could not be disregarded. It had also pointed to the fact that he no longer commanded the resources to engage the Ottomans in open battle. The lesson Mehemed drew from this encounter was that, without the elimination of Hunyadi's and his major allies' strongholds in Serbia, especially Szendrő, Galambóc and Belgrade, he could not expect to venture safely into the northern Balkans.

The internal situation of the Kingdom of Hungary continued to be uncertain. Ulrich von Cilli was recalled by the king to his court to become his confidant once again and the Eizingers were sent into limbo. In April 1455, Cilli renewed his previous alliance with Hunyadi's enemies signing a treaty of mutual aid with Ujlaki and Garai.[51] Hunyadi was all but powerless to influence events at court. Cilli renewed his intrigues against the chief captain, even trying to lure him to Vienna in order to have him murdered. Hunyadi soon made it clear that he wanted nothing to do with the court and he was concentrating on his personal affairs. In July 1455, the king appointed Jiškraz captain of the Körmöc mint and once again placed the northern towns under his jurisdiction.

It is a historical irony that Hunyadi, who had been so adamant about safeguarding royal prerogatives against encroachment by all only a few years before, was now compelled to refuse to accept the full authority of the king in Hungary. This was certainly understandable in personal terms, but not necessarily from the point of view of the interests of the realm. Traditional Hungarian historiography took Hunyadi's side in these matters arguing that this was really a contest between Hunyadi and Cilli and that the latter's personal ambitions were harmful to the Hungarian national interests. This argument was advanced, however, at a time when national interests were very different from those of the fifteeenth century. As far as Hunyadi's military plans were concerned, he was indeed a champion of the defense of the Kingdom of Hungary, but Cilli's efforts on behalf of the king—and, of course, himself—were comparable to those of Hunyadi on behalf of Wladislaw I. It is true that Hunyadi still considered that the best defense was in attacking Ottoman-held lands in the Balkans. It is also true that Cilli did not have the same dedication to defense as did the chief captain, but the lack of resources argued against Hunyadi's approach and not necessarily against Cilli's. In the final analysis, neither Hunyadi nor Cilli was a "Hungarian patriot" as some historians would have us believe. Each of these great lords was looking out for his own interests.

In June 1455, Hunyadi tried once again to interest the great lords in an anti-Ottoman campaign. At a session of the diet he argued that he would recruit 20,000 men in addition to his own 10,000, at the expense of royal revenues. He also recommended that the prince of Burgundi be asked to send another 10,000 men and the pope to contribute 20,000 soldiers to the common enterprise. If the Italian states jointly sent 30,000 and Branković contributed another 10,000 soldiers, he would have an army of 100,000, certainly large enough to expell the Ottomans from Europe. This army would have to be provided with only three months' worth of provisions. After that, it would be able to feed itself from requisitioned food.[52] This was, of course, wishful thinking, and Hunyadi must have been aware of it. It was more typical of this meeting that Giovanni da Capistrano, who was soon to play an important role in Hungarian affairs and who was also present at the diet, would have the temerity to

Struggle for Survival 153

suggest to Djuradj Branković that he should convert to Roman Catholicism if he wanted help against the Ottomans. At this, the old despot left the diet in anger.[53]

In the meantime, Cardinal Széchi had received instructions from Rome that he should vigorously pursue a course leading to the reconciliation between Hunyadi and his rivals. Capistrano was instructed to help the cardinal in this effort. As the result of their concerted prodding, a tentative agreement was reached on July 25, 1455, according to which the king would come to reside in Buda as soon as possible and further negotiations would be conducted under his personal supervision.[54]

While the great lords of László V bickered among themselves, Branković felt compelled to act. Since it was now obvious that he could not expect serious help from the Hungarians, and since he had no resources left to defend himself, he proceeded to conclude an agrement with the sultan that made him, in fact, a vassal of the Ottoman Empire. The sultan was for the moment engaged in the reorganization of his army and administration and was glad of the agreement. He had created a navy that embarked on the systematic conquest of the islands in the Mediterranean. His troops finally defeated Skanderbeg, and the sultan was now in control of the entire Dalmatian seacoast. Mehemed II, the Conqueror, felt that the time had arrived for the elimination of the last great foe on the European continent and the subjugation of the Kingdom of Hungary, stretching across the route of possible expansion of his empire into East Central Europe. Thus, he ordered the assembly of the imperial army from Europe and Anatolia in the spring of 1456 at Edirne. His first target was the fortress of Belgrade. He proclaimed that, once this fortress was taken, he would be able to eat his suppers in peace at Buda in less than two months' time.

The Hungarians received the news of the sultan's plans and were, as usual, unprepared for it. The king spent most of 1455 in Vienna. The great lords did not heed Hunyadi's warnings about the approaching danger. Typically, Garai notified Hunyadi that, because of the epidemic sweeping through his lands that spring, no troop movements were possible. The plague was indeed a serious matter—among others, it killed the intended bride of Mátyás Hunyadi, Elisabeth Cilli—but it was a lame excuse for not getting ready for the coming Ottoman onslaught.

The fearful summer of 1456 was, therefore, fast approaching without a glimmer of hope of stopping the seemingly invincible forces of the Ottoman Empire. Only Hunyadi refused to accept the "inevitable."

IX

THE PHOENIX

There were unconfirmed reports from various sources in the Balkan Peninsula as early as February 1456, that the sultan was preparing his army for an all-out assault on Szendrő or Belgrade.[1] Logically, this was to be expected. The sultan was now lord of the ancient Byzantine capital of Constantinople, but his empire was not yet secure in the north. Besides Venice and a possible coalition of the Italian city states, his only remaining opponent was the Kingdom of Hungary. The Holy Roman Empire was in no position to offer effective resistance, and the sultan was confident that he could now eliminate the Hungarians as a threat to his domination of the Balkans.[2] In February it was not yet clear whether the sultan intended to attack Serbia or Belgrade. The latter seemed the likely target. After Buda, it was the most important fortress in the path of Ottoman expansion, and its walls were reputed to be not as strong as those of Buda or Constantinople. It was not until April, however, that the Hungarians could be sure that the sultan had set his sights upon it.

The Hungarians were well aware of the danger. King László V called upon the diet to meet at Pest on January 13 to discuss a possible anti-Ottoman campaign. He was in Vienna when the call went out and promised to be present when the diet met.[3] But no one was in a hurry, not even the king. He left Vienna only in early February. When he arrived at Buda, only a few nobles were present at Pest, and he had to issue another urgent call to all the counties to assemble by the end of the month. We do not know when the diet finally began its deliberations, but by April 6 it was ready to vote on a resolution. This stipulated that, because the bad harvest of the previous year had made the supplying of an attacking force in the Balkans uncertain, no campaign against the Ottomans would start before August 1.[4] The sultan, however, was not prepared to oblige the Hungarians. The next day, April 7, news reached the diet of the gathering of the Ottoman forces at Edirne and the target of these forces—Belgrade.

The Hungarian lords, including Hunyadi, who was present at the diet, turned to Cardinal Carvajal, who was also in attendance, and urged him to send an immediate message for help to Rome. They also suggested that the pope send a naval force to Constantinople to keep Mehemed II from using all his forces against Hungary. At the same time, the king ordered the general mobilization of the lesser nobility and the strengthening of the defenses of the Danube line. Most of the great Hungarian lords were, however, too buys with other matters. Only a few, Hunyadi foremost among them, had the will to stand up to the might of the Ottoman sultan. It seems that Carvajal, the papal legate, did intend to intervene in Rome on Hungary's behalf, recommending a naval threat against Constantinople.[5] The king was apparently more worried about his empty treasury than about the need for soldiers and arms; on the same day that the news of the impending attack was received, he asked for and received from Hunyadi a loan of 8,000 florins, bringing his debt to him to 20,000 florins. In exchange, he gave Hunyadi the fortress of Temesvár and appointed him count of Temes County.[6]

As soon as it became apparent that the sultan's preparations were in earnest, the king fled as far west as he could go. Under the pretext that he was going hunting, he and Count Cilli hurried away from Buda, avoiding the major roads, and reached Vienna in a few days.[7] What a contrast his behavior presented to the actions of another young king of Hungary less than a decade before! One often finds excuses in the writings of historians for László V—that he was too young, that he was under the influence of Ulrich von Cilli, who could not have cared less for the interests of the realm, that since his treasury was empty he could not have done anything anyway. In the end, however, there remains the cold fact that the king ran away, leaving Hunyadi to do the best he could, without the king's moral authority behind him, to save his kingdom from the Ottomans.[8]

Hunyadi, who had spent the winter in Transylvania, had begun gathering his forces in early February, moving along the Maros River with his *banderium* in the direction of the Great Plain. After attending the diet in Pest, he returned to his troops and continued his preparations. Carvajal declared a crusade in the lands for which he was a legate, offering a full range of indulgences to all those who took up the cross or contributed financially to the success of the enterprise.[8] He also instructed Capistrano to began concentrating on the recruitment of crusaders. Capistrano, with Gabriel of Verona, combed the countryside for recruits but they were slow to assemble. Those who joined were mostly peasants and craftsmen, and their armament consisted mostly of rusty swords, clubs, straightened-out scythes, and other makeshift weapons. The better-armed possessed bows and arrows, but there were only a few of these,[10] but they improved with time, and the number of recruits began slowly to increase. They gathered near the town of Szeged, designated for their assembly by Hunyadi. He himself arrived there in late April. Soon thereafter, Carvajal also arrived, but Hunyadi persuaded him to return to Buda to urge the lords there to join the campaign. In this effort Carvajal was largely unsuccessful. The cowardice of László V had set a bad example for the barons, most of whom opted to stay away from Belgrade. The cardinal considered sending Capistrano to the Holy Roman Empire to expand his recruitment campaign, but Hunyadi convinced him that Capistrano should remain in Hungary instead.[11]

In the middle of June, Hunyadi took some of his soldiers to the delta of the Morava River, hoping to stop Mehemed's northward advance by preventing his crossing of the Danube. However, he had no information about the marching order of the Ottoman army, and his troops were in any case insufficient in numbers to face the oncoming enemy alone. Thus, he sent urgent appeals to the counties and to Carvajal for more men and asked the Saxons to join him immediately.[12]

The preparations of the Ottomans proceeded according to the sultan's instructions. Besides assembling his troops at Edirne, he established foundries at Üsküb for the manufacture of large cannon, using some of the bells captured in the churches of Constantinople.[13] These cannon were loaded on ships that sailed north on the Danube toward Belgrade. But the sultan's preparations did not go as smoothly as he intended, and he had cause to worry about what he was leaving behind. Rumors

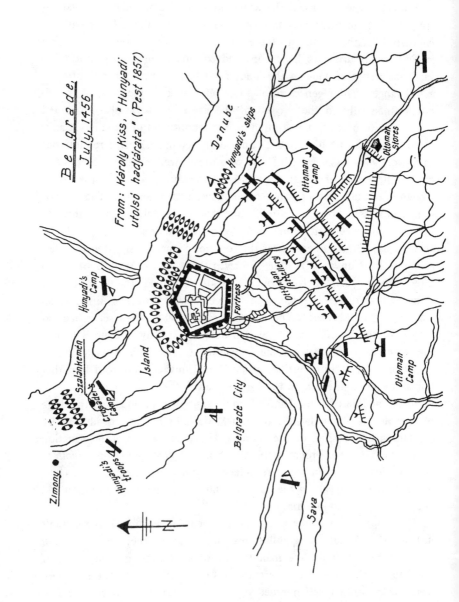

had reached him about Carvajal's appeal to Rome for a naval force to sail to Constantinople, and he did not dare to leave his new capital city entirely undefended. Therefore, he left behind a sizable contingent, a step that may have contributed to the ultimate outcome of his campaign.[14]

Mehemed divided his army and moved it in separate groups toward Belgrade. He also sent his fleet up the Danube, carrying both provisions and siege guns. It is possible that some isolated Serbian detachments tried to interfere with his progress without much success. He eventually bypassed Szendrő and marched straight to Belgrade.[15]

Belgrade was one of three great strongpoints in East Central Europe and the Balkans. One of these, Constantinople, had already fallen. The other, Buda, could not have withstood the Ottomans if Belgrade had been taken. The fortress was described by Brocquiere in 1433 as follows:

> Belgrade is surrounded by high walls. Along the walls on one side flows the Sava River, and on the other side is the city, on the bank of the Danube. The fortress is, therefore, located in a triangle formed by the two rivers. The land is high on all sides except on the land-side where it is so flat that one can walk all the way up to the moat. . . . The fortress, which is very strong on account of its location, is surrounded by a moat and a double wall; both follow the countours of the land. Five strongpoints compose the fortress, three of them built on a promontory and two along the riverfront. The two lower ones are well-fortified, but the three others are really strong. There are a great many Serbians in the city, but most of them are not permitted to enter the fortress. The strongpoints are well stocked with artillery. I noticed three bronze cannon, one of them so huge that I have not seen its like anywhere. The inner diameter of its mouth was 42 inches; however, I thought that it was too short in comparison with its width.[16]

We do not know Hunyadi's route to Belgrade from the mouth of the Morava. What seems certain is that he crossed the Danube during the last few days of June and, constantly fighting the advance troops of the Ottoman army, reached the vicinity of Belgrade in early July.[17] His brother-in-law, Mihály Szilágyi, was the commander of Belgrade. His subordinate commanders included János Geszti and Joannes Bastida, both members of Hunyadi's *familia*.[18]

When the Ottoman army arrived at Belgrade, it was immediately arrayed in battle order. Its three lines were staggered behind each other, the first of them only a few hundred yards from the walls. They contained three hundred cannon of various sizes as well as huge stone-throwing catapults, and the bombardment of the walls began immediately.[19] Mehemed II, seeking to isolate the fortress completely from its surroundings—as he acted at Constantinople three years earlier—ordered the establishment of a naval blockade on the Danube. The Ottoman ships, numbering some 60 larger and, perhaps, 150 smaller vessels and barges, were tied together with heavy chains about a kilometer-and-a-half upriver.[20] The sultan also sent some troops across the river to secure his army from that direction, but these troops dispersed in looting and foraging in the area. According to Nesri, Taji Karadsa, the commander in chief of Rumeli, suggested to the sultan that a large contingent be shipped across the Danube to prevent the Hungarians from resupplying the garrison. This recommendation was not accepted.[21] The sultan, perhaps misled by the reports about the size of Hunyadi's *banderium,* did not want to weaken the siege by further dividing his army. The Ottoman army was by no means as powerful and large as some eyewitnesses maintained. An epidemic that it had brought with it from Asia Minor had caused it serious losses on the way, and a large number of desertions had further reduced its numbers.[22]

Hunyadi was left alone by the Hungarian barons; only László Kanizsai, János Korógyi and Rajnald Rozgonyi came to his support.[23] Capistrano proved his most reliable ally. He arrived at Belgrade with five shiploads of men just before the siege began on July 2, and his crusaders continued to come throughout the siege. Hunyadi also received some help from the cities, who sent him arms and some troops.[24] The chief captain established his camp near Zimony (Zimun) at the village of Szalánkemén. The fortress had already been surrounded on the land side, and the naval blockade stopped reinforcements from the Danube. Hunyadi immediately recognized that the key to a successful defense was the breaking of the blockade. In a short time, he collected about 200 vessels of all sizes.[25] He also sent a message to Szilágyi, ordering him to be ready to attack the Ottoman ships from the rear on July 14. Szilágyi complied; he had nearly 40 vessels, and he loaded them up with Serbs "who were excellent bowmen."[26]

When the appointed day arrived, the attackers were ready. Hunyadi's vessels carried nearly 3000 men, mostly crusaders, and the shore was crawling with others ready to prevent the escape of Ottoman sailors. The chain holding the Ottoman ships together was soon broken, and individual contests between ships ensued. The battle lasted for over five hours and ended in victory for Hunyadi. Three large Ottoman vessels were captured and three others were sent to the bottom. It was reported that nearly 1000 Ottoman sailors were either wounded or killed. In the end, the Ottomans made a run for it, and the blockade was broken. The sultan ordered the remaining vessels burnt in order to keep them out of Hunyadi's hands.[27]

On the 15th, Hunyadi was able to enter the fortress. He took 3000 of his troops with him to relieve the defenders and replace the dead and wounded. The wounded were shipped out, and the badly damaged walls were repaired as well as they could be. Hunyadi ordered the crusaders to move closer to Belgrade, and they occupied the left bank of the Sava opposite the city, where they would be ready to reinforce the defenders as needed.[28]

The defeat of his fleet did not discourage the sultan. His canon continued to pound the walls with terrible efficiency. By the 20th of July, the outer walls had been almost completely demolished. The Ottoman army also worked hard at filling the moat with logs and branches that had been brought along from great distances for this purpose.[29] The sultan and his commanders closely supervised the siege. During one of these inspections, Taji Karadsa Pasha was killed by a cannonball fired from the fortress. He was the first of the sultan's high command to die at Belgrade.[30]

On the afternoon of the 21st Mehemed ordered an all-out attack on the fortress. The janissaries pressed the attack with great vigor, and there seemed no way that the defenders would be able to stop them. By nightfall, the janissaries had entered the city and were fighting in the streets. They pressed the defenders on the bridge that connected the city with the strongpoints of the fortress and scaled the walls of the citadel. But Hunyadi did not lose heart. He directed the defense with great resourcefulness. He ordered the defenders to throw tarred wood, sulfur-saturated blankets, sides of bacon and other flammable material into the moat, which swarmed with Ottoman soldiers and set them afire. Soon a wall of flames separated the janissaries fighting in the city from their comrades outside the walls. Those caught in the moat were burned to death or seriously injured, and the janissaries inside the city were massacred. By the morning of the 22nd, the city had been saved. A lull in the fighting set in[31] and reinforcements poured in from across the river to relieve the defenders.

During the two days' of fighting, Capistrano had been inside the city —he may have been in one of the towers guarding the citadel—and had encouraged the defenders during the street fighting. When, on the 22nd, the lull set in, he returned to his crusaders across the Sava River. Hunyadi, assessing the situation, observed that the Ottoman camp was still there and the enemy simply resting. Anticipating further attacks, he ordered the craftsmen to work on the fortifications, repairing them as well as possible, and forbade anyone to leave the fortress. He must have been aware of the fighting spirit of the crusaders that were freshly brought across the river and did not want them to go beyond the walls challenging the Ottomans to a fight. He may also have been worried that the repulsion of the attack the previous night had instilled too much self-confidence in the defenders and wanted them to be ready for all eventualities. Nothing could hold back the crusaders, however. They obeyed only Capistrano and his friars, and these were now on the other side of the river.

At first, it is said, four or five crusaders crept out from under the demolished ramparts, taking up a position not far from the first Ottoman line, and began trading insults and arrows with the Osmanli. No one really paid much attention to them on the enemy's side; they were a nuisance to be ignored. Then other crusaders began joining the first five, encouraged by the "fun" that their fellows were having. From the other side of the river Capistrano, who obviously knew about Hunyadi's order, tried to stop them without success.[32] He soon became so exasperated at this insubordination that he himself and his adjutants—the friars Giovanni de Tagliacozzo, Ambrose of Aquila, and Peter, the crusaders' flagbearer— shipped back across the river to talk to them.[33] Here Capistrano was himself carried away by his men's exuberance. As he stood there, surrounded by them, more and more crusaders gathered around him and he preached them about their crusade. It seems that some of these men became impatient with all the talk and began attacking the nearest Ottoman line. Capistrano then raised his staff and began walking forward, drawing the rest of the troops with him. The Ottomans in the front line were so surprised by this development that they panicked and ran, leaving their cannon and catapults to the crusaders, who promptly turned them against the enemy. The ensuing panic overtook the second and third lines, and the fighting became universal and terribly confused.

At this point the sultan himself took a hand and ordered the janissaries to counterattack. However, the feared vanguard of the Ottoman army refused to obey his order. They must have been exhausted by the night's fighting, and many of them were wounded. When the sultan abused the pasha of the janissaries, he bravely plunged into the thick of the fighting and was promptly killed. Hunyadi rode with his troops out of the fortress and entered the melee. The fighting went on all afternoon. By evening, 6000 fresh sipahis, who had ben away on a raiding expedition, returned, but they were unable to sway the fighting. In the confused battle the sultan himself killed an enemy soldier and was himself wounded. The commander of the Anatolian troops and the khan of the Mongol auxiliaries were killed.[34] With the coming of dusk, the fighters rested, but it was obvious to the sultan that his army was in no shape to resume the fighting the next morning, especially since he expected that fresh crusaders would be brought across during the night from the other side of the river. Therefore, under cover of darkness, he ordered a general retreat. The battle was over, Belgrade was saved, and the conquest of the Kingdom of Hungary prevented. As Nicholas da Fara reported: "All the stores of the magnificent camp of Mehemed fell into the hands of the Hungarians. The Turks' losses are not exactly known, nor is it known how many of them had actually participated in the two-day battle . . . ."[35] Hunyadi wrote Frederick III that the Hungarians had captured twelve bombards, each of them 60 inches long, and many stone-throwing catapults. He also stated that there were twenty-two large galleys among the Ottoman vessels.[36]

Europe rejoiced upon receiving news of the victory. There was a general expectation that Hunyadi would follow up his victory with further efforts to expell the Ottomans from the Balkans but nothing came of this expectation. On August 11 Hunyadi suddenly died. He had probably contracted the plague that was rampant in the Ottoman camp and even in the city of Belgrade. Thus ended the life of one of the most fascinating characters in European history.

* * *

Given the abundance of eyewitness accounts of the siege and the great interest that the defense of Belgrade aroused throughout Europe, one would think that no more controversies would remain unexplored for today's historians. This is far from being the case. Two of the issues worth further exploration are the sizes of the armies that faced each other in July 1456 and the roles played by Hunyadi and Capistrano.

Given wildly exaggerated numbers about soldiers participating in battles was an excellent propaganda technique in the fifteenth century. If a gigantic army was defeated, the valor and prestige of its opponent were vastly enhanced. Why would propaganda be called for in this case? For one thing, the Minorities considered Capistrano a potential saint, and the "miracles" he had allegedly performed could not hurt their cause. One of these "miracles" was the fact that a huge Ottoman army had come to Belgrade and was driven away in shame. For another, Hunyadi's family and their friends were interested in enhancing his reputation as a victorious general, and for his last victory to have been over a giant Ottoman army could not but add to his prestige.

There can be no doubt that the Ottoman army arrived at Belgrade in great strength. The sultan had, however, been forced to leave behind a sizable contingent to guard Constantinople against possible attack by the Western maritime powers. When the Ottoman host began to move in the early summer, it marched in two major and possible several small groups. In Franz Babinger's phrase, "they gradually moved from the south toward Belgrade in dense swarms."[37] Since no real opposition was expected until the army reached the major strongholds of the enemy such as Szendrő or Belgrade, it did not have to be concentrated and could therefore follow different routes to the north.

Western estimates of the Ottoman army at Belgrade ranged from 150,000 to 400,000 men,[38] but it is likely that even the lower number is an overstatement. Norman Tobias has examined the limitations on army sizes in the early eight-century siege of Constantinople, and his findings seem relevant for other armies in the preindustrial age. According to his findings, an army marching into battle on the fringes of Europe could not have exceeded 60,000-70,000 fighting men. This limit was a consequence not so much of limitations on provisions and fodder it could carry with it or acquire through robbery from the local population (in military terms, "requisitioning") as of finding sufficient drinking water for men and animals. Men can endure thirst for a considerable length of time if they have to; animals cannot. Since armies in the fifteenth century used a large number of pack and draft animals, and since the horses that they rode on were also means of warfare, their daily water requirements were large. Thus, an army either had to follow a river, move in groups several days' distance apart, or take different, perhaps parallel, routes simultaneously. In the latter two cases it was exposed to attack while its forces were divided and might lose the war even before reaching its destination.[39]

The answer to this dilemma in the Balkans was to follow the course of several rivers crossing the peninsula. For the army of Mehemed II to have followed the Danube, however, would have meant a long detour and waste of precious time. Thus, the sultan decided to send his army north in sections. He himself moved with perhaps 60,000 men along the northern slopes of the Balkan Mountains, while another contingent of about 20,000 soldiers took the rote along the southern slopes. Smaller contingents must have followed the main groups at staggered intervals. Besides making the army's provisioning easier, this arrangement also secured the eastern flank of the troops against surprise attack—a wise move in view of Hunyadi's attempt to stop it at the mouth of the Morava.

Armies in this period carried along a large number of auxiliaries. We know, for instance, that Mehemed II had the support of Mongol troops under the leadership of their khan at Belgrade. They also attracted all sorts of camp followers. An army of this size needed wagon- and pack-animal drivers, barbers and barber-surgeons, musicians and soothsayers, water-carriers and equipment repairmen, personal servants for the officers and bodyguards for the headmen, whores and their procurers, all adding to its number. This army of about 80,000 might have only included 55-56,000 fighting men, still a formidable force even if its size fell far short of the estimates of frightened Western reporters.[40]

A letter from Bernhard von Kraiburg, chancellor to the archbishop of Salzburg, dated Vienna, August 25, 1456, shows that this was close to the actual size of the Ottoman army at Belgrade. Kraiburg reported that a reliable eyewitness (probably a soldier of the Viennese contingent of crusaders)[41] stated that about 100,000 "Turks" came to Belgrade. They had thirty-one ships carrying provisions for the army. The dead came to about 4-5,000 men on both sides. Hunyadi's troops, including the mercenaries recruited for the defense, came to about 16,000 men, only half of whom took part in the fighting. Only thirteen cannon were captured, including one of enormous size.[42] However, even this report should be considered exaggerated. If the opposing forces came to nearly 150,000 men (since the crusaders were supposed to have numbered more than 30,000), then 4-5,000 dead appears a small number of casualties indeed. On the other hand, the number of ships mentioned by Kraiburg's informant seems too small. It is possible that the eyewitness spoke only of large vessels, discounting barges, of which there may have been a considerable number.[43]

This brings us to the size of Hunyadi's army. It is very unlikely that more than 16,000 soldiers were involved at one time or another in defending the fortress. Eyewitnesses reported that Hunyadi sent 5,000 of his own men to reinforce the defenders before the siege began. In addition, he had another 5-6,000 men in the *banderium* he led to Belgrade from the Morava. We know that at least one other *banderium*, that of Korógyi, military governor of Macsó (Mačva) was also present and that perhaps parts of the armies of László Kanizsai, Rajnald Rozgonyi, and Joan Bastida participated. Capistrano was active in recruiting crusaders in Hungary and Carvajal did the same in the Holy Roman Empire and Austria. It seems that some crusaders were prevented by various obstacles from reaching Belgrade in time; long after the siege was over, they continued to arrive.[44]

One of our problems in this instance is that there was no standard size for a *banderium*, and the number of soldiers they contained depended upon several factors. These included the wealth, influence, and attractiveness of their owners and the requirements of the occasion. We know that Hunyadi usually augmented his *banderium* by hiring mercenaries and that he spent considerable amounts of money to do so.[45] We do not know how much he spent for recruits in 1456. Unless he received at least part of the special tax offered by the diet (of which there is no trace in the documents), his *banderium* must certainly have consisted of less than 10,000 men.[46]

Another problem is presented by the estimated number of crusaders recruited by Capistrano and his fellow Franciscans. Although a smaller number than those actually present would have given greater prestige to the victors, it would have reflected badly upon Capistrano's charisma. At one time or another, the friars asserted that 30,000 crusaders were present at Belgrade, most of them recruited in Hungary. This number would not be out of line with the actual size of the population of the Kingdom of Hungary. If, as we have suggested, there lived about 3.2 million peasants in the realm, then 30,000 would come to about 0.9 percent of the total, an entirely realistic number. But no one ever counted these volunteers. Kraiburg's statement that only about 8,000 of the crusaders actually fought at Belgrade is probably accruate. It would probably be wrong, however, to underestimate the effectiveness of the crusader's army. Two independent sources, without providing an estimate of the size of this mob, do permit us to evaluate their contribution to the defense. Mihály Szilágyi, commander of Belgrade before the arrival of Hunyadi, declared that he would never have believed that there were so many men available for war in Hungary until he saw their multitudes swarming over the river banks.[47] Thuróczi, the chronicler, reported with unmistakable glee that the conceited sultan who had intended to eat his supper in peace at Buda two months after he conquered Belgrade, had been driven away in shame by simple peasants.[48] The solution to this problem is in the fact that the crusaders also arrived at Belgrade in swarms and continued to come, as I have said, even after the siege was over. As late as November 1456, when László V finally gathered enough courage to inspect the battered city, he was accompanied by a large retinue of German crusaders.[49] All in all, it is most likely that far fewer than the reported 70,000 crusaders came to Belgrade. Their number was probably less than half of this.[50]

Who was mainly responsible for saving the fortress is the subject of conflicting claims. The participating Franciscans had already been building a case for Capistrano's beatification before the siege began, and the undoubtedly important role he played came in handy for this purpose. Hunyadi's biographers were equally adamant about building a case for his singlehandedly having saved Belgrade. What the records indicate, however, is that all those who were present were called upon to exert themselves almost beyond their capacities to stop the conqueror of Constantinople.

Capistrano's role has often been evaluated on the basis of his activities prior to the defense of Belgrade, as a papal inquisitor of heretics and schismatics, and these are irrelevant here. As an inquisitor appointed in

1451, he was certainly not interested in endearing himself to liberal-minded historians of any age. His fellow friars, driven by their conviction of Capistrano's sainthood, did not hesitate to provide fanciful descriptions of his behavior and its alleged effects on the Ottoman enemy during the fighting.[51] Capistrano was 71 years old in 1456. He had come to Hungary in 1455 primarily to pursue heretics;[52] Cardinal Carvajal, who considered his major task the recruitment of crusaders, had a difficult time convincing Capistrano to help him.[53] It was only in February 1456 that Capistrano finally embarked on a recruitment campaign. Frail and old as he was, he crisscrossed the Kingdom of Hungary in pursuit of volunteers.[54] Most of his recruits probably came from the directly threatened southern districts—Serbs, a great many Hungarians, and even Greeks—but there were also crusaders from Germany, Bohemia, Poland, and Austria. What was most remarkable about them was their discipline, reflecting the high degree of self-control of the Franciscans. It is also possible that this was a sign of the popularity of the anti-Ottoman war among the long-suffering population of southern Hungary.[55]

Capistrano himself, as we have seen, directly participated in the battle. His presence in the fortress was certainly inspiring, and in the final battle he played a major role. Although his fellow Minorities were in no way modest in describing this role, their words do ring true when shorn of the alleged appearance of firey angels flying over Capistrano's head as he marched against the Ottoman lines. He definitely showed courage and determination during the siege. It is an entirely different matter to consider him the one man mainly responsible for saving Belgrade as his admirers claimed. That role must definitely be attributed to János Hunyadi. He provided the fortress with the best possible equipment and a commander who could be trusted not to give up the fight easily. He masterminded the naval engagement and the overall defense of the fortress during the last critical days of the siege. He was responsible for the resourceful use of flammable material that saved the fortress on July 22. It is true that he entered the last engagement relatively late, after the crusaders had already broken through the Ottoman lines, and that the crusaders acted against his orders in leaving the fortress. Without Hunyadi's final intervention, they would probably have been massacred by the Ottoman cavalry and the battle would have been irretrievably lost. Hunyadi was, therefore, the decisive factor in preventing Belgrade from falling to the Ottomans.[56]

With Hunyadi's victory at Belgrade, his life work was complete. He departed from this world a remarkable success, a man whose achievements would be remembered by future generations. He left behind two sons, one of whom was destined to become a great Renaissance king of Europe, His story, however, belongs to another book.

X

EPILOGUE

The news from Belgrade produced joy and consternation in Vienna. The city had been saved; but the man who had engineered the victory, and on whose shoulders the defense of the kingdom had rested for almost two decades, was dead. What would happen to the southern defenses now that the guiding spirit behind them was gone? Hunyadi's sons were too young to step into his shoes; at least this was the impression at the royal court. Would another man come foreward to claim the mantle worn so lightly by the former regent and chief captain of the realm? Ulrich von Cilli had no doubt that he should be the man to inherit Hunyadi's power. One of the reasons behind his enmity for János Hunyadi was his resentment at having been bypassed in the diet of 1446 for the regency. László Garai also thought of himself as a likely successor; in a purely military sense Mihály Szilágyi considered himself the logical heir. All of them thought of László, the older son of the former regent, as a temporary stand-in who would soon be replaced.

When the news of Hunyadi's death reached Cilli, he rejoiced at the chance to step forward and claim his place in the sun. He sent a message of congratulations to the king for having been freed of so great an obstacle to his rule in the Kingdom of Hungary, suggesting that he, Cilli, was ready "to exterminate this house of dogs,"[1] namely, the sons of Hunyadi. He also sent a letter to his father-in-law, Branković, notifying the old despot that he would send him soon "two balls" the like of which he had not seen before, with which he would be able to play to his heart's content.² Thus, he openly vocied his threat to have Hunyadi's sons killed.

Cilli advised the king to move immediately to Hungary in order to establish his control over the Kingdom. The fact that László Hunyadi had begun the rebuilding of the fortifications of Belgrade without asking for royal permission was reason enough to hasten the move. At the end of August 1456, therefore, the king sailed for Buda on the Danube, while a mixed army of German crusaders and Cilli's mercenaries marched alongside on the shores. He was accompanied by Otto, the prince of Bavaria, Henrik Rosenberg, the Sternberg brothers, the Lichtensteins, and, of course, Ulrich von Cilli.

The king did not stop at Buda for long. He alredy called for the session of the diet to assemble at Futak, and he moved there with his troops and entourage. He issued an invitation to László Hunyadi to join him, since he wanted the older son of the dead chief captain at his court.³ While at Futak, the king visited the ailing Capistrano. The friar was exhausted by his exertions before and during the siege and was living at Ujlak, the major residence of Miklós Ujlaki. When the king visited Capistrano, the old man was feverish and suffering from diarrhea that he had contracted during the siege. He did not have long to live; on October 26, he died and was buried at Ujlak.⁴

When the session of the diet opened, the king demanded that the nobles swear a new oath of allegiance to him. He felt that this was necessary in the new situation. Then he appointed Cilli the new chief captain of Hungary, and in the absence of the king from the country, regent; but he also appointed László Hunyadi captain of the city and fortress of Belgrade.⁵ The young Hunyadi was apparently satisfied with the turn of events. He invited the king to be present when Belgrade was to be transferred to his command and hurried ahead to prepare a worthy reception for his sovereign.

At this point Cilli's letter to Branković about the "balls" that he was going to send to the despot was intercepted, and it was immediately apparent that he was speaking of the heads of Hunyadi's sons. Belgrade was still under the command of Mihály Szilágyi, and he had the letter read aloud to the assembled friends of the Hunyadis, including bishop Vitéz. When the cleric was asked his opinion, he answered that, although he was a peaceful and a tolerant man and could not condone the assassination of the count (if this was what Szilágyi was contemplating), if it were to take place, he would not condemn it.⁶

Cilli himself was a master intriguer. He sent the royal counselor Friedrich Lambert to Belgrade ostensibly to inspect the condition of the chambers intended to be used by the king but in fact to see if a trap was being laid for Cilli. Lambert reported everything to be in order; he saw few soldiers in the fortress and detected no preparations for an ambush. But he was deceived. Szilágyi had hidden his troops, about 1,500 men, in various buildings in the citadel, and they were ready for any eventuality.⁷

On November 8, 1456, the king and his retinue, accompanied by the crusaders and Cilli's soldiers, reached Belgrade. The king was greeted with great respect; László Hunyadi waited on him at the gates and handed him the keys of the city. The king graciously accepted them and returned them to László, signifying that Belgrade was now entrusted to his care. About one hundred festive knights, commanded by Rajnald Rozgonyi, followed the king into the city. Behind them, and in the face of the rest of the royal retinue, the gates were suddenly shut. As Hunyadi explained to the surprised king, Hungary's laws forbade the entry of foreign troops into the fortresses of the frontier districts.⁸ The stage was now set for the reckoning between Cilli and the Hunyadis, and the odds favored the latter.

Cilli was naturally frightened; he suggested to the king that László Hunyadi was after his crown and that the only way out of the trap was to kill him.⁹ This conversation was overheard and reported to Hunyadi. The next day, while the king and Cilli went together to a mass, a council of Hunyadi's friends was called, and they agreed to kill Cilli. While the mass was still in progress, Cilli was called out, and an argument ensued between him and László Hunyadi. Both reached for their swords, and Cilli wounded his young rival. At this, the friends of Hunyadi, hiding in an adjoining room, ran out and Mihály Szilágyi cut off the head of the resisting count.¹⁰ Thus ended the line of the Cillis, Counts of the Holy Roman Empire, because Ulrich had no male heir. His body and later his head were delivered to his soldiers outside the fortress to be returned to Cille for burial.

The king was horrified and expected that his turn would be next, but László Hunyadi did not rapproach him; showing the king Cilli's intercepted letter, he tried to explain the reasons for the murder and asked

Epilogue 173

for the king's pardon. In fact, he suggested to the young sovereign that being freed of the influence of his uncle truly made him king. Characteristically, Piccolomini, no friend of the Cillis, later suggested that László Hunyadi had done as much for the Christian cause in killing Ulrich von Cilli as his father had done in all his anti-Ottoman wars, because the count was an enemy within the gates.[11] This was, of course, unjust, since Cilli was neither better nor worse than any other great Renaissance lord, but the contest that had plagued Hungary for almost two decades had finally ended. The Hunyadis were victorious, and the king accompanied László Hunyadi to Temesvár. He was feted there with great pomp, and at a mass celebrated at the cathedral he embraced Hunyadi's mother, proclaiming her his mother and her sons his brothers. Then he placed his hand on the sepulchre and swore that he would never avenge Cilli's death.[12] Afterwards, he appointed László Hunyadi master of the royal stables and chief captain of Hungary.

The years 1456-1457, therefore, marked a decisive turning point in the history of the Kingdom of Hungary and the entire area of East Central Europe. The two heroes of Belgrade, János Hunyadi and Giovanni de Capistrano had died within a month of each other in 1456. Ulrich von Cilli had died in that same year. László Hunyadi's turn was to come in the spring of 1457. Djuradj Branković had died in that same year, and the death of the young Habsburg king, László V, followed shortly thereafter. László Garai, the last member of his illustrious family, had only two more years to live. A new generation was coming onto the political scene, bringing new ideas and new principles to guide their actions. Only the enduring emperor, Frederick III, survived into the next decade, representing a continuity of prevarication and indecisiveness that was not typical of the new generation.

The Kingdom of Hungary emerged from these decisive years in a strange position. Although the Balkans were now completely lost to the Ottomans, since most of the fortresses, except, of course, Belgrade, were in their hands, Hungary saw a period of greatness that matched earlier periods of stability. But it was not to last long.

Although internal peace was to be restored by King Mátyás Hunyadi (Corvinus), the loss of the Balkan fortresses augured badly for the safety of the Kingdom. But that is a subject for another study.

NOTE ON THE SOURCES

I believe that it is not necessary to provide a separate, detailed bibliography for this work, since each chapter includes bibliographic information relevant to its contents in the notes. However, some titles have been abbreviated in the notes, and listing them separately here will provide the reader more detailed information than is available in the notes. These sources are as follows:

Bonfini:	Antonius Bonfini, *Rerum Hungaricarum Decades.* of the many editions, the 1767 one, issued in Pozsony, was used.
Chalcocondylas, *Historiarum:*	Laonici Chacocondylas Atheniensis, *Historiarum Libri Decem* (Interprete Conrado C. Tigurino) (Venetis, 1729).
Dlugosz:	Joannis Dlugosz seu Longini, *Historiae Polonicae Libri XX,* 2 vols. (Leipzig, 1711-12).
Fejér, *Genus:*	Georgius Fejér, *Supplementa, Indices, at Genus, Incunabula ac Virtus Joannis de Hunyad* (Buda, 1844); vol. 11 of Fejér, *CDH.*
Katona, *HCR:*	Stephanus Katona, *Historia Critica Regum Hungariae* 42 vols. (Pest, 1790).
Kupelwieser, *Kämpfe:*	Ludwig Kupelwieser, *Ungarns Kämpfe mit den Osmanen bis zur Schlacht bei Mohćcs* (Vienna, Lepzig, 1895).

Pray, *Annales:* Georgius Pray, S.J., *Annales Regum Hungariae ab anno Christi 997 as annum 1564* 4 vols., (Vienna, 1766).
Ranzanus in SCHWANDTNER: Pietro Ranzanus, "Epitome Rerum Ungaricarum," in Schwandtner, below.
Székely, *Tanulmányok:* György Székely, ed., *Tanulmányok a parasztság történetéhez Magyarországon a XIV. században* (Studies on the History of the Peasantry in Hungary in the Fourteenth Century) (Budapest, 1974).
SCHWANDTNER: Joannes Georgius Schwandtner, ed., *Scriptores Rerum Hungaricarum Veteres,* 3 vols. (Vienna, 1767).
Teleki: József Teleki, *Hunyadiak kora Magyarországon* (Age of the Hunyadis in Hungary) 12 vols., of which 6-9 are Dezső Csanki's *Történeti Földrajz a Hunyadiak korában* quoted above (Buda, 1863).
Thuróczi in SCHWANDTNER: Joannis Thuróczi, *Chronica Hungarorum. Ab origine Gentis... ad annum usque Christi 1464* in Schwandtner as above.
Thury: József Thury, ed., *Török-Magyarkori emlékek: Török történetirók* (Documents of the Hungarian-Turkish Relations. Turkish Historians) 2nd series. 4 vols. (Budapest, 1896).
Zichy-oklevéltár: Codex Diplomaticus domus senioris Zichy de Zich et Vásonkeő 12 vols. (Budapest, 1870-1899).

NOTES

Notes to Chapter I

1. Ulrich and Herman von Cilli were named counts of the Holy Roman Empire by Charles IV in 1372. Herman's wife was the daughter of Stepan Twartko, prince of Bosnia. The Ulrich in question here was their great-grandson, and he had married Katherina Branković, daughter of the despot of Serbia. For the history of the family see "Crhonica der edlen Grafen von Cilli" in Friedrich Hahn (ed.), *Collectio monumentorum veterum et recentiorum* (Braunschweig, 1725), 2:676, 748, and 754. See also Franz Krones, *Die Freien von Saneck und ihre Chronik als Grafen von Cilli* (Graz, 1883); László Allecker, *A Cilli grófok és Cille városa* (The Counts of Cilli and the Town of Cilli) (Nyitra, 1892); Viktor Lug, *Das Verhältnis des Grafen Ulrich von Cilli zu König Ladislaus Posthumus* (Reichenberg, 1904); Bruno Schwicker, *Az utolsó Cillei grófok és viszonyuk Magyarországhoz* (The Last Counts of Cilli and Their Relations to Hungary) (Budapest, 1884).

2. For more on this murder, see "Epilogue."

3. Michail Beheim's poem, published by Theodore von Karajan in "Zehn Gedichte Michail Beheims zur Geschichte Oesterreichs und Ungarns," *Quellen und Forschungen zur vaterlandischen Geschichte, Literatur und Kunst* (Vienna, 1849), gives a vivid description of events leading up to the murder. Jakab Bleier analyzed the validity of Beheim's claims in "Beheim Mihály élete és művei a magyar történelem szempontjából"

Notes to Chapter I 177

(The Life of Michail B. and His Works on Hungarian History), *Századok* (Budapest) 36 (1902): 216-32, 347-64, and 444-63. For the murder scene see pp. 451-58.

4. This is clear from a decree issued by László Hunyadi, "*banus* (military governor) of Dalmatia and Croatia," dated Nagyida, August 24, 1453 in *OL*. D1. 44,702.

5. Thuróczi in SCHWANDTNER, 2:29.

6. Several patents issued by Queen Erzsébet describe the rise of the Garais during the late fourteenth century and stress their kinship to the queen. See, for instance, *OL.D1*. 86,367.

7. According to Beheim, the group consisted of István Várdai, archbishop of Kalocsa; László Garai, the palatine; Miklós Ujlaki, the military governor of Transylvania; Thomas, count of Corbavia, Rajnald, János, and Oswát Rozgonyi; Pál Bánfi, László Pálóci, the lord chief justice; László Buzlai, the royal cupbearer; Conrad Holzer, royal treasurer; Georg Volkenstorff; and Johannes Mulveder (Karajan, *Quellen und Forschungen*, pp. 25-27). This list, when compared with the supporters of the Hunyadis, shows that most of the prominent lords took sides with the king.

8. Teleki, 10:553.
9. Ibid., 2:508. See also, Thuróczi in SCHWANDTNER, 1:279.
10. Teleki, 2:509.
11. See Stephanus Kaprinai, S.J., *Hungaria diplomatica temporibus Mathiae de Hunyad, Regis Hungariae*, part 1 (Vienna, 1747), pp. 147-49. See also Teleki, 10:545. In the document, dated March 14, 1457, the king informs the cities of Krems and Stein in Austria of the events of the day. See also Beheim in Karajan, *Quellen und Forschungen*, p. 63.
12. Beheim in Karajan, *Quellen und Forschungen*, p. 26.
13. Kaprinai, *Hungaria diplomatica*, pp. 150-51; he jumped to his feet and exclaimed, "ego mortem evasi, testem innocentiae habeo Deum; quoquiam tertio ictu percussus adhuc supersium, quartum infligi vetant iura." See also Petrus Ranzanus, "Epitome rerum Ungaricarum per indices descripta," in SCHWANDTNER, 1:494.
14. Bonfini, liber 8, p. 498.
15. The letter, dated April 16, 1457, was published by Lajos Kropf, "Egykoru tudósítás Hunyadi László haláláról" (Contemporary Report about the Death of László Hunyadi) *Századok* 35 (1901): pp. 180-81. Mesner mentions the presence of Branković, but this is unlikely.

16. In the document, dated Buda, March 21, 1457 (Teleki, 10:546-53), the king declared his protection of the participants in László Hunyadi's death. For another report on the alleged conspiracy against the king, see Ernst Birk, "Hofmär von Ungarn; Beiträge zur Geschichte der Königin Elisabeth von Ungarn and ihres Sohnes König Ladislaus," in *Quellen und Forschungen* (Vienna, 1849), pp. 253-57.

17. See her letter to her brother Mihály urging him to organize the resistance (Fejér, *Genus,* pp. 234-36). A strange outgrowth of these events was the conclusion of an alliance in Szeged on January 17, 1458, between Erzsébet Szilágyi and her brother, on the one hand, and László Garai and his wife Anna, on the other, in which both parties promised to work for the elevation of Mátyás Hunyadi to the throne of Hungary and his marriage to the Garais' daughter, Anna. (Teleki, 10:565-69).

18. Robert von Lilienkron, *Die historische Volkslieder der Deutschen,* 2 vols. (Leipzig, 1876), 1:489-503. See also Frantisek Palacky, *Zugenverhör über den Tod König Ladislaus* (Prague, 1856).

19. See the letter of Pope Calixtus III to Cardinal Juan de Carvajal (Fejér, *Genus,* pp. 236-37).

20. Bonfini decas 3, liber 3, p. 290. This legend was embellished by Gáspár Heltai in *Chrónika az Magyaroknak dolgairól* (Chronicle about Matters Concerning Hungarians) (Kolozsvár, 1575). Even Chalcocondylas in *Historiarum,* pp. 257-58, thought it worth mentioning.

21. See János Karácsonyi, "Adalékok Hunyadi János származásához" (Data Concerning the Origins of János Hunyadi), *Turul* (Budapest) 17 (1901): 49-53. See also Mór, Wertner, *Turul,* pp. 142-44: *Teleki,* 10: 347-63; Gyula Moravcsik, "A Szibinyáni Jank mondához" (On the Legend of Jank Szibinyáni) *Ethnographia* (Budapest) 37(1923): 96-99; Mihály Romanecz, "A Szibinyáni románckör a szerb népköltészetben" (The Romantic Cycle about Szibinyáni in Serbian Folk Poetry), in *A pancsovai Állami Főgimnázium Értesitője az 1889-1890. tanévről* (Yearbook of the State Gymnasium of Pancsova for the Academic Year 1889-1890) (Pancsova, 1890), pp. 3-24.

22. *OL. Dl.* 13,604 K.B.A. fasc. 1524, no. 12; also *Dl.* 14, 605, dated Pozsony, January 30, 1453.

23. "Jangus genere natus erat non admodum obscuro. Patria fuit Choniate sive Huniadi Ardelii oppidum unde profectus venit ad Tribalorum Ducem." (*Historiarum,* p. 256).

24. Gyula Foster, "Hunyadi János származása és családja" (The Origin and Family of János Hunyadi) *Budapesti Szemle* no. 469 (1916): 390-410, and nos. 473-74, pp. 36-51. See also Arisztid Oszwald, "Hunyadi János ifjusága" (The Youth of János Hunyadi), *Történeti Szemle* (Budapest no. 4 (1916): 354-65; János Karácsonyi, "Mátyás király ősei" (The Ancestors of King Mátyás) in *Mátyás Király emékkönyv* (Kolozsár, 1902), pp. 9-17; Mór Wertner, "A Hunyadiak" (The Hunyadis), *Hunyadvármegye történelmi és régészet társulat évkönyve* (Yearbook of the Historical and Archeological Society of Hunyad County) 11 (1907): 89-96; Samu Borovszky, *Temes vármegye története* (History of Temes County), (Budapest, 1894), pp. 295-301; János Melich, "Szibinyáni Jánk," *Magyar Nyelv* (Budapest) 52 (1956): 129-38.

25. The patent (*OL. Dl.* 37,591; see also Fejér, *Genus*, p. 33; Teleki, 10:1-10) states: "...Prelatorum Baronumque nostrorum consilio ac novae nostrae donationis titulo et omni eo iure quo eadem ad nostram spectant collationem, memorato Woyk, militi et per eum Magos et Radul carnalibus, ac Radul patrueli fratribus, nec non Joanni filio suis, ipsorumque haeredibus et posteritatibus universis dedimus, donavimus et contulimus...." Another document issued by László Batizi "royal man" and notary of the cathedral chapter of Hátszeg, dated October 28, 1409, attests to the installation into the property without objection (Teleki, 10:1-10). This was a substantial grant; the estate included about forty villages and a market town (oppidum). See Dezső Csánki, "Hunyadmegye és a Hunyadaik" (Hunyad Count and the Hunyadis) *Századok* 21 (1887): 8-31. The original document erroneously located the estate in Fejér County and failed to mention that Hunyadvár was a fortress.

26. "...illum partibus de Transalpinis suum traduxisseret in Dominum...." Thuróczi in SCHWANDTER, 1:397.

27. Hahn in *Chronica*, 2:704.

28. See, for instance, Imre Áldor, *Hunyadi János és kora* (János Hunyadi and His Age), (Budapest, 1876); Iván Nagy, *Magyarország családai cimerekkel és nemzedéki táblákkal* (The Families of Hungary with their Coats of Arms and Generation Tables) 13 vols. (Pest, 1857-68), 5:186-89. Also Georgius Pray, *Annales Regum Hungariae* (Vienna, 1766), 2:176; Teleki, 1:52. Another version was presented by Bálint Hóman in Bálint Hóman, Gyula Szekfű, *Magyar Történet* 5 vols. (Budapest, 1936), 2:431. According to him, Hunyadi was of South Slavic descent. (See also, Melich, "Szibinyáni Jánk".)

29. Teleki, 1:11; Georgious Fejér, *Codex Diplomaticus Hungariae, Ecclesiasticus ac Civilis* 42 vols. (Buda, 1844), 11:258.

30. It was Melich's view that this woman might have been a Szapolyai, and Elemér Varju, who examined and deciphered the impressions, since obliterated, of a coat of arms on a grave in the cathedral of Gyulafehérvár, supported this interpretation. See his "A Hunyadiak siremlékei" (Gravestones of the Hunyadis), *Magyarország műemlékei* (Memorials of Hungary) (Budapest, 1905), 1:95. Also, Junius (Béla Zilahi-Kiss), "Hunyadi János édesanyja" (The Mother of János Hunyadi), *Budapest Hirlap* (Budapest), June 5, 1902, p. 3, and Vilmos Frankói, "Hunyadi János származása és a vajdahunyadi freskók" (The Ancestry of János Hunyadi and the Frescoes of Vajdahunyad), *Turul*, (1914), p. 479.

31. For King Sigismund's acknowledgment of one such loan, see Teleki, 10:37.

32. Two works by Erik Fügedi provide important proof of this: "Hungarian Bishops in the Fifteenth Century: Some Statistical Observations," *Acta Historica* (Budapest) 11 (1965): 375-89, and *A 15. századi magyar arisztokrácia társadalmi mobilitása* (Social Mobility of the Fifteenth-Century Hungarian Aristocracy), (Budapest, 1972). Fügedi shows that lowly origin was not necessarily an obstacle to high church office, and that twenty-five of the wealthiest aristocratic families were mostly of foreign origin during the reign of King Sigismund. Hóman in *Magyar történet*, 2:383, points out that in this period even families of Hungarian origin had many foreign relatives by marriage.

33. One example is the case of a burgher of Buda who was appointed *miles aulae* by King Sigismund in 1412. See Károly Czimer, *A magyar királyok udvari katonái a XI.-XVI. században* (The Court Soldiers of Hungarian Kings during the Eleventh and Sixteenth Centuries) (Szeged, 1913).

34. Oszwald, "Hunyadi ifnusága," p. 494, and Varju, "A Hunyadiak siremlékei," pp. 93-94.

35. The patent is dated Pozsony, February 1, 1453 (*OL. Dl.* 24,762).

36. Thuróczi in SCHWANDTNER, 1:397. Alos Gyula Szekfű, *Szerviensek és familiárisok* (Servants and Retainers), (Budapest, 1912).

37. A patent of László V granting the fortress of Látha to János Hunyadi and his sister (*uterina soror*, that is, on his mother's side), the widow of Pongrác Dengelegi, and her sons László, János, and András, seems to confirm her existence. This document, in turn, has raised questions about

a possible second marriage for Hunyadi's mother and the existence of another sister. Foster, in "Hunyadi ifjusága," p. 400, argued that since the alleged sisters were not named in the document of 1419 they must have been born after that date, but János Karácsonyi, in "Hunyadi származása" p. 50, casts doubt on the authenticity of that document and held that János Hunyadi had two full sisters.

38. Oszwald, "Hunyadi ifjusága," p. 495, and Foster, "Hunyadi származása," p. 399.

39. A letter written in his name by János Vitéz in "Epistolae," SCHWANDTNER, 2:53, was long accepted as proof of the date of Hunyadi's birth. It stated that ". . . iam supra sexuaginta numeramus annos, quibus paene continuis furia illam. . . ." (that is, of the Ottomans). Since the letter was written in 1448, it was assumed that Hunyadi was over sixty years old at that time, but it is more than likely that he was referring to Hungary's long struggle with the Ottomans." Thuróczi, in SCHWANDTNER 1:449, stated that Hunyadi was still a relatively young man when he died in 1456. Aeneas Sylvius Piccolomini, in *Historia Bohemica,* p. 174, emphasized the difference between Hunyadi's and Capistrano's ages.Andreas Pannonius called Hunyadi *iuvenis* when he was appointed a *miles aulae* in 1428.

40. His gravestone at Gyulafehérvár, now destroyed, contained the following inscription; "hic est tumulus Johannus vocatus, frater Gubernatoris sit iunctus celicis choris. Anno Domini MCCCCXXXVV" (Foster, Hunyadi ifjusága," p. 43). A patent issued by László V on May 12, 1456, mentions that Hunyadi had lost not only some of his closest friends but his brothers in the struggle with the Ottomans (*OL. D1.* 14,604).

41. That Hunyadi did not know Latin is proven by the fact that his oath as regent had to be translated into Hungarian for him. A document in Teleki, 10:248-56, stated that he mistakenly signed some papers because he did not understand their Latin content. Culture in the Middle Ages was not, however, necessarily exclusively Latin-based. See the enligthening article on this issue by Franz Bäuml, "Varieties and Consequences of Medieval Literacy and Illiteracy," *Speculum* 55 (1980): 239-65. The statement of Vilmos Fraknói in *Vitéz János esztergomi érsek élete* (The Life of János Vitéz, archbishop of Esztergom) (Budapest, 1879), p. 37, that "in the fourth year of (Hunyadi's) regency, he lived in the athomosphere of the Renaissance. He studied the classics, read satyrical and sparkling

pamphlets of daily literature, and maintained relations with Italian humanists," is somewhat exaggerated since translations of such works were scarcely available. The essence of this statement, however, that Hunyadi had varied interests, is probably correct.

42. Thuróczi in SCHWANDTNER, 1:397.
43. *Historiarum*, p. 256. Also Fejér, *CDH*, 11:16.
44. Karácsonyi, "Hunyadi származása," p. 51. However, he is mistaken when he mentions Becse, Tokaj, and Munkács as likely ones, since these were given to Branković only in 1433, when Hunyadi was already serving in Italy.
45. As the patent quoted above (n. 42) stated, "Hunyadi was admitted to membership in the royal court during the reign of King Sigismund and he soon became a counselor of the king." Hóman in *Magyar történet*, 2:432-33, gives a different sequence of these early actitivities. According to him, Hunyadi began as a herald of György Csáki, and became close friends with Ferenc, the count's son, and eventually godfather to his second son, Mátyás. Then he moved on to the court of Lazarević, where, according to legend, he laid the foundations of his family's wealth by finding a treasure trove in a Bulgarian fortress or a convent. Hunyadi may also have served the Counts Cilli. Much of this is based on Hunyadi's presumed advanced age as misinterpreted from the letter quoted in n. 39.
46. Ferenc Bánfi, "Philippo Scolari és Hunyadi János," *Hadtörténeti közlemények* (Budapest) 47 (1930): 125-30. Also Gusztáv Wenzel, *Ozorai Pipo: Magyar történetmi jellemrajz Zsigmond király korából* (Pipo of Ozora: A Historical Biography from Hungary in the Times of King Sigismund) (Pest, 1863); by the same author, "Okmánytár Ozorai Pipo történetéhez" (Archive to the History of Pipo of Ozora), *Történelmi Tár* (1884): 1-31, 220-47, 412-37, and 613-27.
47. There is disagreement on this point among historians. Teleki, 1: 176, maintains that Hunyadi married Erzsébet Szilágyi before moving to court in 1428 and that their first son was born in 1431. Hóman, in *Magyar történet*, 2:433, believes that he married her only after his return from Italy and that László Hunyadi was born in 1436, but this is unlikely. When the older Hunyadi boy was beheaded in 1457, he was about twenty-four years old; if Hóman were right he would have been only twenty-one and would hardly have had time to serve as *banus* of Croatia and Slavonia, which he did after 1453. See also Károly Goóth, "Mikor született Mátyás

Király?" (When Was King Mátyás Born?) Kolozsvári Szemle (Kolozsvár) 3(1943), no. 3, p. 176.

48. Vilmos Fraknói, "Szilágyi Mihály élete" (The Life of Mihály Szilágyi), *Budapesti Szemle* (1911), p. 162.

49. Decas 3, liber 4:178.

50. In SCHWANDTNER, 1:274.

51. Bonfini, decas 3 liber 9:371.

52. Bonfini, decas 3, liber 4:290.

53. Andreas Pannonius, *Libellus de Virtutibus Matthiae Corvino De-Dicatibus, 1467* see Vilmos Fraknói, "Andreas Pannonius élete és munkái" (The Life and Works of Andreas Pannonius), in Vilmos Fraknói and Jenő Ábel (eds.) *Két magyarországi egyházi író a XV. századból* (Two Clerical Writers in Hungary in the Fifteenth Century) (Budapest, 1886), p. 29. In this sense, Hunyadi's character corresponded to that of the ideal nobleman so well described by Marc Bloch: "The noble loved first and foremost the display of physical strength of a splendid animal, deliberately maintained by constant exercise, begun in childhood: . . . to this quality we must add courage as well: . . . the devotion to the chief, the passionate desire for glory . . . the fatalistic acquiescence in the face of ineluctable destiny . . . finally, the hope for reward in another world" [*Feudal Society*, 2 vols. (Chicago, 1961)], 2:295. But the patent of László V is also worth quoting here: "he trained his body to endure any sort of labors and hardship, and the difficult service of the soldier. With all these efforts he laid the foundation of his later military exploits and he made himself worthy, through his noble spirit, for appointment to various high offices" (*OL. Dl.* 14,604).

54. Ranzanus in SCHWANDTNER, 1:481-82.

55. Bonfini, decas 3, liber 4:448. Also Ferenc Bánfi, Hunyadi János milánói tartózkodása" (János Hunyadi's Stay in Milan), *Erdélyi Muzeum*, 1934, p. 265, and Teleki, 1:123.

56. This is the explanation for Hunyadi's ability to lend 1,200 gold florins to King Sigismund on January 17, 1434 (*OL. Dl.* 12,707; and a copy in *OL. Dl.* 13,088).

57. Vitéz, introspective and moody, was an excellent scholar and a good writer. His ancestors, under the name of Sáfár de Chew, had received properties from King Charles Robert in the early fourteenth century. The family had its ups and downs; during the interregnum of 1382-87 it had

sided with the enemies of the future king, Sigismund of Luxemburg and Brandenburg, and lost its properties. In 1428, when János was twenty-one years old, his father changed the family's name to Vitéz. János was born in Ózredna (Srednya) in Kőrös County, Croatia. He studied at the University of Padua and was appointed to King Sigismund's chancellery in 1433. During the brief reign of Albert I (1437-39), Vitéz advanced to the position of chief royal notary. After the king's death, Vitéz sided with the supporters of Wladislaw I and was a member of the delegation that went to Cracow to invite the young king of Poland to be king of Hungary as well. Vitéz actually wrote the document in which the king announced his acceptance of the Hungarian throne. By then he had added the title of *canonicus* of Zagreb to that of chief royal notary. Shorterly thereafter, Vitéz was named provost of the cathedral chapter of Nagyvárad in Transylvania. After the battle of Varna in 1444, Hunyadi was instrumental in having him named bishop of Nagyvárad. When Hunyadi became regent in 1446, Vitéz acted as his diplomatic representative abroad on several occasions and conducted his correspondence. He took part in the second battle of Kosovo in 1448, and in 1453 he bacame head of the chancellery of László V. He was named archbishop of Esztergom in 1465 and died in 1472. Vitéz's last biography was written by Vilmos Fraknói and is now out of date. His collected letters are in "Epistolae Joannes de Zredna," in SCHWANDTNER, vol. 2. They have recently been translated into Hungarian and published in *XV. századi magyar humanisták levelei* (Letters of Fifteenth-Century Hungarian Humanists) (Budapest, 1976). See also Frigyes Pesty, "Vitéz János emberismerete" (The Knowledge of Human Nature by János Vitéz) *Századok* 13 (1879): 613-15; Gyula Prokopp, "Vitéz János Esztergomban" (János Vitéz in Esztergom) *Vigilia* (Budapest) 30 (1965), no. 9, pp. 528-30.

58. Bonfini, decas 3, liber 9:371. It is likely that Bonfini, writing in he 1490s, confused Hunyadi with his father who was, however, long dead at the time.

59. Thus, Hunyadi missed the great peasant revolt in Transylvania. As *milites aulae,* the Hunyadi brothers advanced further loans to their king (*OL. Dl.* 14,472).

60. Josef Hammer-Purgstall, *Geschichte des osmanischen Reiches* 4 vols. (Pest, 1840), 1:648. See also, Dlugosz, liber 12:708.

61. Katona, *HCR,* 5;854. Also, Pray, *Annales,* 2:329; Hyeronimus Pez, *Scriptores rerum Austriacarum* (Leipzig, 1721), vol. 1: "Chronicon Monasterii Mellicensis," column 257.

62. According to Jenő Rónai-Horváth, *Magyar hadi krónika: A magyar nemzet ezeréves küzdelmeinek hadi története* (Hungarian Military Chronicle. Military History of the Thousand-Year Struggle of the Hungarian Nation) 2 vols. (Budapest, 1895), 1:247.

63. "Alberti Romanorum Hungariae, Bohemiae, etc. Regis, literae, quibus Joannem et alterus Joannem utrosque filios Olah de Hunyad, banus de Severino, possessione donat," in Fejér, *Genus,* p. 34.

64. Elekes, p. 108.

65. This is reported in a document issued by King Albert I on September 27, 1439 (the day of his death!) (*OL. Dl.* 13,439).

66. It is likely that the Hunyadi brothers employed the tactics described in 1437 in a report, destroying every village they encountered and burning every house. See János Karácsonyi, "Az első magyar hadijelentés 1437-ből" (The First Hungarian Battle Report from 1437), *Hadtörténeti Közlemények* 11 (1910):15-22.

67. *OL. Dl.* 39, 290, dated September 17, 1439, at Titel.

68. Ibid.

Notes to Chapter II

1. Even in the organization of his major instrument, his private army, which he shaped according to the needs of the age and in which he used infantry in an imaginative way, he followed centuries of military tradition. See József Deér, "Zsigmond király honvédelmi politikája" (Military Policies of King Sigismund), *Hadtörténeti Közlemények* 37 (1936): 37-57, 169-83; Elemér Mályusz, *A magyar rendi állam Hunyadi korában* (The Hungarian Feudal State in the Age of Hunyadi) (Budapest, 1958), p. 1; Gyula Szekfű, *A magyar állam életrajza* (The Biography of the Hungarian State) (Budapest, 1917), pp. 78-9; Hóman in *Magyar történet,* 2:241.

2. Elemér Mályusz, "Zsigmond király központositási törekvései Magyarországon" (The Efforts at Centralization of King Sigismund in Hungary) *Történelmi Szemle* 3 (1960):162-63 described it this way: "Anyone looking at the medieval Hungarian state from a distance (of hindsight) would consider it a strong institution. The country's territory was

unified: . . . the offices of state were not inherited; . . . (office holders) were appointed by the king and served at his pleasure. He also appointed the officers of the counties the so-called *comites* (or counts); he received large revenues from customs duties, the salt-monopoly, the mints, and levies on the cities; he owned the largest estates, the most serfs. His unquestioned authority and his prestige as king gave him direct jurisdiction over the nobles and the people who were obliged to take up arms (at his call). He was the supreme judge and, relying on his privilege as the supreme patron of the church, he exercised the broadest authority (over the religious institution). . . . But real life was different. . . . "

3. The first Ottoman raids into Hungary's dependencies in the northern Balkans began immediately after the first disaster of Kosovo in 1389 and intensified after King Sigismund's defeat. In 1420 the records of the city of Brassó in Transylvania attest to their devastating effects: "Amurathes, Imperator Turcarum, vulgo Murabek, terram Barczensem (i.e., the area of the Barcaság of which Brassó was a part) ferro et igno vastat, senatum Coronensem (i.e. Brassó) abducit, residuo populo in arce montis conservato . . . . " (in SCHWANDTNER 3:210). On the contemporary borders of the Kingdom of Hungary, see Miklós Kring (Komjáthi), "A magyar államhatár kialakulásáról" (About the Evolution of the Borders of the State of Hungary) *A Gróf Klébelsberg Kunó Magyar Történetkutató Intézet Évkönyve* (Vienna) 4 (1934):3-26.

4. The Hungarian *regnum* in the fifteenth century (this term was used in the sense of the privileged orders and as designating the territorial entity of the Kingdom of Hungary) had little in common with what Heinz Lubasz has called the "modern state." (*The Development of the Modern State,* New York, 1967, 2d ed., p. 1). Its most important permanent fixture was the institution of kingship; it had no stable diplomatic or bureaucratic institutions. The king was the source of law, together with customs and the church. As Gerhard Ritter observed in *Der Neugestaltung Europas im 16. Jahrhundert* (Berlin, 1950), p. 21, "(the king) was neither sovereign nor all-powerful: . . . he shared public authority with his feudatories, especially with the great feudal aristocracy . . . . "

5. Max Weber, *Wirtschaft und Gesellschaft: Grundriss der Sozialökonomik* (Tübingen, 1922), pp. 725-32. Marc Bloch's study *Le societé feodal: La classe et le gouvernement des hommes* 2 vols. (Paris, 1939-40) (English translation by L. A. Mangold, *Feudal Society* (New York-London,

1961) refined Weber's concepts in describing the Hungarian version of feudalism. The individual's relations to the *regnum* were determined by the notion of a set of privileges and obligations that had to be respected. Most struggles took place over this issue. Individuals and groups had different privileges and obligations. See László Makkai, "Feudalizmus és az eredeti jellegzetességek Európában" (Feudalism and the Original Characteristics in Europe) *Történelmi Szemle* 17 (1976):257-77.

6. See, for instance, the contract between Paulus de Majthen of the fortress of Éleskő, on the one hand, and György and Sebestyén Rozgonyi, on the other, for the former's services as *familiaris;* dated October 27, 1453, in *Haus- Hof- und Staatsarchiv* (hereafter *HHSTa*) (Vienna) Handschrift Weiss, no. 158, p. 446, and another typical contract, between István Ethre *familiaris,* on the one hand, and his lord the bishop of Vác, on the other: dated April 24, 1452 in *OL. Dl.* 44,630 (Muz. Ta). Rewards for retainers were often given in kind. For instance, Imre Marcali signed a contract with one of his retainers promising to pay him 80 florins, 150 measures (?) of grain, 18 sides of bacon, 8 cattle fattened for sloughter, and 800 measures of wine. A contract between Miklós Gersei, count of Zala County, and his retainer Osvát Rumi provided the latter with flour, fodder, half the produce collected from four villages, 600 chickens, 400 *denarii,* 10 barrels of wine and, in addition, 100 florins to be paid at a later date [József Holub, *Zala megye története a középkorban (History of Zala* County in the Middle Ages) (Zalaegerszeg, 1929)], p. 142.

7. The church was also a means of upward social mobility, but a sermon of Pelbárt of Temesvár proclaimed: "the first rule of a servant is voluntary subordination (to his lord)" V. Sándor Kovács, ed., *Temesvári Pelbárt válogatott írásai* (The Selected Writings of Pelbárt of Temesvár) (Budapest, 1982), pp. 25-26.

8. Elemér Mályusz, "A magyar társadalom a Hunyadiak korában," (Hungarian Society in the Age of Hunyadis) in *Mátyás király emlékkönyv* 2 vols. (Kolozsvár, 1942), 1:216.

9. Sinkovics, *A magyar nagybirtok,* pp. 18-23.

10. Until almost the end of the fourteenth century, kingship had been a family affair. See Ferenc Eckhart, *A Szentkorona eszme története* (History of the Concept of the Holy Crown) (Budapest, 1941), p. 44. The theory of continuity was provided by the church, using the example of St. István as the ideal king, his son, St. Imre as the ideal heir apparent, and

St. László as the warrior king fighting for the faith. An excellent illustration of this idea can be found in the sermons of Pelbárt of Temesvár (Kovács, *Temesvári Pelbárt,* especially pp. 168-200). See also, Imre Szentpétery, "Az országtanács 1401-ben" (The Council of State in 1401) *Századok* 38(1904):759-67. On the punishment of king Sigismund by the barons, see Fejér, *CDH,* series 10, 4:75.

11. *The King's Two Bodies* (Princeton, 1961). Emma Bartoniek ["Corona et regnum," *Századok* 68(1934):315-29)] also pointed to the existence, almost from the beginning of Hungarian kingship, of a certain separation between the person of the king and the institution of kingship. The concept of the *regnum* meant both the geographic entity of the state and the king and the privileged orders as mentioned above. During the fifteenth century the lesser nobles were gradually transformed from subjects of the crown into its "members." Eventually, therefore, the *regnum* came to symbolize the community of the privileged, while the crown developed into the symbol of not just the kingship but also the realm. Internally, the realm was held together by the person of the king but the crown as the symbol of the realm was elevated above his person. This was essential because international treaties needed a more secure base than the mortal person of the king. For a valuable recent analysis of this concept see János M. Bak, *Königtum und Stände in Ungarn im 14.-16. Jahrhundert* (Wiesbaden, 1973), especially pp. 6-10 and 33-35. The similarities in the application of this concept in the Holy Roman Empire and Bohemia were pointed out by Eckhart (*A Szentkorona,* p. 33).

12. According to Emma Léderer, "A magyar királyválasztási jog a középkorban" (The Hungarian Rule of the Election of Kings) *Századok* 70 (1936):369, the end of the maleline of the Árpád dynasty in 1290 produced two views on the rule of succession. One of these advocated the right of the *regnum* to elect a new king whenever one died, while the other would have given the right of selection to the pope. In either case, however, there was no dispute over the right of inheritance of the members of the House of Árpád, but even its female line died out by 1302.

13. See king Albert I's decree dated May 29, 1439, containing thirty-five articles including the "laws of the *regnum*" and his promise to observe them in *OL. Dl.* 59,243 and 13,381.

14. The struggle over the kingship of László V hinged, at least on the surface, upon the issue of election vs. inheritance. See W. Wostry, *König*

Albrecht II, 1437-1439 (Prague, 1907); also Vilmos Fraknói, "Az első Habsburg király trónrajutása Magyarországon" (The Risign of the First Habsburg King to the Throne of Hungary) *Századok* 47(1913):258.

15. Szabolcs Vajai, "Az Árpád-kor uralmi szimbólikája" (Symbols of Rule in the Age of Árpáds), in János Horváth and György Székely, eds., *Középkori kútfőink kritikus kérdései* (Critical Questions of Our Medieval Sources) (Budapest, 1974), p. 342.

16. József Deér, *Die heilige Krone Ungarns* [Österreichische Academie der Wissenschaften, "Dankschriften" 90 (1966)], pp. 27-28; also Tamás Bogyay, "Problémák Szent István koronája körül" (Problems Concerning the Crown of St. István) *Uj Látóhatár* (Munich) 13 (1970):105-15; Theodor Reussig, "Die heilige Krone Ungarns" *Zeitschrift für Kunstgeschichte* (Munich-Berlin) 31(1968):162-65.

17. See n. 11.

18. For the statement of the privileged orders in this instance see Martin G. Kovacsics, *Supplementa* 1:262. See also, Márton Sarlós, "A szentkorona-tan kialakulásához: A XV. századi államfelfogás és szellemtörténeti jogtörténetünk" (On the Evolution of the Concept of the Holy Crown: The Fifteenth-century Concept of the State and Our Juridical History) *Jogtudományi Közlöny* (Budapest) 14(1959): 357-66; Gyula Szekfű, *Állam és nemzet* (Budapest, 1942), pp. 302-8; Szekfű, *Magyar történet* 3:289; Sándor Domanovszky, *A harmincadvám eredete* (Origins of the Customs Duties) (Budapest, 1916).

19. Ignácz Acsády, *Magyarország pénzügyei I. Ferdinánd uralkodása alatt* (The Finances of Hungary during the Reign of Ferdinand I) (Budapest, 1888), p. 10.

20. Hóman in *Magyar történet,* 2:406-9.

21. Mályusz, "Zsigmond király központositási," p. 168.

22. Pál Engel, *Király hatalom és arisztokrácia viszonya a Zsigmondkorban, 1387-1437* (Royal Authority and Its Relations to the Aristocracy in the Age of Sigismund, 1387-1437) (Budapest, 1977).

23. Mályusz, "A magyar rendi állam," pp. 332-34.

24. Ibid.

25. That the communications between the council and the rest of the country were not easy was shown by a report dated Ság, April 13, 1439, in *OL. Dl.* 63,953, from the local convent to king Sigismund (then dead by almost a year and a half) on the execution of one of his orders. If the

news of the king's death took such a long time to filter down to the convents that acted as notaries public, one can imagine the time it took for events of lesser significance.

26. Even the king's marriage plans were approved by the council in 1403. See Mályusz, "A magyar rendi állam Hunyadi korában" in Sándor Domanovszky, *Magyar művelődéstörténet* (The Hungarian Feudal State in the Age of Hunyadi) (History of Hungarian Culture), 5 vols. (Budapest, 1942), 2:28-32.

27. As was the case in 1444 when King Wladislaw's embassy to Edirne was accompanied by the personal envoys of Branković and Hunyadi. See Oscar Halecki, *The Crusade of Varna. A Discussion of Controversial Issues* (New York, 1943), pp. 13-31.

28. Bódog Schiller, *Az örökös főrendiség eredete Magyarországon* (The Origin of Perpetual Baroncies in Hungary) (Budapest, 1890), p. 37. There were, of course, exceptions. For instance, the Garais succeeded in holding on to the office of palatine for three generations. A patent of queen Erzsébet, by then a widow, dated Buda, December 14, 1439 (in *OL. Dl.* 13,464) described the Garais' path to power.

29. The king's hands, however, were tied more than one way, one of these being the various baronial alliances (called leagues) established with their reluctant approval [see Edmund Berzeviczy, "Adalékok a Sárkányrend történetéhez" (Data for the History of the Order of the Dragon) *Turul* 14(1893):93-96, including a copy of the founding letter which includes the membership]. The latter reads like a contemporary "Who's Who in fifteenth-century Hungary."

30. *Brevis, vera tamen notitia et cognito Banorum et Banalis officii, HHSTa,* Handschrift Weiss, no. 157. In the area that is part of today's Yugoslavia there was a *banus* for Ozora and Só, and another for the district centering on the fortress of Jajcza; in Serbia proper, there were *bani* for Macsó and Belgrade; in Wallachia, the area bordering on the Olt River up to the Iron Gate on the Danube was the district of Szörény (Szekfű, *A magyar állam,* pp. 82-83). The *voivode* of Transylvania was not only the supreme judge in the province, but also appointed the heads of counties. Similar power was given to the *banus* of Croatia and Slavonia. The *voivode* was also Székely *comes.* It is, therefore, no wonder that during the interregnum of 1444-1452 the *voivode* (Hunyadi) and the *banus* of Croatia and Slavonia (Ulrich von Cilli), were the major contestants for power in the kingdom.

31. There were sometimes shifts in the ranking of these officials. While in the fourteenth century the most important royal attendant was the cupbearer, in the fifteenth, the steward took his place. The latter took over the handling of revenue derived from royal estates, while the former became the appelate judge of the free royal cities. By the end of the fifteenth century, the treasurer shared his responsibilities with the cupbearer. See László Erdélyi, *Magyar történelem: Művelődés és államtörténet* (Hungarian History: History of Culture and the State) (Budapest, n.d.), 2 vols. 1:388).

32. Ibid.

33. Imre Szentpétery, "A királyi titkos kancellária történetéhez" (On the History of the Royal Secret Chancellery) *Századok* 48 (1914): 440-45; also Lóránt Szilágyi, "A királyi kancellária szerepe az ország kormányzatában" (The Role of the Royal Chancellery in the Governance of the Country) *Turul* 44 (1930): 45-83. According to Szilágyi, the chancellery represented a transition between the feudal court and the premodern bureaucracy of the monarchy. Since there was no stated budget, all these activities had to be financed from the private resources of the king. See Béla Grűnwald, "A régi Magyarország" (Old Hungary) *Nemzetgazdasági Szemle* (Budapest) 11 (1887): 691-729.

34. The Spanish traveler Péter Tafur, who visited Buda in 1438 or 1439, described the new palace in detail (Lajos Kropf, "Régi utazók Magyarországon" (Early Travelers in Hungary) *Századok* 41 (1907): 92-3.

35. Lajos Elekes, "Királyi és főuri udvar" (Royal and Baronial Courts) in Domanovszky, *Magyar művelődéstörténet* 2:243-80.

36. Ibid., 280-89.

37. Here and there, however, one still comes across documents showing the survival of ancient judicial customs; in *OL. Dl.* 13,393, for example, a duel is used as a means in determining the truth between opponents.

38. Imre Szentpétery, "Nemesi és polgári életforma" (The Style of Life of the Nobles and Burghers) Domanovszky, *Magyar művelődéstörténet*, 2:320-21.

39. Szekfű, *Szerviensek,* pp. 50 and 67, and Mályusz, *A magyar rendi állam,* pp. 330-331. On the evolution of the judicial system, see Tibor Hajnik, "A királyi biróság személyes jelenléte és ennek helytartója a vegyesházi királyok korszakában" (The King's Personal Presence and His

Representatives During the Age of Kings from Various Houses) *Akadémiai értekezések a történeti tudományok köréből* (Budapest, 1892), and Lóránt Szilágyi, "Irásbeli supplicatiok a középkori magyar adminisztrációban" (Written Requests in the Medieval Hungarian Administration), *Levéltári Közlemények* 10 (1932): 157-70.

40. See, for instance, king Albert's patent granting László Garai the right to judge his serfs at his own court except in capital cases (Teleki, 10:41-43), and the grant of king Sigismund to the baron Blagay of permission to set up the gibbet and pass the death sentence on offenders in his court [Lajos Thallóczy and Samu Barabás, eds. *A Blagay-család oklevéltára* (Archive of the Blagay Family) (Budapest, 1897), pp. 218-23.] In a document dated Buda, January 16, 1441 (*OL. Dl.* 55, 235) King Wladislaw I ordered László, son of István Losonci, to return properties he had taken from Italian merchants and specified that if he disobeyed, the military governor whose retainer László was, was to give satisfaction to the injured party.

41. Imre Hajnik, *A magyar birósági szervezet és perjog as Árpád- és Vegyesházi királyok alatt* (The Hungarian Judicial System and the Right of Justice under the Árpád Dynasty and the Kings from Various Houses) (Budapest, 1899), pp. 25-26.

42. A whole series of patents were issued by various kings granting this right to great lords among them *OL. Dl.* 13,435 and 102,471.

43. This development is reflected in a document issued by the palatine on February 9, 1438 at Buda (*OL. Dl.* 25,926), confirming the decision of the lord chief justice against the king in a property suit. See also István Bertényi, "Az országbirói intézmény története az 1380-as években" (History of the Institution of the Lord Chief Justice in the 1380s) *Századok* 107 (1973): 391-405; József Gerics, "A magyar királyi kuriai biráskodás és a központi igazgatás Anjou-kori történetéhez" (On the History of the Judicial Functions of the Royal Curia and the Central Governing System during the Rule of the Anjous) in *Jogtörténeti Tanulmányok* (Budapest) 1 (1966): 298-301.

44. On the possible evolution of the nobility from the clans of the tribes see Bálint Ila, "Település és nemesség Gömör megyében a középkorban" (Settlements and Nobility in Gömör County in the Middle Ages) *Turul* 54 (1940): 56-57.

45. Péter Ágoston, *A magyar világi nagybirtok története* (History of

the Secular Esates in Hungary) (Budapest, 1913), p. 67. For other important apsects of the laws see István Szabó, "Az 1351. évi jobbágytörvények" (The Serf Laws of 1351) *Jobbágyok, parasztok. Értekezések a magyar parasztság történetéből* (Serfs and Peasants: Studies on the History of the Hungarian Peasantry) (Budapest, 1976), pp. 137-66, and "Az 1351. évi XVIII. törvénycikk" (Article XVIII of the Law of 1351), ibid., pp. 123-36.

46. Restricted only by the laws of 1351. The exemption from paying the tithe remained a matter of dispute. See, for instance, a letter of protest by the nobles of Petróc to the cathedral chapter of Szepes, dated August 20, 1441 (in *OL. Dl.* 39,738).

47. Engel, *Királyi hatalom*, p. 89.

48. Sinkovics, *A magyar nagybirtok*, pp. 30-31.

49. Ibid., p. 22.

50. E. Molnár, *A magyar társadalom története a Honfoglalástól Mohácsig* (The History of Hungarian Society from the Conquest to Mohács) 2 vols. (Budapest, 1949), 2:272.

51. Bálint, Ila, "A Szentgyörgyi és Bazini grófok birtokainak kialakulása" (The Evolution of the Properties of the Counts Szentgyörgyi and Bazini), *Turul* 44 (1927): 37-71.

52. Mályusz, "A magyar társadalom," *Mátyás király emlékkönyv* 2:339-40. There were eight royal free chartered cities in Hungary during this time: Buda, Sopron, Pest, Pozsony, Nagyszombat, Kassa, Bártfa, and Eperjes. At the end of the century (1498) Lőcse and Zagreb were added to the list.

53. Molnár, *A magyar társadalom*, 2:272-75.

54. A document dated Veszprém, March 15, 1439, lists Simon Rozgonyi, bishop of Veszprém, "the perpetual count of Veszprém county" (*OL. Dl.* 13,274), and one dated Tyrnawa, April 13, 1453, mentions Dénes Széchi as "comes perpetuus" (*OL. Dl.* 14,671, Tyrn. Mon. fasc. 14, no. 19).

55. Fügedi, *A 15. századi*, p. 72.

56. Among the various ways by which the barons gathered wealth was the acquisition of the right to mint coins; see the patent of Wladislaw I, dated Szerdahely, December 28, 1441 (in *OL. Dl.* 13,656) and another granting the same right (in *OL. Dl.* 44,313).

57. Mályusz, "A magyar társadalom," *Mátyás király emlékkönyv* 3: 337. The barons usually tied their retainers to themselves by land grants.

See, for instance, the patent issued by Miklós Ujlaki to Mihály Oszkói and László Dyczi, his court judges (in *OL. Dl.* 95,361).

58. Molnár, *A magyar társadalom,* 2:264-65.

59. In *Borsod vármegye története a legrégibb időktől a jelenkorig* (History of Borsod County from Ancient Times to the Present) (Budapest, 1909), p. 66.

60. Szentpétery, "Nemesi és polgári életforma," pp. 330-32.

61. Ibid., p. 333.

62. See György Győrffy, "A magyar nemzetségtől a vármegyeig, a törzstől az országig" (From the Hungarian Clans to the County and from the Tribe to the Country) *Századok* 92 (1958): 12-87. Earlier studies that are still useful include: Imre Palugyai, *Megye alkotmány* (County Constitution) (Pest, 1864); Károly Tagányi, "Megyei önkormányzatunk keletkezése" (The Origins of the Autonomous Government of the Counties) *Értekezések a Történeti Tudományok Köréből* (Budapest 18 (1899), No. 6:397-99.

63. The count was originally the royal intendant, governing the royal estates. By the fifteenth century, however, he headed the county administration. Sometimes a single count controlled several counties simultaneously. See Elemér Mályusz, "A középkori magyar nemzetiségi politika" (Medieval Hungarian Nationality Policies) *Századok* 73 (1939): 404-405.

64. József Holub, *Zala megye története a középkorban* (History of Zala County in the Middle Ages) 3 vols. (Nagykanizsa, 1929), 1:101-2; also, Ákos Timon, *Magyar alkotmány és jogtörténet* (History of Hungarian Constitution and Jurisprudence) (Budapest, 1906). Bishop Pietro Ranzanus, an envoy from Naples to Hungary in 1448, mentioned that Hungary had 73 counties but he could name only 55, since no one he spoke to could name them all. In SCHWANDTNER, 1:495.

65. Antal Foglein, "A vármegyei jegyzőkönyvek" (Record Books of the Counties) *Levéltári Közlemények* 16 (1938): 142-67; also Géza Istványi, "A megyei levéltárak első nyomai a 14. században" *Levéltári Közlemények* 15 (1937): 245. Both of these authors suggest that county administrations originated in the local need for courts of justice. On the development of the judicial functions that the counties eventually performed, see Imre Nagy, Farkas Deák, and Gyula Nagy, eds., *Hazai Oklevéltár* (Archive of the Homeland) (Budapest, 1879), pp. 389-99.

66. Dőry, et al., *Decreta,* 2d decree, articles 10, 14-16.

67. The counties were not always able to protect non-nobles against the lords. Abuses often occurred; see, for example, *OL. D1.* 13,200.
68. Dőry, et al., *Decreta* 2d decree of 1435, articles 4 and 5.
69. Many documents attest to the counties' willingness to act against the aristocrats. For instance, Szatmár County notified the king of the recovery of expropriated land for the lawful owners in March, 1435. (*OL. D1.* Q.29, 62,265, Ibrányi 1vt.) A similar report by the county of Közép-Szolnok is *OL. D1.* 65,036 and 65,037 (Becsky cs. lta).
70. Dőry et al. *Decreta* 2d decree, articles 3 and 7. The control of the great lords over the lesser nobility was still extensive.
71. Frigyes Pesty, *Oklevelek Temes vármegye és Temesvár város történetéhez* (Documents on the History of Temes County and the City of Temesvár) 2 vols. (Pozsony, 1896), 1:282.
72. Elemér Mályusz, "Zsigmond király központositási törekvései Magyarországon" (The Centralizing Efforts of King Sigismund in Hungary) *Történelmi Szemle* 3 (1960): 162-92; Lajos Elekes, *Rendiség és központositás a feudális államokban: Problémák a kérdés keleteurópai vonatkozásainak kutatásában, különös tekintettel a XV. századi Magyarország viszonyaira* (Feudalism and Centralization in the Feudal States: Problems in Research on the Issue in Relation to the East European States, with Special Attention to Conditions in Fifteenth Century Hungary) (Budapest, 1962).
73. Held, "Military Reform in Early Fifteenth Century Hungary," *East European Quarterly* 11 (1977): 129-39; also, Deér, "Zsigmond király honvédelmi politikája" especially pp. 169-70.
74. Mályusz, *A magyar rendi állam,* p. 19.
75. Ibid., p. 25.

Notes to Chapter III

1. János Karácsonyi, *Magyarország egyháztörténete főbb vonásaiban* (The Major Elements of Hungarian Church History) (Nagyvárad, 1915), p. 15.
2. The original of the document is in *OL. D1.* Filmarchiv, fasc. 579, no. 53. See also Katona, *HCR,* 11:614-18; Fejér, *CDH* series 10, 4:303-6; Vilmos Fraknói, *Oklevéltár a magyar királyi kegyuri jog történetéhez* (Archive for the History of Patronage Rights of the Hungarian

Kings) (Budapest, 1899), pp. 8-11; Dőry, et al., *Decreta*, pp. 180-82.

3. A copy of the document whose original was lost, was discovered by Béla Iványi in 1931 in the archives of the city of Eperjes and published by him in *Eperjes szabad királyi város levéltára* (The Archive of the Free Royal City of Eperjes) 2 vols. (Szeged, 1931), 1:71. Hungarian historians apparently did not realize the significance of this copy until Elemér Mályusz discussed and published it in full in *A konstanzi zsinat és a magyar főkegyuri jog: Értekezések a történeti tudományok köréből* (The Council of Constance and the Hungarian Right of Royal Patronage: Studies on Historical Sciences) (Budapest, 1958).

4. For instance, Robert de Cavalcantibus, a canon of Florence and chaplain of St. Peter's church in Rome, issued an order to "all clerics of the bishopric of Esztergom and of the city of the same name subpoenaing János and István Keéri to appear before him in a case concerning the properties of the nuns of the Island of Rabits at Pest (*OL. Dl.* 13,348). Although it is possible that the case had first been tried in some Hungarian clerical court and the examiner was acting on an appeal, this would probably have been mentioned in the document if it were so. A more direct challenge to royal control over the church is represented by Pope Martin V's appointment of György, the deacon of Szepes as bishop of Transylvania in 1419, rejecting the election of another cleric to the post by the cathedral chapter of Gyulafehérvár (Antal Beke, "Római emlékek a magyar egyház XV. századi történetéből" Documents from Rome about the History of the Hungarian Church in the Fifteenth Century) *Történelmi Tár* New series, 1 (1900): 2.

5. István Barta, *Egyház és állam viszonya Magyarországon a középkor végén* (The Relations of State and Church in Hungary Near the End of the Middle Ages) (Budapest, 1935), pp. 34-36.

6. Ferenc Kollányi, *A magánkegyuri jog hazánkban a középkorban* (The Private Patronage Rights in Our Country in the Middle Ages) (Budapest, 1906), pp. 18-19; also János Reiner, "A magánkergyuri jog hazánkban a középkorban" (Rights of Private Patronage in Our Homeland in the Middle Ages) *Századok* 41 (1907): 498-99.

7. The archbishop of Esztergom supervised the bishops of Győr, Eger, Pécs, Vác, Veszprém, and Nyitra and the vicar of the Cumans. The archbishop of Kalocsa was responsible for the bishops of Csanád, Translyvania, Nagyvárad, Zagreb, Bosnia, Belgrade, and the Szerémség. The

latter three bishoprics had been lost to the Ottomans early in the fifteenth century, and their bishops were living in the Kingdom of Hungary.

8. Fügedi's statistical observations on the social origins and tenure of Hungarian bishops ("Hungarian Bishops, p. 388), are surprising:

Diocese	bishops	years	barons	nobles	commoners	peasants	unknown
Esztergom	7	122	2(57)	2(24)	1(6)	1(24)	1(11 years)
Eger	11	112	4(42)	2(12)	1(6)	1(7)	3(45)
Gyor	9	127	2(46)	4(58)	1(4)	2(19)	---
Nyitra	14	125	4(48)	4(13)	---	---	6(64)
Pecs	8	146	4(104)	2(15)	1(16)	---	1(16)
Vac	10	113	2(36)	4(40)	---	1(10)	3(27)
Veszprem	12	104	4(27)	4(62)	3(14)	---	1(1)
Kalocsa	12	109	3(26)	2(22)	3(49)	1(2)	3(10)
Csanad	9	124	3(53)	2(21)	1(7)	---	3(43)
Transylv.	14	119	3(42)	6(48)	---	1(1)	4(28)
Nagyv[rad	16	120	2(18)	3(38)	4(39)	1(6)	6(19)
Zagreb	9	119	1(12)	4(74)	2(11)	---	2(22)
Total	131		34(511)	39(427)	17(152)	8(69)	33(281)
%	100		26.00	31.00	9.00	9.00	30.00

Please note that some bishops held more than one see at the same time, and that it is very likely that some of the bishops whose origins are unknown came from the lower strata of the population.

9. The archbishops maintained two *banderia* each and the bishops of Eger, Nagyvárad, Pécs and Transylvania one each; the other bishops also had substantial contingents of soldiers under their command. See Elemér Mályusz, *Egyházi társadalom Magyarországon a középkorban* (Clerical Society in Hungary in the Middle Ages) (Budapest, 1971), p. 171; also Bálint Hóman "A középkori királyság bomlása" (The Dissolution of Medieval Kingship) *Magyar középkor* (Budapest, 1938), p. 39; Oszkár Bárczay, *A hadügy fejlődésének története* (The History of the Development of Military Affairs) (Budapest, 1895), 3 vols., 2:475-84) discusses the military obligations of the bishops in the Kingdom of Hungary.

10. Ottokár Székely, "Az egyházi nemesség" (The Church Nobility), *Jahrbuch der Wiener ungarischen historischen Institut* 5 (1935): 29; also

József Ozorai, "Az egyházi vagy prédiális nemesek és birtokuk" (The Clerical or *Praedialis* Nobles and their Properties), *Uj Magyar Sion* (Budapest) 17 (1886): 16-39.
11. Hóman in Hóman-Szekfű, *Magyar történet,* 2:200-201.
12. Fejér, *CDH,* series 10, 4:756.
13. Ibid., 753-55.
14. Székely, "Az egyházi," p. 43.
15. Béla Máyer, "Pápai bankárok Magyarországon a középkor végén" (Papal Bankers in Hungary at the End of the Middle Ages) *Századok* 57/58 (1923/24): 650-51; also, Pongrácz Sörös, "Pápai adófizetés Magyarországon különös tekintettel a bencés apátságokra" (Papal Taxation in Hungary with Special Reference to the Benedictine Abbeys) *Uj Magyar Sion* 16 (1902): 185-87.
16. August Theiner, *Vetera monumenta historica Hungariam sacram illustrantia,* 2 vols. (Rome, 1859-62), 1:601.
17. Fügedi, "Hungarian Bishops," p. 379. According to him (p. 390), the yearly *servitium* and income (in florins) of Hungarian bishops at the end of the fifteenth century as reported by a Venetian diplomat, Vincenzo Guidotto (Quoted by István Balogh, *Velencei diplomaták Magyarországról 1500-1526)* (Venetian Diplomats' Reports of Hungary, 1500-1526) (Szeged, 1929), p. 79 was as follows:

Diocese	servitium	income	(corrected)*
Esztergom	4,000	35,000	25,000
Eger	800	22,000	
Gyor	800	13,000	4,000
Nyitra	275	???	
Pecs	3,300	25,000	
Vac	500	4,000	
Veszprem	900	12,000	
Kalocsa	2,000	20,000	
Transylvania	1,500	24,000	
Csanad	900	3,000	
Nagyvarad	2,000	26,000	
Zagreb	2,000	18,000	
Szeremseg	100	5,000	

Notes to Chapter III

* In the two "corrected" instances, the diplomat counted the private income of the bishops as part of their clerical revenue. It seems obvious from this list that there was little correlation between the revenues of specific bishoprics and the *servitium*. See also Nándor Knauz, "A magyar érsek- és püspökségek jövedelmei" (The Revenues of Hungarian Bishoprics and Archbishoprics) *Uj Magyar Sion* 3 (1865): 554-90.

18. György Székely, "Az egyházi tizedkizsákmányolás" (The Clerical Exploitation through the Tithe) *Tanulmányok a parasztság*, pp. 320-21; by the same author, "Az egyházi nagybirtok ujjászervezése" (The Reorganization of the Large Estates of the Church), ibid., p. 337. The collective properties of the church were larger than the holdings of any single baron or of the king. The accumulation of these estates was illustrated by the case of the Benedictine abbey of Pannonhalma; *Estates Acquired:*

century	royal/private		donation	purchase	total	lost	remain
11th	18	2		13	33	3	30
12th	3	23		3	29	11	18
13th	11	16		57	84	44	40
14th	--		1	14	15	22	-7
15th	--		2	8	10	19	-9
Total	32	44		95	171	99	72

Pongrácz Sörös and Tibold Rézner, "A pannonhalmi főapátság története. Harmadik korszak" (History of the Abbey of Pannonhalma: Third Period), in László Erdélyi (ed). *A pannonhalmi Szent Benedek rendi kolostor története* (History of the Cloister of St. Benedict of Pannonhalma) 3 vols. (Budapest, 1905), 1:564-69, 3:423-27.

19. Dated Gyulafehérvár, January 13, 1440 (*OL. Dl.* 74,073).
20. Dated Tasnád, August 1, 1440 (*OL. Dl.* 55,219).
21. Samu Barabás, ed., *A római szent birodalmi Gróf Széki Teleki család oklevéltára* (The Archive of the Family of Count Széki Teleki of the Holy Roman Empire) 3 vols. (Budapest, 1895), 1:532, and an order for the postponement of a trial in a similar case, ibid., p. 533.
22. Vince Bunyitay, *A váradi püspökség története* (History of the Bishopric of Nagyvárad) 3 vols. (Nagyvárad, 1883-84), 2:3. Also Mályusz, *Egyházi társadalom,* pp. 174-75. According to Fügedi ("Hungarian Bishops"

pp. 378-79), out of 75 bishops 36 (48 percent) attended a university. Only one of the bishops of peasant origin did not receive a university education. Ten bishops of noble origin were really public servants; they served as royal secretaries, officials of the king's administration, or even as chancellors. According to Fügedi, this might point to the possibility that a university education was becoming a requirement for appointment to high church office in Hungary.

23. Andor Csizmadia, "Galvano di Bologna pécsi működése és a középkori magyar jogi oktatás egyes kérdései" (Galvano di Bologna at Pécs and Several Questions Concerning Legal Education in Medieval Hungary) *Jubileumi tanulmányok a pécsi egyetem történetéből* (Jubilee Studies on the History of the University of Pécs) 2 vols. (Pécs, 1967), 1:114-15; also, Zoltán Miklósy, "Hiteles hely és iskola a középkorban" (Notary Public and Schools in the Middle Ages), *Levéltári Közlemények* 18/19 (1940/41): 170-78; Eugen Ábel, "Ungarische Universitäten im Mittelalter" *Ungarische Revue* (Leipzig-Berlin-Vienna), (1936), pp. 496-514.

24. Remig Békefi, *A magyarországi káptalanok megalakulása és Szent Chrodegang regulája* (The Emergence of the Cathedral Chapters in Hungary and the Regulation of St. Chrodegang) (Budapest, 1901), pp. 20-24.

25. Mályusz, *Egyházi társadalom,* pp. 97-99. Also Fejér, *CDH* series 3, 1:108-109; Holub, *Zala megye,* 1:392-97.

26. Miklósy, "Hiteles hely," p. 170.

27. Ibid., p. 171. Also Pál Tóth-Szabó, "A jászói konvent mint hiteles hely" (The Convent of Jászó as Notary Public) *Turul* 21 (1903): 110-19.

28. Béla Iványi, *A győri székeskáptalan régi számadáskönyvei* (The Old Account Books of the Cathedral Chapter of Győr) (Budapest, 1918), pp. 21-22.

29. Remig Békefi, *A káptalani iskolák története Magyarországon* (The History of the Schools of Cathedral Chapters in Hungary) (Budapest, 1910).

30. Miklósy, "Hiteles hely," p. 175.

31. János Jerney, "A káptalanok és konventek története" (History of the Cathedral Chapters and Convents) *Magyar Történelmi Tár* 2 (1855): 23-25.

32. Pál Lukcsics, *XV. századi pápák oklevelei* (Patents of Popes of the Fifteenth Century) (Budapest, 1931), no. 1333.

33. László Fejérpataky, "A veszprémi káptalan kincseinek összeírása"

(The List of the Treasures of the Cathedral Chapter of Veszprém) *Történelmi Tár* (1887): 173-92; also, Antal Horváth, *A csornai konvent hiteleshelyi működése* (The Activities of the Convent of Csorna as Notary Public) (Keszthely, 1943); Fejér, *CDH,* series 2, 2:55.

34. According to a report of a visitation to the cathedral chapter of Esztergom in the late fourteenth century, there were 39 canons and 12 substitutes under its jurisdiction. From the cathedral alone, the chapter received the revenues collected at 12 chapels and altars in addition to its share of the tithe [Ferenc Kollányi, "Visitatio capitoli E. M. Strigoniensis, anno 1397" *Történelmi Tár,* New series, 2 (1901): 71-106.]

35. Mályusz, *Egyházi társadalom,* p. 124. In general, there had to be at least three canons in a cathedral chapter in order for it to operate; the average was 12.

36. Ibid., 125.

37. See note 16 above.

38. See the documents in *Történelmi Tár,* New series, 2 (1901): 253-55.

39. Jenő Házi, *Sopron középkori egyháztörténete: Győr egyházmegye multjából* (The Medieval Church History of Sopron: From the Past of the Bishopric of Győr) 5 vols., (Sopron, 1939), 4:95, 103, 113, and 203; also, Sörös and Rézner, "A pannonhalmi" 2:173. A typical donation is recorded in a document dated January 19, 1449 *(OL. Dl.* 36,391, fasc. 49, no. 1); János, son of Tamás, son of Farkas Homonnai, bequeathed 100 florins and other goods to the church at Zezarma named for St. Michael. An unusually large donation of 2,000 florins was made to the chapel of St. Peter in the cathedral of Eger (Lukcsics, *XV. századi pápák,* 2:37). Smaller donations were, however, more common. For instance, in 1439, János, son of Miklós, son of Péter Benchányi, having chosen the church of St. Lambert at Apácavásárhely as his burial place, donated his serf plot to the monastery there (Pál Lukcsics, *A vásárhelyi apácák története* (History of the Nuns of Vásárhely) 2 vols. (Budapest, 1934), 1:35.

40. According to a document issued in 1387, there was a large Gothic church in the market town of Nagybánya whose parish priest employed 11 chaplains and one preacher. The church also maintained a school whose master's salary was paid by the town (Mályusz, *Zsigmondkori Oklevéltár* (from now on: *ZsO*) (Archive for the Age of Sigismund) (Budapest, 1958-63) 3 vols., 1:150; also Fejér, *CDH,* series 10, 8:233-34).

41. Károly Schrauf, *Magyaroszági tanulók külföldön* (Students from Hungary Abroad) 2 vols. (Budapest, 1892-1902), 2:356-58. Also, Andreas Veress, "Matricula et acta Hungarorum in Universitate Pataviana," in *Fontes Rerum Hungaricarum* (Budapest, 1815), 1:1-129; Vilmos Fraknói, *Magyarországi tanárok és tanulók a bécsi egyetemen a XIV-XVI. században* (Hungarian Professors and Students at the University of Vienna in the Fourteenth to the Sixteenth Century) (Budapest, 1896); Sándor Bálint, "Szeged egyetemi műveltsége a középkorban" (The University Education of Szeged in the Middle Ages), *Felsőoktatási Szemle* (Budapest) 10 (1961): 238-41; Pál Nyáry, *A krakkói egyetem és magyar diákjai a 14. -16. században* (The University of Cracow and its Hungarian Stuents in the Fourteenth to the Sixteenth Century) (Budapest, 1942); Endre Kovács, "L'université de Cracovie et la culture hongrois aux XVe-XVIe siècles," *Nouvelles études historiques* (Budapest, 1957).

42. Erik Fügedi, "Koldulórendek és városfejlődés Magyarországon" (Mendicant Orders and the Development of Cities in Hungary), *Századok* 106 (1972): 74.

43. Mályusz, *Egyházi társadalom,* p. 209. For the exceptions see Elek Jakab, "Apátságok Erdélyben" (Abbotries in Transylvania) *Magyar Történelmi Tár* 13 (1867): 3-21.

44. During the thirteenth century, 170-180 convents existed in Hungary. The new houses that emerged after that time were mostly built by the mendicant orders and they numbered 145. (György Balanyi, *A szerzetesség története* (History of the Regular Clergy) (Budapest, 1923), p. 17.

45. Sörös and Rézner, "A pannonhalmi," 3:76. What all the orders needed was to open their doors for schools and the involvement of the monks with the cultural and educational advancement of prospective clergymen and secular people. Of the 18 Benedictine monasteries that maintained the office of notary public only seven seems to have maintained some sort of school. Of the Cistercian cloisters, only four had schools within their walls. Most monastic schools apparently belonged to the mendicant orders, especially to the Dominicans and Franciscans. See Miklósy, "Hiteles hely," p. 177.

46. Sörös and Rézner, "A pannonhalmi," 3:63, reported that, in 1439, revenues came to about 10,000 florins. The difference may reflect the discrepancy between the actual income an that reported by the lay overseers.

47. Lukcsics, *A vásárhelyi apácák,* p. 27. Countless documents illustrate the despolitation of the old monasteries. See, for instance, *OL. Dl.* 13,980, Prep. de Saagh, fasc. 32, no. 68, dated Buda, October 11, 1446; also Belitzky, *Sopron vármegye,* 1:926-27.

48. Sörös and Rézner, "A pannonhalmi," 3:21.

49. There were, however, undoubtedly some problems with discipline even in the mendicant orders. For instance, a document dated Vamus, May 17, 1453 (*OL. Dl.* 44,665 Muz. Ta.), records that Mihály Bencze, a vicar of the Minorite friars in Hungary, admitted his wife, son and daughters as members of his order. Although the document does not show if Bencze joined the order late in his life, given his high position in the order, this seems unlikely.

50. Fügedi, "Koldulórendek," pp. 69-95.

51. Sándor Bálint, *Szeged reneszánsz kori műveltsége* (The Culture of Szeged in the Age of the Renaissance) (Budapest, 1975), p. 21.

52. Mátyás Fehér, *A hétszázados vasvári Szent Domonkosrendi kolostor története, 1241-1941* (The History of the Seven Hundred Years Old Cloister of St. Dominic of Vasvár) (Budapest, 1942), p. 27; also, Antal Harsányi, *A domonkosrend Magyarországon a reformáció előtt* (The Dominican Order in Hungary before the Reformation) (Budapest, 1965).

53. Mályusz, *Egyházi társadalom,* p. 279.

54. Bálint, *Szeged reneszánckori,* p. 25.

55. Emil Kisbán, *A magyar pálosrend története* (History of the Hungarian Order of Paulists) (Budapest, 1938).

56. Fügedi, "Koldulórendek," p. 75.

Notes to Chapter IV

1. László Makkai, "Agrarian Landscapes of Historical Hungary in Feudal Times," in *Études historiques hongroises* 2 vols (Budapest, 1980), 1:195; also István Szabó, *A magyar mezőgazdaság története a XIV. századtól az 1530-as évekig* (The History of Hungarian Agriculture from the Fourteenth Century to the 1530s) (Budapest, 1975); Gyula Prinz and Pál Teleki, "A magyar munka földrajza" (Geography of Hungarian Labor) in Jenő Cholnoky, ed., *Magyar föld, magyar faj* (Hungarian Land, Hungarian Race) 6 vols. (Budapest, 1941), 2:157.

2. Rodney Hilton's definiton of a serf was only partly valid for

fifteenth-century Hungary. According to him, "they were the peasants who were not only dependent on other men, in the sense that they were tenants on land which they did not own, but they were also restricted by law in various ways...." (*Bond Men Made Free: Medieval Peasant Movements and the English Rising of 1381* [London, 1973], p. 55.) Hungarian serfs were, in general, less dependent on others than their Western European counterparts. Among their freedoms was the right to move after fulfilling their obligations, to marry as they wished, sometimes even to noble women, and to leave their private property to their designated heirs. In certain cases they had the right to sell land that they had opened up for cultivation. An early but still useful work on medieval Hungarian peasants is Ignácz Acsády's *A magyar jobbágyság története* (History of Hungarian Serfdom) (Budapest, 1907). Of the many later works, see István Szabó's *A falurendszer kialakulása Magyarországon a XV.-XVII. században* (The Development of the Village Network in Hungary during the Fifteenth to Seventeenth Centuries) (Budapest, 1967); Ferenc Maksay, *A magyar falu középkori településrendje* (The Order of Settlement in the Medieval Hungarian Villages) (Budapest, 1962); the works of Márta Belényesy to be cited below; János Major, "A telektipusok kialakulásának kezdetei Magyarországon" (The Beginnings of the Development of Serf Plots in Hungary) *Településtudományi Közlemények* (Budapest) 12 (1959): 34-55.

3. This term applied not just to foreigners or to internal migrants, regardless of their ethnic origin. Any free man could be a *hospes* in the sense that he could legally move as he pleased (Fejér, *CDH*, series 3, 2: 237).

4. There is a multitude of documents in the Hungarian National Archive on this issue. For instance, in *OL. Dl.* 13,675, dated April 24, 1442, the new settlers of the village of Kistótfalu were given a year's exception from all obligations if they moved into abandoned houses. If they built new dwellings, the exemption was extended to twelve years. They had the right to elect their own judge, who was to render judicial decisions on the basis of the privilege of the city of Nagybánya. In *OL. Dl.* 106,450, dated April 1439, the new settlers of the village of Halápcs were granted exemption from all levies for twenty-five years except if they moved into abandoned houses; they all had to pay the tithe. In *OL. Dl.* 24,730 dated April 24, 1440, the great-grandson of Beanus Marichidai granted his estate, Misztótfalu, the rights of a market town in order to repopulate it.

5. Hilton, *Bond Men*, p. 56. For another view, see Max Weber, *The Theory of Social and Economic Organization* (New York, 1941), pp. 378-81; also Eric Wolf, *Peasants* (Somerset, N.J., 1966). Peasant obligations in general consisted of the following: (1) *servitium*, or labor service; in general, one or two days of labor a year on the noble's land plus occasional duties in repairing roads and bridges as required; (2) cash payments such as the *census* and *subsidium*, the latter originally an emergency levy for the defense of the state; (3) rents in kind; (4) gifts on special occasions and (5) a tithe to the church and a ninth of the harvest to the landlord—the last two of these regularized by the laws of 1351. See Zsigmond Pál Pach, "The Development of Feudal Rent in Hungary in the Fifteenth Century," *Economic History Review* (London) 19 (1966):5. On the laws of 1351, see Dőry, et al. *Decreta*, pp. 127-40, and discussions in Szabó, *Jobbágyok, parasztok*, pp. 137-66. I am grateful to János M. Bak for permitting me to see his as yet unpublished study on the social background of these laws.

6. According to Pach ("The Development of Feudal Rent," p. 4), "like the contemporary English manor, the French *seigneurie*, and the German *Grundherrschaft*, the Hungarian large estate was not a large-scale farm, but...a conglomerate of numerous small tenantcies, an organization with the function of collecting dues and contributions from dependent peasants over an immense area, a network of feudal rents."

7. Wenzel, *Magyarország mezőgazdaságának*, p. 286. The *portal* tax was similar to the taille in France and the tollage in England. It was collected by *dicatores* who operated independently of the county authorities. They used rectangular blocks of wood on which they carved the number of *portae* in each village. Half of this block was given to the village judge (who usually could not read) as a receipt after the collection [(József Kovacsics, *A történeti statisztika forrásai* (Sources of Historical Statistics) (Budapest, 1957)], p. 31. There is no monograph on *portal* taxation in fifteenth-century Hungary, although studies do deal with this tax in later periods. See Lajos Juhász, *A porta története* (History of the *Porta*) (Budapest, 1936); Ignácz Acsády, *A jobbágyadózás* (The Taxation of Serfs) (Budapest, 1894) and *A magyar adózás története* (History of Taxation in Hungary) (Budapest, 1896). The *portal* tax was a fixed amount that changed over time. Based on serf plots, houses, or even the number of chimneys, it was a yearly levy. During most of the fifteenth century,

nobles who had the duty to send at least fifty armed peasants, or one for every thirty-three *portae* they controlled at the time of general mobilization, were granted the right to collect the *portal* tax for the state and to use it to maintain their soldiers [(Ignácz Acsády, *Magyarország pénzügyei I. Ferdinánd korában* (Hungary's Finances at the Time of Ferdinand I) (Budapest, 1880), pp. 21-22.)]

8. Ignácz Acsády, "A dicális összeirások gyüjteménye az országos levéltárban" (The Collection of Dical Censuses in the National Archive) *Magyar Könyvszemle* (Budapest) New series, 1 (1893): 195-264.

9. István Szabó, "Magyarország népessége az 1330-as és as 1526-os évek között" (Hungary's Population between the 1330s and 1526), in József Kovacsics, ed., *Magyarország történeti demográfiája: Magyarország népessége a honfoglalástól 1949-ig* (The Historical Demography of Hungary: Hungary's Population from the Conquest to 1949) (Budapest, 1963), pp. 77-78.

10. György Győrffy, *Einwohnerzahl und Bevölkerungsdichte in Ungarn bis zum Ende des XIV. Jahrhunderts* (Budapest, 1960).

11. Fügedi, *A 15. századi,* pp. 35-71. In "A középkori Magyarország demográfiájának mai állása" (Current Status of the Demography of Medieval Hungary) *Demográfia* (Budapest) 12 (1969): 502, he notes that mortality rates were 35 per 1000 and infant mortality 40 percent of all deaths.

12. Fügedi, "A középkori," p. 504.

13. Molnár, *A magyar társadalom,* 2:250-55. His reasoning went like this: "in the area of the country researched by (Dezső) Csánki, extending over 230,000 square kilometers, 18,547 settlements were traced. There were, therefore, 8 settlements per 100 square kilometers. If we projected this ratio to the entire territory of the country or roughly to an area of about 330,000 square kilometers, the total number of settlements would come to 25,040. Deducting 3.3 percent for settlements of "noble peasants" (lesser nobles) we arrive at 265,000 *portae* and a population of 2,738,000 peasants.... There were, on an average, 26 families in each village. Of these, 6-7 families were *inquilini,* 19-20 families lived on serf plots. The average land area of each village was 12.4 square kilometers or about 2,155 *holds* (3,060 acres)." Molnár's population estimate by stratum was as follows:

landholding nobles	40,000	1.2%
peasant-nobles (owning 1 plot)	74,000	2.2%
clerics	30,000	0.9%
city-dwellers	100,000	2.9%
other privileged	382,000	11.2%
serfs with plots	2,054,000	60.4%
inquilini	685,000	20.2%
others	34,000	1.0%
total	3,400,000	100%

According to Molnár, there were 501,000 serf families, 167,000 familes of *inquilini,* and 18,000 families of what he called "peasant nobles" altogether 686,000 peasant families.

14. Elemér Mályusz, "A magyarság és a nemzetiségek Mohács előtt" (Hungarians and the Ethnic Nationalities before Mohács) in Domanovszky, *Magyar művelődéstörténet,* 2:124.

15. One of the few cases in which we have direct evidence of the growth of the population relates to Kolozsvár. [(László Makkai, *Társadalom és nemzetiség a középkori Kolozsváron* (Society and Nationalities in Medieval Kolozsvár (Kolozsvár, 1943), pp. 15-16).] Of course, the mushrooming of market towns in this century in itself indicates a general increase in the number of town-dwellers.

16. Márta Belényesy, "Anyagi kultúránk a XV. században: A munkaközösség öt esztendeje" (Our Material Culture in the fifteenth Century: Five Years of Work by Our Collective) *Agrástörténeti Szemle* (Budapest) 1 (1957): 73-79.

17. Dezső Csánki, *Magyarország történeti földrajza a Hunyadiak korában* (The Historical Geography of Hungary in the Age of the Hunyadis) (Budapest, 1896-1913) 4 vols., 1:5; also Lajos Glaser, "A Dunántúl középkori úthálózata" (The Road Network of Medieval Transdanubia), *Századok* 63 (1929): 138-67.

18. Szabó, *A falurendszer,* p. 187; also "Hanyatló jobbágyság a középkor végén" (Declining Serfdom at the End of the Middle Ages), *Századok* 73 (1938): 16-21.

19. Acsády, *A magyar jobbágyság,* p. 137.

20. The excavation of medieval villages has often revealed such a pattern. See Ilona Sz. Czeglédy and Tibor Koppány, "A középkori Ecsér

falu és temploma" (The Medieval Village of Ecsér and its Church) *Archeológiai Értesitő* (Budapest) 91 (1964): 46, 47; also István Néri, "Beszámoló a Tiszalök-Rázompusztai és a Túrkeve-Mórici ásatások eredményeiről" (Report on the Results of Excavations at Tiszalök-Rázompuszta and Túrkeve-Móric), *Archeológiai Értesitő* 81 (1954): notes 2 and 27.

21. Jenő Szűcs, *Magyarországi városok és városfejlődés a XV. században* (Hungarian Cities and their Development in the Fifteenth Century) (Budapest, 1955), and Erik Fügedi, "Mezővárosaink kialakulása a XV. században" (The Development of Our Market Towns in the Fifteenth Century) in *Kolduló barátok, polgárok, nemesek* (Mendicant Friars, Burghers and Nobles) (Budapest, 1981), pp. 336-63; "Városok kialakulása Magyarországon" (The Emergence of Cities in Hungary) ibid., pp. 311-35 and "Középkori Magyar városprivilégiumok" (Medieval City Privileges) ibid., pp. 238-310.

22. Szabó, "Hanyatló jobbágyság," p. 23 has suggested that the movement of relatively large numbers of people into the market towns was a serious economic blow to the landlords; he also believed that "there was increased pressure on the fewer serfs remaining in the villages... as they had to replace those who had died of the plague or been attracted to the towns." However, in my opinion, this did not lead to increased tensions, since no nation-wide disturbances occurred in this period.

23. Molnár, *A magyar társadalom*, 2:253. For the various ways serfs divided their plots, see *Zichy oklevéltár* (Budapest) 12:344-64. According to Szabó, *A magyar mezőgazdaság*, p. 41, "There was a natural process in operation here in that the sons of peasants established their own households upon marrying and took part of the family's lands with them;" but we do not know the amount of land cleared in the lifetime of each generation or the rate at which abandoned land was taken up by newly established families.

24. Fernand Braudel, *Lés structures de quotidien: Le possible et l'impossible* (Paris, 1979), 1:18-19.

25. Property was measured in several ways. One of these was the so-called *ekealja* (plowshares) or *aratrum*, probably the amount of land that could be plowed with four oxen in an agricultural season. Another was the *mansio* or *sessio* or serf plot which varied with the ability of the peasant family to work it in a given season, and its size varied between 18 and 200 *holds* (25.5-284 acres). The price of land declined in this

period, since it was so readily available. (Péter Ágoston, *A világi nagybirtok története* (History of the Secular Large Estates) (Budapest, 1913), p. 77.

26. The convent of Lelesz reported in 1414 that one of its serfs was robbed of three oxen, three cows and a great deal of grain (Fejér, *CDH*, 6+137). From a single village in Békés County, robbers had driven away a hundred horses, four hundred heads of cattle, and three thousand sheep. (István Sinkovics, "Mezőgazdasági viszonyok," (Agricultural Conditions) in Domanovszky, *Magyar művelődéstörténet*, 2:150. A document in *OL. Dl.* 93,127, dated Tormanfölde, December 15, 1448, attested to the fact that robbers had taken eight oxen, 5 cows, three calves and other valuables from a serf called Pál Bodó, causing 100 florins' worth of loss in the village of Tolmács. Such documents abound in the archive.

27. For instance, the palatine Lőrinc Hédervári reported from Buda on June 19, 1446, that some serfs from the market town of Vasvár were robbed of 220 florins' worth of property on the road (*OL. Dl.* 93,018, Festetics család); another document dated Pest, June 2, 1446, complained about a robbery netting four horses and other property valued at 300 florins from some *hospites* on their way to the fair at Székesfehérvár (*OL. Dl.* 93,033); still another report of a robbery of a serf from the town of Márk in Bereg County lists 3,000 florins' worth of loss (*Zichy oklevéltár*, 4:535).

28. Szabó, *A magyar parasztság*, p. 37; also Sándor Takáts, "A magyar üveg, magyar üvegesek" (Hungarian Glass and Glassmakers), *Századok* 41 (1907): 630-47.

29. Lajos Huszár, "Pénzforgalom és pénzértékviszonyok Sopronban" (Money and Its Values in Sopron) *Századok* 105 (1971): 1150-84. The relations between wages and prices are difficult to establish because they were not uniform throughout the country, and the value of the currency was often changing. During the reign of Lajos I (1342-1382), currency values were relatively stable. The florin equalled one-fourth of a silver mark, whose weight was 245.5 grams of pure silver. One florin was worth 100 silver *denarii*. Since the *denarius* was a unit too large for everyday use, two *obuli* were equal to one *denarius*, but this was still a cumbersome arrangement. Thus, one gold florin was valued varriously at 200, 300 or even 400 silver *denarii* which, naturally, meant the debasement of the precious metal content of the *denarius*. In 1430, the silver content

of 400 *denarii,* the equivalent of one florin, was reduced from 38-42 grams to 24.9 grams. By 1435, it contained only 2.7 grams of pure silver, and this was one reason for the peasant revolt in Transylvania in 1437-1438. According to Molnár, *A magyar társadalom,* 2:182-84, the weight of a gold florin was 3.4 grams of 0.997 percent pure gold. On the relation between wages and prices in the area around Buda, see András Kubinyi, "A mezőgazdaság története a Mohács előtti Budán: Gallinczer Lénárt számadáskönyve 1525-ból" (Data on Agricultural History at Buda before Mohács; The Account Book of Lénárt Gallinczer for 1525) *Agrártörténeti Szemle* 8 (1964): 37-401. Molnár (2:185) lists some commodity prices from this period: one *hold* (1.42 acres) of plowland cost about 2.24 florins, a fattened hog 19.91, an ox 3378 florins, a hundredweight of salt 6.08 and leather for a pair of boots 9.04 gold florins. He reports that the wages of a day laborer were about 12 *denarii* a day during harvest, while 8 *denarii* bought 13 kilograms of wheat. An average laborer, who made only 8 *denarii* a day, was paid 16 gold florins a year for 200 workdays. The cost of food for a servant family at the abbey of Pécsvárad was 8.75 florins and clothing cost 1.39 florins; wine for the family came to 2.5 florins. See also István Baraczka, "A hazai pénzrendszerek és pénzek történetéhez" (About the History of Money Systems and Money in Hungary) *Levéltári Közlemények* 36 (1965):235-300.

30. Mályusz, *ZsO* 1:461-62. For another example see Kálmán Géresi, *A Nagykárolyi Gróf Károlyi család oklevéltára* (Archive of the Count Károlyi Family of Nagykároly) 4 vols. (Budapest, 1883) 1:163.

31. Szabó, "Az 1351. évi," p. 499; also Hóman, Szekfű, in *Magyar történet,* 2:226-27.

32. See, for instance, the letters of king Albert to Zala County, dated Buda, August 31, 1438 *(OL. Dl.* 13,284), and to the convent of Kapornok dated June 19, 1438 *(OL. Dl.* 61,540); see also the letter of Lőrinc Hédervári, dated June 15, 1438 *(OL. Dl.* 61,538), and others. Documents attesting to the desire of lords and even towns to gain new serfs for their lands are: Mályusz, *ZsO,* 1:9; *OL. Dl.* 13,899, N.R.A. fasc. 7, no. 50.

33. I wish to thank Leslie Domonkos of Youngstown University for permitting me to see his as yet unpublished manuscript entitled "The Multi-Ethnic Character of the Hungarian Kingdom in the Latter Middle Ages," presented as a lecture at the Duquesne University History Forum in October 1981.

Notes to Chapter IV

34. For a sixteenth-century description of these, see Nicholaus Olahus, "Hungaria-Attila" (Pozsony, 1735), in *Bibliotheca Scriptorum medii recentique aevorum* (Budapest, 1938), pp. 1-34. Szekfű (*Állam*, p. 88) asserted that 80 percent of the population of Hungary proper was ethnically Hungarian. Such percentages were probably unstable, however, because of internal migration, immigration into the country from the Balkans and warfare.

35. Mályusz, "A magyarság és a nemzetiségek," in Domanovszky, *Magyar művelődéstörténet,* 2:107. He also stated that within Hungary proper 86 percent of the people were ethnically Hungarian. In this, however, the same reservation as above (n. 34) stands.

36. Mályusz, "A magyarság és a nemzetiségek," p. 118.

37. Dezső Csánki, "Máramarosmegye és az oláhság a XV. században" (Máramaros County and the Wallachians in the Fifteenth Century) *Századok* 23 (1889): 27-56.

38. Jenő Szűcs, "A nemzetiségi ideológia középkori históruma" (Medieval Historical Elements of Ethnic Ideology) *Valóság* (Budapest) 11 (1968): no. 6, pp. 40-41. In this, of course, Hungary did not differ from other European monarchies. See Federico Chabod, "Y a-t-il un état de la Renaissance?" *Actes due Colloque sur la Renaissance organise par la Société d'histoire moderne* (Paris, 1958), pp. 57-58.

39. Kálmán Eperjessy, *A magyar falu településtörténete* (The History of Settlement-patterns of Hungarian Villages) (Budapest, 1940), p. 24. However, this village network had not developed uniformily. For instance, in Gömör County in the highlands, there is no trace of settlements of Hungarians as late as the early thirteenth century (Ila, "Település és nemesség," pp. 5-6).

40. Néri, "Beszámoló," p. 138, points out that the peasants had learned a lesson from previous catastrophies and deliberately sought areas in which nature provided some protection; thus, settlements established after 1241 were seldom built on old foundations. See also Maksay, *A magyar falu,* p. 84, and Molnár, *A magyar társadalom,* 2:257. There were, however, exceptions. Belitzky (*Sopron vármegye,* 1:614) observed that "serf villages in Sopron County were built without protection in mind, scattered according to the fertility of the land. They liked to build their villages on the banks of rivers or streams providing advantages of fishing and the watering of animals." An explanation of this contradiction.

may lie in the fact that Sopron County, located in Western Hungary, was not as exposed to attacks as were the eastern and southern counties.

41. Maksay, *A magyar falu,* p. 84; Eperjessy, *A magyar falu,* pp. 71-72.

42. Eperjessy, *A magyar falu,* p. 72.

43. Fejér, *CDH,* 7:815.

44. István Éri and Alajos Bálint, *Muhi elpusztult középkori falu tárgyi emlékei* (Material Remains of the Medieval Village of Muhi) (Budapest, 1959), p. 4; also Julia Kovalovszky, *Régészeti adatok Szentes környékének településtörténetéhez* (Archeological Data for the Settlement History of Szentes and Its Environment) (Budapest, 1957), p. 27; Néri, "Beszámoló," p. 140. The last of these shows that most villages in the Great Plain were built either on the edges of swamps or on high ground in their midst.

45. Néri, "Beszámoló," p. 140. Móric consisted of thirty-one houses in the sixteenth century. An Ottoman *defter* from 1572 enumerated thirty-one heads of households living in thirty houses and one church. See also Károly Kondra, *Adatok az egri egyházmegye történetéhez* (Data for the History of the Bishopric of Eger), 2 vols. (Eger, 1855), 1:536.

46. Borovszky (*Borsod vármegye története,* p. 66) noted that before 1526 most villages in the county consisted of only a few houses, five to ten or, at the most twenty, and many had no churches of their own.

47. István Győrffy, *Magyar falu, magyar ház* (Hungarian Village, Hungarian House) (Budapest, 1943), pp. 84-90; also, Eperjessy, *A magyar falu,* pp. 52-53.

48. István Győrffy, "A Nagykunság és környékének népi épitkezése" (Folk-building Patterns of Nagykunság and Its Environs) in *Magyar Nép, Magyar föld* (Budapest, 1942), p. 63.

49. Zsigmond Bátky, István Győrffy, and Károly Viski eds., *A magyarság tárgyi néprajza* (Materials on the Folklore of the Hungarians), 4 vols. (Budapest, 1936-40), 2:314.

50. Néri, "Beszámoló," p. 140.

51. Ibid., p. 141, n. 23. In Móric no evidence of such fences was found.

52. Ibid., p. 140, n. 19. Néri lists ten fully excavated villages and notes that the village of Móric was more than a kilometer long. Brocquière noted in 1433 that the "large village" (really a market town) of Szeged

was more than a mile long (*Ouvrage, extrait d'un manuscrit de la Bibliotheque national par le grand d'Aussy* (Memoires de l'Institut national des Sciences morales et politiques) (Paris, n. d.), p. 16.
53. Szabó, *A magyar mezőgazdaság*, p. 41.
54. Belitzky, *Sopron vármegye*, p. 618.
55. Ibid., p. 619.
56. Belényesy, "A földművelés," p. 91 n. 61.
57. Márta Belényesy, "A permanens egymezős földhasználat és a két- és háromnyomásos rendszer kialakulása Magyarországon a középkorban" (The Permanent One-Field System and the Evolution of the Two- and Three-Field Systems in Medieval Hungary) *Ethnographia* 71 (1962): 81-106.
58. György Székely, "A parasztság szerepe az árutermelésben" (The Role of the Peasantry in Producing for the Market) in *Tanulmányok*, 124-25.
59. Marc Bloch's observations (*Feudal Society*, 1:135) is valid for fifteenth century Hungary; in Hungarian villages casual brutality and callousness existed side by side with strong family ties. Erik Fügedi [("Kapisztránói János csodái: A jegyzőkönyvek társadalom-történeti tanulságai" (The Miracles of János Kapisztránói: The Socio-Historical Lessons of the Records), *Századok* 111 (1977): 180)] describes a moving example of the cohesion of a village community in saving the life of a child who had fallen into a deep well, concluding that "near and distant relatives or mere acquaintances acted out of the conviction that it was their duty to do all they could for their fellow human being." Oláh (*Hungaria-Attila*, 1938) reported that the village of Simánd, in the district of Arad-Jenő in Transylvania, consisted exclusively of lame, blind, or otherwise crippled people. They would not permit a healthy person settle among them. Furthermore, they deliberately crippled their own children, created a special language among themselves, and made their living by begging. This was, of course, an extreme example of the protectiveness of a peasant community. On occasion, peasant communities of an entire district cooperated. In August 1448, the serfs of the market town of Vasvár in Vas County together with those of Mihályfalva and Gerse villages collectively drove the county authorities out of their meeting. The document attesting to this is dated Vasvár, August 12, 1448 (*OL. Dl. 93*, 102).
60. See my "The Peasant Revolt of Bábolna, 1437-1438," *Slavic Review* 35 (1977): 129-39.

61. On the use of peasants for feudal wars, see *Teleki,* 10:124. On the problems and circumstances surrounding the organization of a peasant militia, see András Borosy, *A telekkatonaság és a parasztság szerepe a feudális magyar hadszervezetben* (The Role of the Militia and the Peasants in the Feudal Military System of Hungary) (Budapest, 1971), especially pp. 15-21 and 24-48.

62. We must note the uncertain nature of the data on peasant life in the fifteenth century in general. See Fügedi, "Kapisztránói," p. 879.

63. Fügedi ("Hungarian Bishops," pp. 375-91) has noted, however, that the six bishops in this century who were of peasant origin lived an average of nine years longer than their aristocratic counterparts. This, of course, has no statistical value but does provide food for thought. On barber-surgeons, see Lajos Fekete, "Adatok a magyar sebészet történetéhez" (Data on the History of Surgery in Hungary), *Történelmi Tár,* Old series, 2 (1878): 87-89, alos Gyula Magyari-Kossa, "Közegészségügy a régi magyaroknál" (Public Health Among Ancient Hungarians) *Közegészségügy* (Budapest) 3 (1921): 127; Tibor Győry, "Monumentumok a magyar orvostörténetből" (Monuments from the History of Medicine in Hungary) *Századok* 35 (1901): 45-46. Methods of surgery were originally taught by the various religious orders, especially the Benedictines, Dominicans, Cistercians and the Hospitallers. Their surgeons were university-trained. A synod held in Buda in 1279 forbade the monks to practice surgery in the country, and practices deteriorated subsequently.

64. Szabó, *A magyar mezőgazdaság,* p. 47.

65. The use of the heavy plow was related to the spread of the two-field and three-field systems. The lands that were left fallow in these systems needed a heavier plow the year in which they were cultivated again and this called for more animals and more cooperation among the villagers than before. According to István Balassa, eight oxen or five horses and three men were required to guide the animals and hold the handles of the plow (*Az eke és a szántás története Magyarországon* (History of the Plow and Plowing in Hungary) (Budapest, 1973), p. 286.

66. Ibid., p. 288.

67. Szabó, *A magyar mezőgazdaság,* p. 47.

68. Brocquière, *Ouvrage,* p. 16.

69. Sándor Takáts, "A magyar malom" (Hungarian Mills), *Századok* 41 (1907): 143-60 and 236-49, "A magyar molnár" (The Hungarian Miller) ibid., pp. 52-56.

Notes to Chapter IV

70. Makkai, "Agrarian Landscapes," p. 195.
71. Ibid., p. 202; also Márta Belényesy, "Der Ackerbau und seine Produkte in Ungarn im 14. Jahrhundert," *Acta Ethnographica* (Budapest) 6 (1958): 107-42.
72. Makkai, "Agrarian Landscapes," p. 195.
73. Zsigmond Jakó, *Bihar megye a török pusztitás előtt* (Bihar County before the Turkish Devastation) (Budapest, 1940), p. 1.
74. Ibid., p. 2; also Lajos Gláser, "Az Alföld régi vizrajza és a települések" (The Old Topography of the Great Plain and the Settlements) *Földrajzi Közlemények* (Budapest) 67 (1939): 216.
75. Jakó, *Bihar megye*, p. 11.
76. Ibid., p. 13.
77. Néri, "Beszámoló," n. 19 and 23.
78. Szabó, *A magyar mezőgazdaság*, p. 49; also *Hazai Okmánytár* 2: 305.
79. Makkai, "Agrarian Landscapes," p. 204.
80. The amount of wine consumed was enormous. For instance, the records of the abbey of Pécsvárad show that the monks drank 560 liters of wine per head per year, or over 1½ liters a day. This cost the abbey 8.22 florins a year per brother. In 1451 a patent issued by bishop János Vitéz of Nagyvárad for the village of Belényes stipulated that the village judge and his jurors must decide suits only during the morning hours, all cases settled after midday being null and void because "by then they were all drunk" (Molnár, *A magyar társadalom*, 1:192, n. 1).
81. Makkai, "Agrarian Landscapes," p. 204. Elaborate rules against thievery in the vineyards were soon created. One such set of rules, issued by the nuns of The Island of Rabbits of Pest, is in *OL. D1.* 19,163.
82. These towns were still overwhelmingly agrarian in character; only a small portion of thier food requirements was filled from outside sources. See Ferenc Kováts, *Városi adózás a középkorban* (The Taxation of Towns in the Middle Ages) (Pozsony, 1900), p. 16.
83. János Belitzky, *A magyar gabonakivitel története 1860-ig* (History of Hungarian Grain Exports up to 1860) (Budapest, 1932), pp. 8-12; also Ferenc Kováts, *Nyugatmagyarország áruforgalma a XV. században* (Circulation of Trade in Western Hungary in the Fifteenth Century) (Budapest, 1902), p. 187; Alexander Domanovszky, "Zur Geschichte der Gutherrschaft in Ungarn," in Gian Piero Bognetti et al., eds., *Festschrift*

zum 70 gebursttag von Alfons Dopsch (Frankfurt a. M., 1966), pp. 441-69.

84. Brocquière (*Ouvrage,* p. 17) reported that in Szeged an excellent stud cost only 10 florins. Yet he also reported that when Hungarians travelled, six or even eight of them crowded into a wagon drawn by a single horse. This was, of course, consistent with the fact that horses were mainly used for war.

85. József Soós, *Magyar néptáplálkozástan* (Study of Hungarian Folk Habits of Eating) (Budapest, 1942), p. 19. Brocquière observed that fish were available in great numbers and that he had seen a market with enormous numbers of wild birds for sale (*Ouvrage,* p. 19). Néri ("Beszámoló, p. 149), notes that the excavation of Móric showed that the inhabitants consumed a great many animals.

86. Néri, "Beszámoló," p. 145.
87. Ibid., p. 147.
88. Ibid., p. 144.
89. Ibid.
90. Brocquière (*Ouvrage,* p. 18) remarked that throughout his trip in the Great Plain he had seen no trees except for a small strip of woods alongside a stream.
91. Sándor Sólymossy, "Hitvilág," in Bátkay, et al., *A magyarság tárgyi,* 4:357.
92. Ibid., pp. 382-83.
93. Ibid.
94. Ibid.
95. Brocquière noted the excellent quality of salt mined in Hungary. He said that it was cut into blocks a foot square that looked like marble slabs (*Ouvrage,* p. 19).
96. János Fegyó, "Középkori lakóház leletmentése Ráckevén" (Saving the Archeological Finds of a House at Ráckeve) *Studia Comitatensia* (Szentendre) 2 (1973): 93-105.
97. Solymóssy, "Hitvilág," 4:349-74, and "Vallásos élet" (Religious Life) ibid., pp. 290-300; also Zsigmond Szendrey, "Jeles napok" (Memorable Days) ibid., pp. 323-41. As Hilton observed (*Bond Men,* p. 19) "many of the thoughts and feelings of peasants must have derived from pre-Christian or non-Christian sources." See also Zsuzsanna Kulcsár, "A tömeges boszorkányüldözések magyarázata és okai" (The Causes and

Explanation for the Mass Persecution of Witches) *Századok* 98 (1964): 158-75; Ferenc Schramm, *Magyarországi boszorkányperek* (Witch Trials in Hungary), 2 vols. (Budapest, 1973); Vince Bunyitay, *A váradi püspökség története* (History of the Bishopric of Nagyvárad) (Budapest, 1883-84), 4 vols., 1:70. (It is worth noting that the mass persecution of witches did not begin in Hungary until well into the sixteenth century.) Hilton points out that the relation between evangelistic heresies and peasant discontent is by no means clear. Hussite teachings certainly had less effect in fifteenth-century Hungary than previously believed. This may point to a great deal less tension in contemporary peasant life than has been attributed to it recently by some Hungarian historians.
98. Kováts, *Temesvári Pelbárt*, pp. 154-55.
99. Solymóssy, "Vallásos élet," 4:297-300.
100. Traian Stoianovich, *A Study in Balkan Civilization* (New York, 1967), pp. 22-25. Béla Gunda, "Ethnography," in *The Hungarian Quarterly* (Budapest) 7 (1942): 285-304, found that particular superstitutions were associated with specific occupations. Different spells and charms were used by herders of cattle, swine and horses as well as by farmers and by those who lived by fishing and hunting.
101. Károly Kozák, "A zalaszántói templon feltárása és környékének középkori története" (The Excavations of the Church of Zalaszántó, and the Medieval History of its Environs) *Archeológia Értesitő* 89 (1962): 223-24.
102. "Calendarium generale et speciale usque A.1400 quod in Hungaria obtinuit," in Fejér, *CDH*, series 7, 2:33-49.
103. Czeglédy and Koppány, "A középkori Ecsér," p. 51; Néri, "Beszámoló," p. 142.
104. Erzsébet Lócsy, "Alhéviz és Békásmegyer középkori temploma" (The Medieval Church of Alhéviz and Békásmegyer) *Archeológiai Értesitő* 94 (1967): 203, 210.

Notes to Chapter V

1. Lajos Thallóczy and Antal Áldásy, *Magyarország melléktartományainak oklevéltára*, vol. 1, *A Magyarország és Szerbia közti összeköttetések oklevéltára, 1198-1526* (The Archive of the Feudal Dependencies

of Hungary. vol. 1. The Relations between Hungary and Serbia, 1198-1526) (Budapest, 1907), pp. 4-6.

2. It is possible that Hunyadi had learned this concept from his mentor Philippo Scolari.

3. Hunyadi organized his army on the pattern of the Italian *condottiere* and added the imaginative use of the battlewagon that he had learned from the Hussites. His battles did not, however, resemble the cautious maneuverings of the Italians; they were all-out fights to the death. See Lajos Elekes, "Hunyadi hadserege" (The Army of Hunyadi) *Századok* 84 (1950): 85-86.

4. Pál Engel, "János Hunyadi: The Decisive Years of His Career, 1440-1444," János M. Bak and Béla K. Király, eds., *From Hunyadi to Rákóczi: War and Society in Medieval and Early Modern Hungary* (New York, 1982), pp. 117-19.

5. Fejér, *CDH*, 11:321-27.

6. A letter dated Buda, June 13, 1440, issued by Wladislaw I, granted safe conduct to some of his opponents, among them László Gari and János Korógyi for a meeting at Buda (*OL. Dl.* 13,554). The supporters of the king who signed it included Lőrinc Hédervári, Matkó Thallóczi, János Perényi, Imre Marcali, and László Pálóci. That Hunyadi's name did not appear on the letter points to the fact that he was not considered important enough to sign it.

7. The arrival of the Hungarian delegation in Cracow and the ensuing negotiations are described in *Codex diplomaticus Regni Poloniae et Magni Ducatus Litvaniae* (Vilnus, 1758), 1:53-54. Members of the delegation included János Vitéz and the lords who signed the letter cited in n. 6. See also *Dlugosz*, 12:615-18.

8. See Wladislaw's declaration dated Cracow, March 8, 1440 and July 20, 1440 (in *OL. Dl.* 13,894 and *OL. Dl.* 39,291). If Wladislaw died without a male heir, László was to inherit the throne: the king also promised to support the marriage of the queen's other daughter to a man of her choice.

9. For this see Chapter I, no. 28. Erzsébet issued patents as "king" (see *OL. Dl.* 86,367, 14,591 and 44,278).

10. The theft is vividly described in Helene Kottannerin, *Aus den Denkwürdigkeiten der Helene Kottannerin*, ed. Endlicher (Leipzig, 1846), pp. 101-103. See also the patent of Wladislaw I dated Buda, November 7,

1440, (in *OL. Dl*. 13,589, 13,588 and 13,570) which describes the circumstances of his trop to Buda and, incidentially, the help that he had received from Simon Rozgonyi, bishop of Eger.

11. *OL. Dl*. 13,589.
12. For example, Elekes, *Hunyadi,* p. 130.
13. See, for instance, Erzsébet's decree dated Pozsony, July 18, 1442, in *Teleki,* 10:114-15.
14. "Historia Friderici Imperatoris" in Adam F. Kollar, *Analecta monumentorum onmis aevi vindobonensia* 2 vols. (Vienna, 1761), 2: col. 915-29 and 988-89.
15. See the patent of Wladislaw I (in *OL. Dl*. 589, 13,588 and 13,570), and for the circumstances of Cilli's release, another document dated Buda, November 6, 1440, (in *OL. Dl*. 92,906), including the count's promise to return the fortresses of Trencsén, Keménd, Márványkő, Kigyókő, Németi and Paks to Wladislaw in exchange for his freedom. A document dated Esztergom, November 11, 1440 (*OL. Dl* 13,590), contains Cilli's grant of the estate of Treuburg in Karinthia to Rajnald Rozgonyi in appreciation for the latter's actions on his behalf while in captivity.
16. On the rejection of the coronation of László V by the nobility see Bak, *Königtum und Stände,* pp. 43-44 and 169-72. For the text of the declaration of the privileged orders assembled in the diet, see *Codex diplomaticus Regni Poloniae,* 1:56-58.
17. See the letter from Erzsébet to Frederick III dated Wienerneustadt, March 3, 1441, in *Teleki,* 10:95-96.
18. The date of his appointment is uncertain. A document dated May 3, 1440 (that is, three weeks before the arrival of Wladislaw I in Buda), already speaks of Hunyadi as *voivode,* but this date may be wrong (*OL. Dl.* 55,236). A letter dated Bogáth, May 14, 1441 from Hunyadi to Wladislaw I is prefaced by the title of military governor (*OL. Dl.* 37,600). The tide was indeed turning in Wladislaw's favor.
19. All this was the result of the energetic action of the joint governors, to which Wladislaw had given his consent; see the document dated Buda, March 25, 1441 (*OL. Dl.* 92,921), confirming the grant to loyal subjects of estates confiscated from an opponent. For similar actions see *OL. Dl.* 36,390 and 36,390 nos. 2 and 3, containing the protests of the nobles of Farnas against Hunyadi's "arbitrary" action in confiscating their estate.

20. A letter (in *OL. Dl.* 36,390 no. 1) from Angelus of Florence protesting the confiscation by Hunyadi of 45 hundred-weights of lead that the merchant had received from the king shows that Hunyadi was not squeamish when it came to matters of revenue.

21. Nesri in *Thury*, 1:55.

22. In *Teleki*, 10:358. For a contemporary account of these events see Chalcocondylas, *Historiarum*, 1:10. See also Armin Huber, "Die Kriege zwischen Ungarn und den Türken, 1440-1443," *Archiv für Österreichischen Geschichte* 68:169.

23. Another version was provided by Rónay-Horváth, *Magyar hadi krónika*, pp. 253-54. According to him, Ishak Pasha was in the habit of prowling around Belgrade, hoping to catch the defenders unaware and capturing the fortress. On one occasion, Hunyadi having learned of his approach in advance, took part of the garrison of the fortress and met the pasha at Császárhalom. After his victory, he pursued him all the way to Szendrő. According to a document issued by László V at Pozsony, dated September 14, 1453, (*OL. Dl.* 14,726, N.R.A. fasc. 178, no. 29), Ujlaki's troops participated in this engagement, but the document does not speak of the participation of Ujlaki himself.

24. Lajos Thallóczy and Lajos Gelcich, eds., *Raguza és Magyarország összeköttetéseinek levéltára* (Archive of the Relations of Ragusa and Hungary) (Budapest, 1887), p. 437. Naturally, the report of a "large scale raid" may have been an exaggeration. Thus, when Kupelwieser (*Kämpfe*, p. 62) maintains that Mezid's army contained eighty thousand soldiers, he is a victim of the imagination of the Ragusans. The letter from Wladislaw I dated Buda, April 17, 1443 (*OL. Dl.* 13,718), describing Hunyadi's victories in some detail, places this contest in the context of a frontier clash.

25. Thuróczi (in SCHWANDTNER, 1:312-15) simply called Mezid an Ottoman *viovode*. Chalcocondylas (in *Historiarum*, 1:253) stated that Mezid was the commander of the European army. Hammer-Purgstall (*Geschichte des osmanischen Reiches*, 1:437) said that he served as the master of the sultan's stables. Finally, Nicolai Jorga (*Geschichte des osmanischen Reiches* [Gotha, 1908]), described him as the bey (lord) of Viddin.

26. Sead-eddin (*Thury*, p. 132) maintained that Mezid was originally sent not to Transylvania, but to Wallachia. According to Rónay-Horváth

(*Magyar hadi krónika*, 1:254-55), Hunyadi was notified by Ujlaki from Transylvania about the impending raid, but he could not bring his troops to the province without leaving the southern borders undefended. Rónay-Horváth goes on to say that Ujlaki's calling the nobility to arms had little effect.

27. Thuróczi in SCHWANDTNER, 1:249-50.

28. *Teleki,* 1:286, quotes a Transylvanian Saxon report: "Mezetis Turci veres contemsit et arma, obsidione dim gravitor vexata, fugamque auxilio Hunyadis moliri compulit hostes...." Chalcocondylas (*Historiarum*, 1:258) speaks of one engagement but says nothing of this one.

29. Ottokár Székely, "Hunyadi János első török hadjáratai" (The First Turkish Campaigns of János Hunyadi) *Hadtörténelmi Közlemények* 20/21 (1919-21): 9. It is worth noting that the Ottoman sources, although mentioning Mezid's victory, either do no mention Hunyadi's part or, like the anonymous chronicle (in *Thury*, 1:18) do not even mention the first battle. According to Rónay-Horváth (*Magyar hadi krónika*, 1:255), the mistake was Lépes's: Hunyadi wanted to wait for an opportunity to seize the Ottomans' booty and free their captives, perhaps in an ambush, but Lépes preempted him by attacking the advance guard of Mezid's troops, and was drawn into the trap laid by the main army.

30. Vilmos Fraknói (*Mátyás király, 1440-1490* [King Mátyás, 1440-1490] Budapest, 1890, p. 8) maintains that the younger János Hunyadi died in this battle, but this is by no means certain. More likely, he died earlier, since his older brother spoke of him as "felices memoriae" in a letter dated January 3, 1442 (*OL. Dl.* 26,393). Fraknói's argument was based on a patent issued by Wladislaw I at Buda on August 9, 1442 (*OL. Dl.* 13,577), stating that the Hunyadi brothers, especially the younger, had shed his blood in Wallachia during the reign of King Albert I and that as joint governors of Szörény they had done the same. It is also possible that the younger János Hunyadi had died as the result of wounds received in another engagement. For the death of Bishop Lépes, see Katona, *HCR*, 13:216.

31. For detailed discussions of these events see my articles "The Peasant Revolt of Bábolna, 1437-1438," pp. 25-37, and "Peasants in Arms," in Bak and Király, *From Hunyadi to Rákóczi,* pp. 81-102.

32. Székely, "Hunyadi első," p. 9.

33. Thuróczi in SCHWANDTNER, 1:251.

34. There is some disagreement over this issue. Chalcocondylas (*Historiarum*, 1:258) mentioned only one battle and said that Mezid had been killed by a cannon ball during the siege of Nagyszeben, but the poem quoted above in *Teleki* 1:286 (n. 28) seems to contradict this version.

35. Thuróczi in SCHWANDTNER, 1:251. Hunyadi's letter (in *OL. Dl.* 37,600) calls him "Symon de Kamonya." *Teleki,* 1:288 said that he was a Kemény, but there is no basis for this in other documents.

36. The patent of László V quoted in n. 23 describes the victory. Hammer-Purgstall (*Geschichte des osmanischen Reiches,* 1:451) embroidered the story by adding that the Ottomans had lost thirty thousand soldiers, a gross exaggeration. Vilmos Fraknói (*A Hunyadiak és Jagellók kora Magyarországon* [The Era of the Hunyadis and the Jagellos in Hungary] Budapest, 1894, p. 26), accepted this legend, as did Kupelwieser (*Kämpfe,* p. 64).

37. Károly Veszely, "Hol verte meg Hunyadi 1442-ben Mezid béget?" (Where Did Hunyadi Defeat Mezid Bey in 1442?), *Századok* 13 (1879): 134 (Appendix).

38. According to Chalcocondylas (*Historiarum,* 1:254), the sultan himself wanted to lead the army to avenge the defeat of Mezid but Sehabeddin (in Chalcocondylas; "Sebatines") persuaded Murad to send him instead. Seadeddin (*Thury,* 1:133) called him Kule Sahin, "the Brown Falcon," adding mischievously that he was also called the gelded Sehabeddin Pasha. See also Ármin Vámbéry, "Hunyadi János hat legnagyobb csatája melyet szultán Murad II és Mohamed ellen vitt" (The Six Greatest Battles of Hunyadi that He Fought Against Sultans Murad II and Mohamed) *Magyar Történelmi Tár* (Budapest) 11 (1862): 201-204.

39. Ivanics in SCHWANDTNER, 2:16. The patent of László V quoted in n. 23 speaks of eighty thousand Ottoman soldiers obviously an overstatement. Chalcocondylas (*Historiarum,* 1:254) also mentions this number.

40. Nesri in *Thury,* 1:56 and Sead-eddin, ibid., 134.

41. For Hunyadi's recruiting methods see *Teleki,* 1:323.

42. Nesri in *Thury,* 1:56.

43. Katona, *HCR,* 13:269.

44. Székely ("Hunyadi János első," pp. 22-23) questions the possibility, since, as he argues, the mountainous terrain did not favor the driving of battlewagons into the fight.

45. Chalcocondylas (*Historiarum,* 1:256) echoes the Ottoman

sources according to whom Sehabeddin was a coward and an incompetent commander. He reports that Sehabeddin, overconfident because of the size of his army, sent the sipahis to raid and loot the countryside, keeping only a few soldiers in his camp. Thus, when Hunyadi attacked it, there were few to oppose him, and when the raiders returned, they were trapped by the Hungarians, see also Nesri (in *Thury*, 1:56), Sead-eddin (in *Thury*, 1:134).

46. Chalcocondylas, *Historiarum*, p. 256.
47. Nesri (in *Thury*, 1:56). Contemporaries, including Chalcocondylas, recognized that the battle's outcome signaled a turning point in the Hungarian-Ottoman struggle.
48. *Teleki*, 10:360.
49. Elekes, *Hunyadi*, pp. 145-46.
50. Ranzanus in SCHWANDTNER, 1:138.
51. A number of documents issued during September, 1441, at Buda attest to Erzsébet's realization that only through negotiations could she salvage something for herself and her son. These documents speak of the appointment of a negotiating team, headed by Simon Rozgonyi (*OL. Dl.* 13,644), the team members' acceptance of their appointment (*OL. Dl.* 39,293), the royal council's consent to the talks (*OL. Dl.* 13,644) and the archbishop Dénes Széchi's approval of the agenda (*OL. Dl.* 44,321), the former queen's reward for the negotiators on November 30, 1442 (*OL. Dl.* 13,645).
52. Fejér, *Genus*, pp. 50-51.

Notes to Chapter VI

1. On the contemporary impact of Hunyadi's early victories see Callimachus in SCHWANDTNER, 1:487, also Chalcocondylas, *Historiarum*, pp. 257-58.
2. Frederick III sometimes acted as if he were Hungarian sovereign. For instance, he issued a patent, dated March 3, 1443, to Stepan Frangepan (Frankopan) and his successors granting them the privilege of coining money (Lajos Thallóczy and Samu Barabás, *A Frangepán-cslád oklevéltára* (The Archive of the Frangepan Family) 2 vols. (Budapest, 1910), 1:339.
3. On Frederick III's attitude towards the Hungarians see the letter

of Casper Schlick in *Fontes Rerum Austriarcarum* series 2, 62:9-12. It would be difficult to agree with Elekes' argument (*Hunyadi*, pp. 183-85) that the Habsburgs actively worked to prevent the Hungarians' anti-Ottoman campaign. On Caesarini's efforts to arrange peace between the emperor and Wladislaw I, see Fraknói, *Egyháznagyok*, pp. 18-21.

4. For Branković's role, see Thuróczi in SCHWANDTNER, 1:488.

5. On the origins of the campaign and Hunyadi's role in its preparation, see Thuróczi, ibid., 1:252-53; also the letter of Wladislaw I to the county authorities of Közép-Szolnok (in *OL. Dl.* 65,057).

6. Callimachus in SCHWANDTNER, 1:487.

7. Béla Iványi, *Bártfa szabad királyi város oklevéltára* (The Archive of Bártfa, Free Royal City) 2 vols. (Budapest, 1914), 1:71-73; also *Teleki*, 10:133, 140 and 330-31.

8. Székely, "Hunyadi János első," p. 28.

9. Michael Beheim, a German folk balladeer who had received first hand information from one Hans Mägest, a participant in the Long Campaign (captured by the Ottomans and freed seventeen years later after the event), stated that Wladislaw's army consisted of fourteen thousand well-armed soldiers (Karajan, "Zehn Gedichte," pp. 35-46, quoted by Bleyer, "Beheim Mihály," pp. 222-46; also *Dlugosz*, 12:779). According to a Czech mercenary who participated in the campaign, Hunyadi had six hundred battlewagons [(A. Jirecek, *Archiv für Österreichische Geschichte* (Vienna, 1886)], p. 198.

10. See Branković's letter to Hunyadi in Fejér, *Genus*, pp. 71-75.

11. *Teleki*, 1:334 says that there were thirty-five thousand soldiers; Kupelwieser (*Kämpfe*, p. 68) agrees; Bonfini (p. 457) mentions fifteen thousand; Fraknói (*Egyháznagyok*, p. 37) says fourty thousand. The composition of the army was truly international. In addition to Wladislaw's Polish soldiers and his Hungarian retainers, and Hunyadi's and Ujlaki's Hungarian armies, there were troops from Bohemia, Moldavia, and Wallachia; there were also Serbs and a small number of crusaders from Germany and Austria. (See *Teleki*, 10:123-25 and *Dlugosz*, 12:685-86.)

12. A letter from Hunyadi to Ujlaki quoted by Elekes (*Hunyadi*, p. 200) as follows: "A great many Bosnians, Bulgars, Serbs, and Albanians are constantly arriving in our camp, bringing all sorts of presents. They have brought us so much fresh food that our provisions are practically untouched." I disagree with the conclusion that Elekes draws from

this letter, namely, that in all his campaigns, Hunyadi sought to forge an alliance with the "peoples of the Balkans" against the Ottomans. Hunyadi did indeed try to interest the feudal princes in a common effort against the Ottomans, but he, like all his contemporaries, did not want the "peoples" to participate.

13. According to *Teleki*, 1:337, the reason for this was that contemporaries mentioned none or two different battles each, while none of them mentioned them all. On the early skirmishes see the letter of Schlick in *Fontes Rerum Austriacarum*, 62:42-44.

14. Letter from Hunyadi to Ujlaki, dated November 8, 1443, in Katona, *HCR*, 13:251, and Fejér, *Genus*, p. 55.

15. See Hunyadi's letter in Katona, *HCR*, 13:674.

16. According to Hunyadi, news of this detachment reached him on November 3. He met it at the end of the Nišava Valley where it barred his way. Its leaders included Ali Bey, son of Tincurtas, Balaban Pasha of Tokat, the beys of Vidin and Sofia, and Mahmud Celebi, brother of Halil Pasha, the grand vizier. Hunyadi estimated its size at thirty thousand men, and he reported that two thousand Ottoman soldiers died in the engagement; ibid.

17. Rónay-Horváth, *Magyar hadi krónika*, 3:262.

18. Székely, "Hunyadi János első," p. 29.

19. Exaggerations about the size of the Ottoman army were frequent. Beheim mentioned two-hundred thousand strong (Bleyer, "Beheim Mihály," p. 222).

20. According to Chalcocondylas' colorful description (*Historiarum*, 1:309-11) Murad II's council restrained the sultan who wanted an open battle, but the bey of Thessali, Turkham Pasha disagreed; he recommended withdrawal and what amounted to a scorched-earth tactic. Jese, son of Evrenos, suggested that the passes should be denied to the Hungarians instead, and when they became exhausted and withdrew, the sipahis should be sent after them. This was the recommendation that finally carried the day. For Hunyadi's letter on the army's march see *OL. Dl.* 30,810. This battle occurred on Christmas Day in 1443.

21. Székely, "Hunyadi János első," pp. 54-56.

22. Chalcocondylas, *Historiarum*, 1:315.

23. According to Beheim (Bleyer, "Beheim Mihály," p. 227), the high ranking captives were turned over to Branković but he returned them

to the king. However, when the Ottoman envoys sought Celebi's freedom, they visited the despot, so he may still have had the Ottomans in captivity.

24. *Századok*, 28 (1894): 679-85.

25. As Hunyadi noted in his letter to Pope Eugene IV, dated May 11, 1445, "all the neighboring rulers, including those of Moldavia, Bulgaria and Albania and even that of Constantinople, offered armed assistance to us and said 'fly faster than the wind, we had already taken care of everything... ,' but we were not given any help, and our supply line was interrupted." ("Epistolae Joannis de Zredna," SCHWANDTNER, 2:17; also V. S. Kovács, *Magyar humanisták*, p. 69).

26. For the memoirs of a Czech soldier describing this mission, see Huber, *Archiv für Österreichische Geschichte* (1886):199.

27. *Teleki*, 1:417.

28. Oscar Halecki, *The Crusade of Varna: A Discussion of Controversial Issues* (New York, 1943), pp. 13-31.

29. *Teleki*, 1:417.

30. Ibid.

31. Hunyadi's letter in "Epistolae Joannis de Zredna," SCHWANDTNER, 2:17.

32. In a letter dated Nagyvárad, May 2, 1444, Wladislaw requested help from the Teutonic Order, remarking that the pope had promised to send thirty-eight galleys of which the Venetians were to supply twelve, the king of Aragon ten, the prince of Burgundi six, that of Milan eight, and the grand master of Rhodes two. This would certainly have been a formidable armada fully capable of closing the Straits of the Hellespont and the Bosporus to the Ottomans (Thallóczy and Áldásy, *Magyarország és Serbia*, p. 144).

33. Halecki, *The Crusade of Varna*, p. 32.

34. David Angyal, "A szegedi béke" (The Peace of Szeged) *Budapesti Szemle* (1910): 144.

35. See the letters of Sultan Mehemed II in József Thury, "A várnai csatáról" (On the Battle of Varna) *Hadtörténeti Közlemények* 5 (1892): 638-41.

36. Although Fejér (*Genus*, pp. 71-75) published a letter presumably written by Branković and the same document was published by Katona (*HCR*, 13:269) and by Thallóczy and Áldásy (*A Magyarország és Szerbia*,

p. 145), the original letter did not survive. However, a patent of the palatine, Hédervári, addressed to the cathedral chapter of Gyulafehérvár, dated Buda, March 10, 1445 (*OL. Dl.* 37,601), noted that János Hunyadi and his sons László and Mátyás had indicated their intention to be installed in the possession of Világosvár in Zaránd County, the estates of Aranyág and Kaladwapataka in Arad County, the towns of Kápolna, Csúcs, Fejérkeresnagybánya, and Kisbánya, and 110 villages including the tolls belonging to their possessor, and five parish churches and their patronates.

37. Angyal, "A szegedi," p. 145; *Teleki,* 1:432.

38. A letter from the Polish privileged orders to Wladislaw to that effect, dated Piotrkow, August 26, 1444, in Thallóczy and Áldásy, *A Magyarország és Szerbia,* p. 146.

39. Thuróczi in SCHWANDTNER, 1:271.

40. The misunderstanding over this issue may have originated in the misreading of a document by Anthony Prochaska, *Uwagi Kryticzne o klesce Warnenskije* (Critical Remarks about the Disaster of Varna) (Cracow, 1900), pp. 1-60. Prochaska quoted Ignácz Bathányi (*Leges Ecclesiasticae,* 1:487) as saying that the king did not sign the peace treaty. But what Bathányi actually said was that the king signed a treaty but not as the result of the arguments of Cardinal Caesarini. Prochaska's view was uncritically accepted by Albrecht Brücker [*Geschichte des polnischen Litteratur,* (Leipzig, 1901), 1:628] and even Halecki was unable to resist its lure in his *Crusade of Varna,* pp. 32-53. For a discussion of Prochaska's sources and his argument, see Lajos Rácz, Vilmos Fraknói, Jakab Bleyer, and József Thury, "Igazság vagy tévedés?" (Truth or Mistake?) *Századok* 36 (1902): 631-53. A whole host of documents refer directly or indirectly to the conclusion of some sort of agreement (most likely a long-term truce), even if, because Islamic law permitted no permanent peace treaty with a non-Islamic adversary, we cannot call it a peace agreement. Thuróczi in SCHWANDTNER, 1:41, Callimachus (ibid., p. 489), Chalcocondylas (*Historiarum,* 1:307) and *Dlugosz* (12:684) all agreed that there was a "peace of Szeged" signed by Wladislaw I, and Ottoman historians referred to it in their works. Andreas Pannonius cautioned the later king of Mátyás Hunyadi against taking his oaths slightly "as Wladislaw I had done at Szeged" (Fraknói, *Irodalomtörténeti emlékek* 1:22; see also Aeneas Sylvius Piccolomini, "Epistolae," *Fontes Rerum Austricarum* 2 (1909): 61-62.

41. For instance, Halecki, mentioned in n. 40.
42. On the negotiations, see *Dlugosz,* 12:699-711.
43. For Wladislaw's declaration, see Hurmuzaki, *Documente,* 1/2: 694-96; also Vilmos Fraknói, "A várnai csata előzményei" (Preliminaries to the Battle of Varna) *Hadtörténeti Közlemények* 2 (1889): 337-88. *Dlugosz,* 12:792-93, stated that Hunyadi's ambition was to become king of Bulgaria, and this influenced Wladislaw's decision. But there is no evidence for this assertion.
44. The declaration of Futak in *Történelmi Tár,* Old series, 8 (1895): 400.
45. *Teleki,* 1:445.
46. Beheim does not mention the "peace of Szeged" in his poem about Varna (Bleyer, "Beheim Mihály," p. 232).
47. Engel in Bak and Király, *From Hunyadi to Rákóczi.*
48. However, two letters, dated January 1445 from the future Sultan Mehemed II asserted that he acted only as regent while the sultan left for Anatolia "in order to contemplate his preparation for eternal happiness." Murad departed, Mehemed stated, because he concluded a truce with all his former enemies (quoted by Thury, "A várnai cstáról," pp. 638-40).
49. *Teleki,* 1:412-18. Wladislaw's behavior seems to indicate reservations about the war to the very end. For instance, after the declaration of August 4, he left Szeged for Nagyvárad, where he spent several weeks [Stanislaw Kwiatowski, *Itinerarum Wladislawa (III) Warnenczyka* (Lemberg, 1879), pp. 26-27]. From Nagyvárad he traveled to Temesvár (In Beheim, to Tumelsburg), where he stayed for several more days. Then he spent two more weeks at Orsova before crossing the Danube (see Bleyer, "Beheim Mihály," p. 348).
50. Kwiatowski, *Itinerarum,* p. 28. According to Rónay-Horváth (*Magyar hadi krónika,* p. 266), six thousand Hungarian and four thousand Polish soldiers accompanied the king to Orsova; only a thousand crusaders were recruited by Caesarini; Hunyadi brought along another four thousand soldiers from Transylvania, and Vlad Dracul joined Wladislaw with four thousand Vlachs. Thus, the army that actually started on this campaign numbered only about twenty thousand men.
51. *Teleki,* 1:430. According to Andreas de Palatio (*Literae de clade Varnensi ad Ludovicum Cardinalem datae* ed. A. Prochaska, Lemberg, 1882, p. 22), the army moved slowly. Beheim mentions the sacking of a city, probably Kladova (Bleyer, "Beheim Mihály," pp. 349, 354). All the

sources flatly contradict the report of Lajos Elekes [("A délkeleteurópai népek összefogása a török hóditok ellen Hunyadi háboruiban" (The Getting Together of the Southeast European Peoples against the Ottoman Conquerors in the Wars of Hunyadi) *Századok* 86 (1952): 96-97)], that Hunyadi consciously promoted some sort of "people's war" against the Ottomans. The fact was that Hunyadi and his allies were motivated by various interests; some of them, such as, for instance, Branković and Dracul, changed sides as their interests indicated.

52. The sacking and burning of Vidin is described by Beheim (Bleyer, "Beheim Mihály," p. 349); Palatio, on the other hand, contradicts this (*Literae*, p. 24).

53. *Dlugosz*, 12:716.

54. Ibid., 12:716-17.

55. Ibid.

56. This was to have serious consequences. According to the anonymous Ottoman chronicler (Thury, 1:58), the bey of Nicopolis followed Wladislaw's army and captured several cavalrymen, whom he sent to Edirne. These revealed Hunyadi's plans, and thus the sultan was able to march directly to Varna without losing time, catching up with his opponent's army within six days after he crossed the Straits. See also Seadeddin in *Thury*, 1:136.

57. Bleyer, "Beheim Mihály," p. 352.

58. Fraknói, "A várnai csata előzményei," p. 379. Thury (A várnai csatáról," p. 645) pointed outthat Murad II had probably used the vessels of Giovanni Adorno, the governor of Genoa's Anatolian possessions, in crossing over to Europe in 1421, when he faced the rebellion of Mustafa, son of Bayazid. After that, the sultan had cultivated his friendship with Adorno, and it is possible that the vessels he used in 1444 were those of his Genoan friend. On this friendship, see Hammer-Purgstall, *Geschichte des osmanischen Reiches*, 1:404.

59. Thuróczi in SCHWANDTNER, 1:278.

60. Angyal, "Murád utja," pp. 252-53.

61. Callimachus in SCHWANDTNER, 1:513-14.

62. A Greek eyewitness to the battle, Paraspondylas Zotikos, erroneously asserted that Hunyadi's army consisted of forty thousand men, while the sultan had two hundred thousand. [Emile Legrand, *Collection de monuments pour servir a l'étude de la langue neo-hellenique* nouvelle

serie, no. 5 (Paris, 1875), and Vilmos Pecz, "Zotikos költeménye a várnai csatáról" (The Poem of Zotikos about the Battle of Varna) *Századok* 28 (1894): 316-37].

63. Pecz, "Zotikos költeménye," p. 320.

64. According to the colorful description of Zotikos, a traitor urged the king to intervene (Pecz, "Zotikos költeménye," p. 335).

65. Andreas of Pannonius asserted, "when Hunyadi returned from the slaughter, he was given the news of the death of the king. He tried to calm the troops but the soldiers lost heart and ran away." (Fraknói, *Irodalomtörténeti emlékek,* 1:13). See also Hunyadi's letter to Pope Eugene IV (*Századok* 3(1869): 570).

66. Hunyadi's letter to the pope, in "Epistolae Joannes de Zredna" SCHWANDTNER, 2:27.

67. Palatio in *Literae,* pp. 459-69. However, Palatio also stated that Wladislaw had cut down and killed Murad II in the battlê.

68. Nicolai Jorga, *Notes et extraits pour servir l'histoire des croisades au XV.-e siecle,* series 4, (Bucharest, 1915), 3:107-10.

Notes to Chapter VII

1. *Dlugosz,* 12:4. See also *Teleki,* 1:457-58.

2. Bonfini, decas 3, liber 6:336. According to Chalcocondylas (*Historiarum,* p. 139), Dracul wanted to settle old scores with Hunyadi. He was thinking of offering him to the sultan or, if his son were captured, in exchange for his freedom.

3. Whether he feared Hédervári or the Western monarchs is unclear; *Teleki,* 1:455-56.

4. Hóman and Szekfű, *Magyar történet,* 2:433.

5. *Teleki,* 10:70, also Katona, *HCR,* 4:415.

6. Hunyadi's correspondence on behalf of Vitéz's appointment to the bishopric was extensive. The letter that broached the subject to Pope Eugene IV is in Joannes de Zredna, "Epistolae," SCHWANDTNER, 2:22-3. In this letter Hunyadi described the conditions of the bishopric of Nagyvárad after the death of bishop Dominici at Varna and gave his reasons for recommending Vitéz for the position. He also wrote to Ludovico Scrampo, Cardinal of Aquileia, ibid., p. 24, Battista, the bishop of Chiet, ibid., Andrea di Santa Croce, a lawyer at the papal court, ibid., p. 25,and Taddeo

de Treviso, a doctor at the Holy See, who accompanied Cardinal Caesarini to Hungary before Varna. Ibid. There are also letters from the nobility of Bihar County to the pope and to the college of cardinals, ibid., p. 26.

7. *Teleki*, 1:467.
8. Ibid., pp. 467-68.
9. Ibid., pp. 469-70.
10. Ibid., pp. 470-71; also ibid., 10:74.
11. *Teleki*, 1:471.
12. Ibid.
13. Kovacsics, *Supplementa*, 2:40.
14. Hunyadi in a letter to Francesco Foscari, doge of Venice, described the conditions created by the dispute with Frederick III (Vitéz, "Epistolae," SCHWANDTNER, 2:39-40). He accused the emperor of illegally occupying several Hungarian fortresses, cities, and estates, and usurping the income of the parish churches in the area under his control. He argued that the Hungarians were entitled to use all the means at their disposal to end this state of affairs.
15. *Teleki*, 1:488.
16. Hahn, *Chronicon*, 2:626.
17. Vitéz, "Epistolae," SCHWANDTNER, 2:27.
18. *Teleki*, 2:16. When Hunyadi became regent, Pope Eugene IV confirmed Csupor in the bishopric, transferring Benedict to Knin. Friedrich von Cilli was in Rome at that time and he threw his weight behind his own candidate. Thus, the pope withdrew Csupor's appointment. In April, 1451, the new pope, Nicholas V, confirmed Csupor's appointment once again, but Benedict continued to occupy the see with the support of the Cillis until his death in 1453. The complex issues of the bishoprics of Zagreb and Eger occupied Hunyadi for a long time. In a letter of Pope Eugene IV (Vitéz, "Epistolae," SCHWANDTNER, 2:36-37) he explained that in the interest of internal peace, he was supporting two candidates for the bishopric of Eger: László Hédervári, brother of the palatine and abbot of the monastery of St. Martin of Pannonhalma (who was also supported by the powerful Rozgonyis), and Tamás Döbrentei, the provost of Veszprém and a protege of Ujlaki. He had to be careful not to alienate either of these two camps.
19. Kropf, "Jehan de Wavrin," pp. 881-903.
20. Katona, *HCR*, 13:445-47.

21. Hahn, *Chronicon,* 1:708; also *Teleki,* 1:505-506, and Vitéz, "Epistolae," in SCHWANDTNER, 2:35.

22. On the election of Hunyadi to the regency see Thuróczi in SCHWANDTNER, 2:258; also Ivanics in SCHWANDTNER, 2:34, and *Teleki,* 1: 511. According to the report of the representatives of the city of Pozsony, the great lords held their meeting separately from that of the diet and then they sent Simon Rozgonyi and László Pálóci to the lesser nobles and the representatives of the cities to vocie their opinion about the election of Hunyadi. (Emma Lederer, "A magyar királyválasztási jog a középkorban" (The Hungarian Rule of the Election of a King in the Middle Ages) *Századok* 7 (1936):398).

23. Letter from the cathedral chapter of Arad, dated July 17, 1448: "quod magnificus dominus Nicolaus de Ujlak, inter ceteres honores Regni Hungariae Vicarius Generalis...." (Pray, *Historia Regni Hungariae,* 2:339).

24. *Teleki,* 1:517.

25. For Hunyadi's oath, see Adam Kollar, "MSS Collectio Adami Franciscus Kollarii, Decreta Regum Hungariae," no. 7, p. 178, in *HHStA,* "In Vulgari." Also János Luczenbacher, "Hunyadi János kormányzói esküje," (The Oath of Hunyadi as Regent) *Tudománytár* (Budapest), series 1, 1 (1834): 229-31.

26. Elekes, *Hunyadi,* p. 331; also Birk, "Adalékok," p. 512.

27. Birk, "Adalékok," p. 513. The most important salt mines located in Transylvania, were under Hunyadi's control as regent. The miners, working for wages, were also permitted each year to work for themselves for a few days and sell the salt so acquired.

28. *Teleki,* 2:275.

29. Elekes, *Hunyadi,* p. 333.

30. The nobility considered the burghers hardly better than serfs. The royal cupbearer had shown his contempt by refusing to sit at the same table with his burgher-jurors and calling them animals (Imre Szentpétery, "Nemesi és polgári életforma" (The Way of Life of the Nobles and the Burghers), in Domanovszky, *Magyar művelődéstörténet,* 2:311.

31. The letter of Joannis de Zredna to Juan Cardinal de Carvajal (in Vitéz, "Epistolae," SCHWANDTNER, 2:40-42) stated that the Dracul-led Ottoman raiders "enslaved four thousand Christians only recently liberated from Ottoman captivity" and that Hunyadi was determined to stop Dracul's adventures once and for all.

32. Vitéz, "Epistolae," in SCHWANDTNER, 2:34-36.
33. *Teleki,* 2:16. Ahrenpeck in Pez, *Scriptores,* 1:1256, estimated that the damage caused to the emperor by Hunyadi came to ten million florins, including the booty.
34. *Teleki,* 2:16.
35. Thuróczi in SCHWANDTNER, 1:258. Also Vitéz, "Epistolae," in SCHWANDTNER, 2:40, and *Teleki,* 2:6.
36. See, for example, *Teleki,* 2:22-23.
37. *Magyar Történelmi Tár* 19 (1883): 64. The document was issued by the bishop of Győr on June 24, 1447. See also Jorga, *Notes,* 3:229. Cardinal Carvajal's role in these negotiations is described in a letter addressed to Cardinal Széchi from the pope in *Teleki,* 2:199-200. See also Jenő Horváth, *Magyarország államszerződéseinek jegyzéke* (The List of the Treaties of the Hungarian State) (Budapest, 1921), p. 16.
38. Kovacsics, *Sylloge,* 2:263; also *Teleki,* 2:39-43.
39. Fraknói, *Magyarország egyházi és politikai,* 2:78.
40. Ibid., p. 79.
41. Ivanics in SCHWANDTNER, 2:49.
42. Ibid., p. 48.
43. Hóman (in Hóman and Szekfű, *Magyar történet,* 2:295) argues that Alfonso did send the promised funds to Hunyadi. This is, however, without proof. For the correspondence with Alfonso see Thallóczy and Barabás, *A Frangepán család oklevéltára,* pp. 350-55. The letter of Alfonso to Hunyadi, dated Casoli, February 2, 1448, is on p. 358.
44. Marino Sanuto, "Vita de duchi Venezia" in Muratori, *Scriptores,* 12:16.
45. Bonfini, decas 3, liber 7:338; also Pray, *Annales,* p. 66.
46. Vitéz, "Epistolae," in SCHWANDTNER, 2:45.
47. Thuróczi in SCHWANDTNER, 1:294. There was, of course, no agreement on the actual size of Hunyadi's army. Chalcocondylas (*Historiarum,* p. 147), mentioned forty-seven thousand men; Piccolomini in *Europa,* p. 396, said they numbered seventy thousand. It is more likely that he had less than thirty thousand.
48. *Teleki,* 2:75.
49. Chalcocondylas, *Historiarum,* pp. 146-47; see also Thuróczi in SCHWANDTNER, 1:294.
50. Lajos Kiss, "A rigómezei hadjárat" (The Campaign of Kosovo-Polje), *Hadtörténeti Közlemények* (8 (1895): 166.

51. Anonymous Ottoman chronicler in Thury, 1:23. According to Nesri (in Thury, 1:62) the sultan had been about to leave Albania in any case when he received the news about Hunyadi. Sead-eddin (in Thury, 1:146-147) maintains, on the other hand, that the news from Branković had reached him in Edirne.

52. Anonymous Ottoman chronicler (in Thury, 1:24). Chalcocondylas (*Historiarum,* p. 357) says that there were 150,000. Thuróczi (in SCHWANDTNER, 1:296) said 200,000, and *Dlugosz,* (12:47) said 360,000.

53. Nesri in Thury, 1:62.

54. Hunyadi's letter to Nicholas Lasocki, in Vitéz, "Epistolae," in SCHWANDTNER, 2:62.

55. Kiss, "A rigómezei," p. 173.

56. Ibid., pp. 454-55.

57. Ibid.

58. Daud Celebi's father had revolted against the ruler and had been blinded as a punishment. In the 1430s, he had fled with his family to Hungary where he was well received by King Sigismund. Daud fought at Varna on the Hungarian side and accompanied Hunyadi to Kosovo-Polje. See József Thury, "Ki volt a vak török császár?" (Who Was the Blind Turkish Emperor?) *Századok* 33 (1893): 839-49.

59. Chalcocondylas, *Historiarum,* pp. 363-64.

60. *Teleki,* 2:94, speaks of the treason of the Wallachians, suggesting that they changed sides during the last phase of the battle but were killed by order of the sultan. Chalcocondylas (*Historiarum,* pp. 366-68) was the originator of this legend. The Ottoman historians are silent about this alleged treason, however, and Hunyadi would certainly have mentioned it in one of his letters if it had indeed taken place.

61. Bonfini, decas 3, liber 9:475.

62. Ibid.; also Thuróczi in SCHWANDTNER, 1:262. The news of Hunyadi's escape reached Hungary remarkably fast. On November 27, László Szepesi, vice-regent and János Szobi, the captain of Buda, jointly notified the city of Pozsony of Hunyadi's escape and his arrival in Szendrő (*OL. D1.* 44,531).

Notes to Chapter VIII

1. Elekes, *Hunyadi,* 345.

2. *Teleki,* 2:114-15.
3. *OL. Dl.* 14,259; also *Teleki,* 10:243-44 and 2:113. The proposal was as follows: The truce was to last for seven years; the Wallachian, Serbian, and Bosnian princes would continue paying the tribute to the sultan and send auxiliary troops to the Ottoman army when required; however, the tribute would be half as much as before, since the lands of these princes had been exhausted. At first, Bosnia would pay its full tribute but not the arrears. The princes in question would retain their Hungarian alliance and their people would be free to move to Hungary. Ottoman merchants could freely trade in Belgrade, Kevi, Harám, Szendrő and Karánsebes, and similar provisions would be made for Hungarian merchants in Ottoman lands. Both parties would retain their territory, and no further conquest would be made. In the case of unauthorized raids, the offenders would be judged in the court of Branković. These agreements would include the Greek emperor. If the sultan rejected this proposal, then the truce that was observed during the reign of King Sigismund would prevail, but merchants would be able to trade only in the designated cities.
4. The letter of Hunyadi to Pope Nicholas V dated October 20, 1449 (in Vitéz, "Epistolae," in SCHWANDTNER, 2:67-68), in which he complained about the internal threat posed by the Hussites and the continuing Ottoman danger. He noted that the "intermediary" (Branković) was reluctant to work for a truce because he feared that, once it was arranged, he would be the next Ottoman target.
5. Ibid.
6. For the letter of Stepan Twartko thanking Hunyadi for his support, see Ivan Kukljević, *Arkiv za povjestniev jugoslavensky* (Archive of South Slavic History) 16 vols., (Zagreb, 1851), 2:35-48.
7. Vitéz, "Epistolae," SCHWANDTNER, 2:63.
8. Jorga, *Geschichte des osmanischen Reiches,* 2:8. It seems, however, that the truce was concluded only for three years. For Hunyadi's letter to the city of Brassó notifying the magistrates of the agreement, dated Buda, February 6, 1452, see *Teleki,* 10:322-23.
9. Hunyadi's letter to Ulrich von Cilli in Vitéz, "Epistolae," SCHWANDTNER, 2:66-67.
10. *Dlugosz,* 13:52. The "eternal peace" between Hunyadi and Jiškraz was dated Kassa, March 31, 1450 (Teleki, 10:256-58).
11. Szentmiklósi was a typical *condottiere,* recklessly brave, insanely

cruel and instiable for booty. He changed sides as frequently as his immediate interest dictated, but he was on good terms with Hunyadi more frequently than not. See Béla Majláth, "Szentmiklósi Pongrácz: életrajz a XV. századból" (Pongrácz Szentmiklósi; A Biography from the Fifteenth Century) *Századok* 12 (1878): 90-118.

12. Dated Buda, June 17, 1450, in *OL. Dl.* 14,379. Also *Teleki,* 10:262-65.

13. *OL. Dl.* 14, 414.

14. Letter from Hunyadi to Pope Nicholas V, followed by letters from Hunyadi to Cardinals San Stephano dei Mori and Juan de Carvajal, and Nicholas Lasocki, his envoy to Rome (Vitéz, "Epistolae," in SCHWANDTNER, 2:81-87.

15. Ibid.

16. A document dated Szendrő, May 9, 1450, may point to such an agreement. It refers to a patent issued by the palatine László Garai about Branković's pawning of several fortresses and towns to Hunyadi and his sons for 150,000 gold florins; Thallóczy and Áldásy, *A Magyarország és Szerbia,* pp. 159-60. A letter from Branković to János Kállói-Lökös, dated Szendrő, April 21, 1450, enumerated the points of disagreement between himself and Hunyadi (*OL. Dl.* Ó. 93.55,456 (Kállay). See also Frigyes Pesty, *Brankovics György birtokviszonyai Magyarországon* (Budapest, 1897), pp. 34-36.

17. The agreement stipulated that László V remain a ward of the emperor until the age of eighteen and that Frederick III would continue to control the properties in question until that time. In exchange, the emperor was not to obstruct Hunyadi in the exercise of the powers of his office (Katona, *HCR,* 6:726; see also Elekes, *Hunyadi,* p. 399).

18. "A dömösi conflictus V. Miklós pápa és Hunyadi János között: egy fejezet a királyi kegyúri jog történetéből" (The Conflict over Dömös between Pope Nicholas V and János Hunyadi: A Chapter from the History of The Right of Royal Patronage) *Századok* 27 (1893): 386.

19. Ibid., p. 389.

20. A royal decree of 1440 published in Kovacsics, *Supplementa,* 1: 212-13, stated that no papal bull would be permitted to be promulgated in Hungary without royal permission, no one except the king would be permitted to request a Hungarian clerical office from the pope, and no one was to initiate a suit in Rome to avoid the jurisdiction of the clerical

courts in Hungary. See also Dávid Angyal, "Az 1440: IV. törvénycikk" (The Decree of 1440, paragraph no. 4) *Századok,* 44 (1910): 590-92.

21. Letter to Pope Nicholas V in Vitéz, "Epistolae," in SCHWANDTNER, 2:77.

22. Hunyadi's letter to Bálint Kapusi dated June 16, 1450, ibid., p. 88. Fraknói's interpretation of these events understandably differed in this case, since he himself was a cleric (*A magyar főkegyuri jog* [The Hungarian Supreme Right of Patronage] Budapest, 1895, pp. 134-36, and "A dömösi conflictus). In both of these works Fraknói, an ardent ultramontane, took the pope's side.

23. Hunyadi issued instructions, of which those to the Saxon leaders in Transylvania survived, prohibiting the trial of secular cases in clerical courts, and empowering the secular authorities to punish offenders against this order, especially in cases in which the last testaments of deceased persons were contested. The document is dated Szászsebes, May 1, 1451, in *Teleki,* 10:292-94. He also wrote a strong letter to Pope Nicholas V protesting his interference in the royal right of patronage in Hungary (Vitéz, "Epistolae," SCHWANDTNER, 2:75-77). This was followed up by a note written by the royal council to the pope, stating that "if your Holiness wants Hungary to continue serving you loyally, you must refrain from interferring with its freedoms." A similar message was sent to the college of cardinals (ibid., pp. 80-81).

24. *OL. Dl.* 37,614, dated Szendrő, April 7, 1451; also in *Teleki,* 10:305-12.

25. This fortress was originally a monastery. See Csánki, *Magyarország történeti földrajza,* 1:91.

26. The conspiracy to humiliate Hunyadi was allegedly disclosed by István Pelsőci, who was wounded in the battle and was supposedly anxious to clear his conscience before his impending death (Bonfini, decas 3, liber 7:344; also Beheim, "Von ehrn Isgraw ain strait den er in Ungarn tet," Karajan, "Zehn Gedichte," pp. 46-48; Thuróczi in SCHWANDTNER, 1:263).

27. *OL. Dl.* 11,959; see also József Szitnyai, "A körmöcbányai békekötés 1452-ben" (The Peace Agreement of Körmöcbánya in 1452) *Történelmi Tár* (1884): 593-612.

28. Hunyadi's letter to Szabolcs County, inviting the representatives of the nobility to a session of the diet at Pozsony, dated February 15,

1452 (*OL. Dl.* 14,518 act. publ. fasc. 46, no. 65), and the resolution of the joint meeting dated Vienna, March 5, 1452 (*OL. Dl.* 44,622 Muz. Ta. and 44,623 Muz. Ta.).

29. The Hungarians expected László V to reside in Buda castle. The royal council sent a large embassy to Vienna to convince him of this necessity. Most barons were members of this embassy. Hunyadi was represented by his elder son, László. See Antal Áldásy, "A magyar országgyűlés követsége V. Lászlóhoz 1452 október havában" (The Delegation of the Hungarian Diet to László V. in the Month of October in 1452), *Századok* 44 (1910): 554-62.

30. *OL. Dl.* 14,604 K.B.A. fasc. k524, no. 12 and no. 14, and 14,605. Other documents enumerating Hunyadi's deeds and virtues are *OL. Dl.* 37,619; 37,617; 24,762 N.R.A.

31. *Teleki,* 2:269-71. It has long been accepted that Hunyadi was the first Hungarian to be named a perpetual baron. See the patent of László V, dated Prague, December 9, 1453, confirming his previous appointment of Hunyadi to the title in *OL. Dl.* 37,629. However, Cardinal Széchi had been a perpetual baron at least since the mid-1440s; see *OL. Dl.* 14,671 Tyrn. Mon., fasc. 14, no. 9.

32. *OL. Dl.* 14,603 and 14,703. The diet seems to have been determined to settle long-simmering problems. It declared void all the grants of Queen Erzsébet and Wladislaw I except those made to Hunyadi; ordered the destruction of all illegally built fortresses; paid off Jiškraz and ordered him out of the highlands; and confirmed Hunyadi's captaincy and his possessions as well as his newly-granted coat of arms. The king's patent, dated Pozsony, February 1, 1453, is in *Teleki,* 10:365-68, and 338-39.

33. In a patent, dated Pertholsdorf, August 15, 1453, the king gave Hunyadi and his sons the estate of Rudystha near Belgrade, with all its possessions including its gold mines and the income from the latter (*OL. Dl.* 14,775).

34. *Fontes Rerum Austriacarum* series 2, 68:177-79.

35. The diet confirmed the appointment of Ujlaki *banus* of Macsó (Mačva) and Slavonia and that of János Rozgonyi as military governor of Transylvania. Rajnald and Osvát Rozgonyi were confirmed as Counts of the Székelys. A document shows the methods used by Cilli to strengthen his position. This is a report by János Vitovecz, "vice *banus* and *comes* of Kőrös County," dated Gereben, May 3, 1453, in which the

Cillis' general explains that he took the town of Rycha and its surrounding estates in order to "protect them" against the depradations of the son of Márton Szerdahelyi-Ders. As it turned out, these properties were owned by the Szerdahelyi-Ders family. Despite the decision of the county court ordering Vitovecz to restore them to their rightful owner, he refused and requested instructions from the count (*OL. Dl.* 14,681). For the grants received by Ujlaki, Cilli's ally, see the document dated Pozsony, September 14,453 (*OL. Dl.* 14,772 N.R.A., fasc. 1711, no. 47).

36. Cilli offered Hunyadi a deal: he could continue to act unofficially as regent and collect the royal revenues if he were willing to send 24,000 florins a year for the maintenance of the royal household and 12,000 florins for Cilli's needs. Hunyadi rejected the deal, but he was still the target of gossip that he had "sold the *regnum* for 36,000 florins" (Piccolomini, *Historia Friderici III Imperatoris* 3:448; also *Teleki*, 2:275).

37. It seems that Hunyadi did not even respond to the royal command. Finally, László V declared that he himself would lead an army against Axamit "in the near future," which was, of course, an empty promise. See *Teleki*, 10:387-90.

38. Ibid., 10:9 and 2:299.

39. The text of the agreement, dated Prague, February 15, 1454, is in *OL. Dl.* 37,631.

40. A document issued by László V, dated Buda, January 25, 1454 (*OL. Dl.* 14,792), discussed the method to be used in case general mobilization was necessary and the types of people who would be required to gather under the command of the chief captain.

41. Elekes, *Hunyadi*, p. 421.

42. *OL. Dl.* 14,839 N.R.A. fasc 1524, no. 23.

43. *Teleki*, 2:317.

44. Hunyadi's letter to Vitéz in *Teleki*, 2:319.

45. *Teleki*, 2:318-19.

46. The agreement concluded between Komorowski and Axamit, on the one hand, and György Rozgonyi acting on behalf of the king on the other, is dated Kassa, December 24, 1454 (*OL. Dl.* 15,307, publ. fasc. 18, no. 7). It stipulated that all fortresses were to be turned over to Rozgonyi in return fo an immediate payment of 4,000 florins and further payments totalling 7,000 florins were to be made within two weeks.

47. Jiškraz's letter to the northern mining centers announcing his new appointment is in *OL. Dl.* 24,376.

48. *Teleki*, 10:430-31. See also Hunyadi's letter to the Saxon cities notifying them of the new Ottoman attack and the sultan's immediate withdrawal to Sofia upon Hunyadi's arrival in *Teleki*, 10:431. See also Thallóczy and Áldásy, *A Magyarország és Szerbia*, pp. 186-87. Hunyadi may have received the news from Branković; at least the letter from Ragusa to Francesco Foscari, the doge of Venice, reported that the sultan had attacked Serbia and that Branković had fled to Hungary with his family (Ibid., pp. 185-86).
49. *Teleki*, 2:330.
50. A letter in Thallóczy and Áldásy, *A Magyarország és Szerbia*, pp. 187-88, dated Srebrenica, October 10, 1454, sent to Ragusa, stated that Hunyadi crossed the Danube on September 20, beat the Ottomans at Kruševac, and was waiting for the armies of Branković and Cilli to join him.
51. Letter of agreement, dated Vienna, April 7, 1455, *OL. Dl.* 24,765, N.R.A.; also, *Teleki*, 10:437-38.
52. *Teleki*, 2:331.
53. Chalcocondylas, *Historiarum*, p. 371; also *Teleki*, 2:338; Hammer-Purgstall, *Geschichte des osmanischen Reiches*, 2:11.
54. Fraknói, *Magyarország egyházi és politikai*, 2:367; also *Teleki*, 2:425.

Notes to Chapter IX

1. Letter of János Koroghi to Giovanni da Capistrano in János Pettkó, "Kapisztrán János levelezése a magyarokkal" (The Correspondence of Giovanni Capistrano with the Hungarians), *Történelmi Tár* 2 (1901) new series, pp. 171-72.
2. Thuróczi in SCHWANDTNER, 1:338. According to Tursun Bey, (*Thury*, 1:77), "Belgrade was the key to the conquest of Hungary."
3. Kovacsics, *Supplementa*, 2:123-24.
4. Letter from King László V to Pope Claxtus III, in Katona, *HCR*, 13:1041-45.
5. Carvajal also wrote to various Western princes soliciting help; see his letter to Prince Sigismund of Austria in *Teleki*, 10:499-501. See also Katona, *HCR*, 13:1045-48, and Thallóczy and Áldásy, *Magyarsáag és Szerbia*, pp. 463-64.

Notes to Chapter IX 241

6. *Teleki,* 10:497-98.
7. Carvajal's letter about the disappearance of the king from Buda in Katona, *HCR,* 13:1059, and *Teleki,* 2:409-10.
8. György Balanyi, "Nándorfehérvár ostroma és felmentése 1456-ban" (The Defense and the Lifting of the Siege of Belgrade in 1456), *Hadtörténeti Közlemények* 13 (1912): 175.
9. Tagliacozzo in Wadding, *Annales,* 12:340-62.
10. Ibid., p. 353.
11. Carvajal's letter to Capistrano instructing him to expand his recruiting campaign in southern Hungary is in Pettkó, "Kapisztrán," p. 214. See also Wadding, *Annales,* 12:331.
12. Hunyadi's letter to Carvajal is in Thallóczy and Áldásy, *A Magyarország és Szerbia,* pp. 464-65. His letter to the Saxons is in *Teleki,* 10:525-26. His urgent message to the Saxons ten days later is in ibid., pp. 526-27, and a further one urging the Saxons "for the love of God" to bring their troops to Belgrade is in ibid., pp. 527-28.
13. Nicholas de Fara (in Wadding, *Annales,* 12:363) asserted that the sultan's foundries at Kruševac were built by renegade Italian, German, and Hungarian craftsmen, who used some of the church bells captured at Constantinople. Tursun Bey *(Thury,* 1:77) shows, however, that this took place at Üsküb, and this is confirmed by Nesri (ibid., 1:64).
14. Letter from Korógyi to Capistrano in Pettkó, "Kapisztrán," p. 193. Jorga in *Geschichte des osmanischen Reiches* 2:7, mentioned that the sultan had a reserve force of 40,000 that he probably left behind to defend Constantinople.
15. According to a letter from Branković to Carvajal in Thallóczy and Áldásy, *A magyarország és Szerbia,* pp. 204-205, the sultan's army did stop at Szendrő and may even have tried a quick attack on the fortress but it failed. The sultan may also have sent some contingents to secure his rear from a possible attack from Albania; see Pettkó, "Kapisztrán," pp. 193-94. If so, he further weakened his forces, and this may explain his later reluctance to send some of his troops across the Danube at Belgrade.
16. Brocquière in *Ouvrage,* 94.
17. Lajos Kropf, "Fullár Erasmus: Adalékok az 1451 és 1456. évek történetéhez" (Erasmus Fullar: Data for the History of the Years 1451 and 1456) *Századok* 30 (1896): 223-27.
18. Pettkó, "Kapisztrán," pp. 216-17.

19. Tursun Bey in *Thury*, 1:77; also Kiss, "Hunyadi János," p. 580.
20. Ranzanus in SCHWANDTNER, 1:486; Fara in Wadding, *Annales*, 12:364.
21. Nesri in *Thury*, 1:65; Tursun Bey in ibid., 1:77.
22. Letter of Tagliacozzo to this effect in Wadding, *Annales*, 12:352; also Thallóczy and Áldásy, *A Magyarország és Szerbia*, p. 382.
23. This issue became controversial, since it was later claimed that more barons were present than was the case. Tagliacozzo mentioned Korógi (in Wadding, *Annales*, 12:352); Kanizsai appears in the account of Thuróczi (in SCHWANDTNER, 1:341). Bonfini (decas 3, liber 8) mentions Sebestyén Rozgonyi, but it was Rajnald who supported Hunyadi at Belgrade.
24. Katona, *HCR*, 13:1060.
25. Tagliacozzo in Wadding, *Annales*, 12:348; also Chalcocondylas, *Historiarum*, pp. 417-18. Most of these ships were barges that had to be prepared for the attack before they could be used for that purpose.
26. Tagliacozzo in Wadding, *Annales*, 12:348.
27. Ibid., p. 349.
28. Ibid., p. 350.
29. Thallóczy and Áldásy, *A Magyarország és Szerbia*, p. 208; also the anonymous Ottoman chronicler in *Thury*, 1:26, Tursun Bey in ibid., p. 65, and Chalcocondylas, *Historiarum*, p. 419.
30. The anonymous Ottoman chronicler in *Thury*, 1:26.
31. Tagliacozzo in Wadding, *Annales*, 12:356-60; also Fara, ibid., p. 365, Thallóczy and Áldásy, *A Magyarország és Szerbia*, pp. 384-85, Thuróczi in SCHWANDTNER, 1:341-42, and Ranzanus, ibid., 2:488.
32. Kiss, "Hunyadi János," pp. 89-91; also Fara in Katona, HCR, 13:1084, and in Wadding, *Annales*, 12:366. It is worth mentioning here than Elekes in "Hunyadi hadserege," p. 471, completely ignores Capistrano's role, since it would not fit his ideological bias.
33. Fara in Wadding, *Annales*, 12:366.
34. Tursun Bey (in *Thury*, 1:79) that "even the dead climbed out of the breaches in the wall, swarmed out of the fortress and fell upon the army of Islam."
35. Ibid.
36. *HHStA*, Handschrift Blau, no. 8.
37. Franz Babinger, *Mehemed der Eroberer und seine Zeit* (Munich, 1953), p. 153.

Notes to Chapter IX 243

38. In 1456, the Ottoman army was reported to have included 12,000 Janissaries and 8,000 cavalrymen who served in the sultan's entourage. The number of sipahis and akinjis was said to have been 80,000 and a reserve of 40,000 was available. See Jorga, *Geschichte des osmanischen Reiches,* 2:7.

39. This paper was delivered at the 16th Annual Conference on Medieval Studies at the University of Michigan, Kalamazoo, Michigan, in May, 1980. Professor Tobias kindly permitted me to study his results.

40. Brocquière wrote in 1433, "the (Ottoman) army usually consists of 100-200,000 men. However, most of them are foot-soldiers and lack either swords, bows and arrows, or maces. Very few of them are fully armed. They impress a great many Christians into service, including Greeks, Bulgarians, Macedonians, Albanians, Slavs, Vlachs, Serbs, and others who are subjects of the Serbian despot." (*Ouvrage,* p. 87.)

41. There were several hundred Austrian crusaders at Belgrade; see A. L. G. Muratori, *Scriptores Rerum Italicarum* 28 vols., (Milan, 1723-1851), 23:59. One of these crusaders was Johannes Goldener, who may have been Kraiburg's source. See Ebendorffer in Pez, *Scriptores,* 2:880.

42. Ibid.

43. Tagliacozzo reported two hundred Ottoman vessels, sixty-four of them seagoing galleys (Wadding, *Annales,* 12:342).

44. Elekes (*Hunyadi,* pp. 447-49) argues that the slow arrival of the crusaders was the result of a conspiracy by the Hungarian lords, who wanted to see Hunyadi defeated. A more likely explanation may be found in a letter from Carvajal to Capistrano, dated Buda, June 14, 1456, reporting that a great many crusaders were gathering in Germany but were delayed for lack of anyone to lead them to Belgrade (Pettkó, "Kapisztrán," pp. 214-15).

45. *Teleki,* 1:316; also Katona, *HCR,* 13:1067-71; Fejér, *CDH, Genus,* pp. 71-75.

46. The Ottoman Sead-eddin noted that Hunyadi sent 5,000 of his men into the fortress before the siege began (*Thury,* 1:153). This would correspond to the capacity of the fortress as given by Brocquière (*Ouvrage,* p. 96). On Hunyadi's recruitment of Hungarian, Czech, and Polish mercenaries, see *Teleki,* 2:423.

47. *Teleki,* 2:424.

48. Thuróczi in SCHWANDTNER, 1:273; also *Teleki,* 2:412.

49. *Teleki,* 2:417.

50. Tagliacozzo's letter of July 28, 1456, stated that the number of crusaders at Belgrade came to about 27-28,000 men (Thallóczy and Áldásy, *A Magyarország és Szerbia* p. 381). However, a few days later, the friar spoke of 60,000 (Wadding, *Annales,* 12:359).

51. Tagliacozzo fantasized about Capistrano's shooting molten lead and lightning bolts from his eyes at the Ottomans (Wadding, *Annales,* 12: 338). An equally prejudiced but opposite account of Capistrano's role, this time from a Marxist historian, is that of Elekes (*Hunyadi,* p. 471) who goes so far as to suggest that it was not Capistrano but Hunyadi who was responsible for the recruitment of the crusading peasants who came to Belgrade.

52. Pettkó, "Kapisztrán," pp. 187-88.

53. Elekes (*Hunyadi,* pp. 445-46) asserted that Carvajal and Capistrano disagreed over the aims of their institution in Hungary, hence the delays in recruitment.

54. Thomas Ebendorffer described the composition of the crusading army in almost lyrical terms: "Behold! Unarmed peasants, blacksmiths, tailors, carters, artisans, and students march at the head of armies, believing themselves to have been called by God to great deeds on behalf of their faith." (Pez, *Scriptores,* 2:880). Thuróczi in SCHWANDTNER, 1:167, reported that "mostly a mass of peasants was recruited;" Fara (in Wadding, *Annales,* 12:362) mentioned; "plowmen and men of the hoe;" Tagliacozzo (ibid., 12:340) spoke of Greeks from Belgrade.

55. I discussed the reasons for the enthusiasm of the peasants at Belgrade in an article: "Peasants in Arms, 1437-1438 and 1456," in Bak and Király, eds., *From Hunyadi to Rákóczi,* pp. 81-101.

Notes to Chapter X

1. Thuróczi in SCHWANDTNER, 1:275, quoting Cilli as saying "ego sum homo ille, qui hoc canile linguagium hac de terra exstirpabo."

2. Bonfini, decas 3, liber 8:317.

3. *Teleki,* 2:456. It seems that László Hunyadi obeyed, but before doing so he asked for, and received, a letter of assurance that he would not have to answer for the fact that his father was unable to give an accounting for his handling of the royal finances because of his untimely death.

4. *Teleki*, 2:457.
5. Hunyadi appeared at the diet with a retinue of selected soldiers. Since, as Ranzanus probably correctly stated, a great many lesser nobles had transferred their loyalty from his father to him (SCHWANDTNER, 2:210), Cilli did not dare openly attack him there. Instead, the count proposed to him that they reach an agreement, and László Hunyadi accepted this proposal. Cilli, thus, adopted László as his son, and both families were to support each other against their enemies, except if they had a dispute with the king.
6. *Teleki*, 2:467.
7. Hahn in *Chronica*, 1:745-46. See also *Teleki*, 2:468.
8. Bonfini, decas 3, liber 8:356.
9. Ibid. See also Hahn, *Chronica*, 2:723; Ebendoffer in Pez, *Scriptores*, 2:882.
10. Hahn, *Chronica*, 2:725; Thuróczi in SCHWANDTNER, 1:287.
11. "...Creditum est no minus filium profuisse, reipublicae Christianae in occasione Comitis, quam patrem in profligatione Mahometis, sum Mahometes et comes hostes religionis essent. Ille externus, iste domesticus." ("Epistolae," quoted by *Teleki*, 2:478, no. 5).
12. Bonfini, decas 3, liber 8:357. Also, Thuróczi in SCHWANDTNER, 1:280; Hahn, *Chronica*, 2:777.

INDEX

Note: words appearing on most pages such as Hunyadi, Hungary, Hungarian etc., have not been included in this Index.

Abbey 116, 141, 142, 143
abbey of Dömös, 137, 141
abbotship, 42
acreage, 68
Acsády, Ignácz, 60
administration, 40
admiral, 94
adzes, 76, 78
Aegean Sea, 76, 78
Ágmándi, Péter, 126
agriculture, 56
agriculturist, 65
akinjis, 88, 89, 109
Albania, 102, 130, 133
Albanians, 108, 111, 128, 132
Albert I (Albrecht II), 8, 12, 13, 15, 20, 24, 27, 81, 116, 118, 121, 143, 149
Alfonso I of Naples, 49
Ali, son of Evrenos, 9, 13
altar, 49, 50
altar boy, 47, 50
altarist, 49, 50, 51, 55
ambassadors, 23, 94
Ambrose of Aquila, 162
amusements, 74
Anatolia, 100, 102, 105, 109, 153

Anatolian divisions, 88
Anatolian troops, 163
András II, 24, 47
animals, 56, 76, 165
animal husbandry, 55, 67, 68, 72, 74
Anjou Lajos I (the Great), 22, 65, 82
Anjou kings, 28, 81
Anna, princess, 90
Arad county, 102
Aragon, 99
Archbishop
  of Esztergom, 19, 83, 126, 142
  of Kolacsa, 42, 126
archives, 45, 48
aristocracy, 8, 20, 23, 30, 33, 38, 40
aristocratic, 8, 24, 25, 35, 40, 64, 138, 142
aristocrats, 2, 8, 12, 20, 25, 29, 30, 31, 35, 36, 39
armistice, 125
armor, 40
Árpád, 20
arrows, 149, 157, 162
artillery, 130, 159

Index

Árva county, 63
asab, 109
Asia, 94, 130
Asia Minor, 92, 95, 96, 100, 102, 160
Asian army, 108
—vavalry, 133
assassination, 171
assimilation, 13
asylum, 71
athleta Christi, 5
Augustinians, 53, 54
Austria, 12, 83, 91, 126, 139, 145, 168
Austrian Alps, 17
—nobles, 123, 146, 148, 150
—revenues, 146
auxiliaries, 165
auxiliary warriors, 70
Axamit, 84, 138, 147, 150
axes, 76, 78
average family, 58
Attendants, 27

Babinger, Franz, 164
Bács county, 10, 36
Baden, city, 123
bakers, 27
Balkan Mountains, 97, 105, 106, 132, 165
—principalities, 137
—Peninsula, 111, 155
Balkans, 5, 6, 17, 54, 58, 64, 86, 89, 90, 92, 99, 100, 101, 102, 103, 104, 105, 111, 112, 124, 128, 129, 130, 135, 136, 137, 143, 147, 148, 151, 152, 156, 159, 163, 165, 173,
balladeers, 28, 33
banderium, 2, 8, 27, 96, 101, 102, 105, 106, 119, 148, 157, 160, 166
Bánfi, Pál, 3
banus, 26

Baranya county, 36, 63, 74
barges, 71, 108, 160, 166
barber-surgeon, 27, 70
Barcaság, 13
barns, 37, 67, 71, 76
barley, 70, 71
baronial alliances, 114
—anarchy, 121
—office, 31, 36, 83
—servants, 68
—usurpation, 122
barons, 14, 19, 26, 27, 31, 32-37, 38, 44, 51, 72, 81, 82, 101, 113, 115, 120, 122, 124, 127, 133, 139, 144, 148, 157, 160
Barta, István, 43
barter, 56
Bártfa (town), 84
Bastida, Joannes, 159
Bátaszék, battle of, 84
Báthori, István, 111
battle of Ménfő (1044), 22
battle of Varna, 118, 123
battle wagons, 12, 81, 89, 95, 96, 106, 108, 130, 132
beans, 70, 71
beds, 38, 76
beef, 74
beer, 70
bees, 78
Béla I, 141
Béla II, 141
Belgrade, 1, 3, 14, 54, 80, 83, 85, 86, 90, 92, 95, 96, 98, 118, 132, 135, 150, 151, 153, 155, 157, 159, 160, 161, 163, 164, 165, 166, 167, 168, 169, 170, 171, 172, 173
Benedict of Zólyom, 118
Benedictines, 51, 52, 53
benefices, 47, 50, 51
Berendi-Bak, János, 144
Berettyó River, 73

Beszterce, 2
Bihar county, 73, 115, 144
bishop, 44, 45, 47, 48, 49, 50, 55, 106
Bishop of Bosnia, 126
Bishop of Eger, 42, 81, 101, 111, 144
Bishop of Knin, 118
Bishop of Nagyvárad, 101, 111, 115, 126
Bishop of Transylvania, 126
Bishop of Vác, 42
Bishop of Zagreb, 118, 136, 144
bishopric, 43, 118, 126
Black Death, 58, 65
black peppers, 72
blacksmith, 62, 71
Blagay family, 138
blankets, 37
blockade, 160, 161
Bodros county, 14
Bohemia, 12, 94, 145, 148, 168
bombards, 163
books, 47
Bonfini, Antonius, 5, 10, 88
Boniface IX, pope, 41
booty, 12, 13, 87, 98, 106, 124
Borostyánkő (fortress), 36
Borovszky, Samu, 37
Borsod county, 63, 65
Bosnia, 15, 132
Bosporus, 94, 100
Botos, András, 84
Bothos, István, abbot, 143
bowmen, 89
bows, 149, 157
Braničevo, 104
Branković, Djuradj, 9, 10, 15, 85, 81, 92, 95, 96, 98, 100, 102, 104, 105, 108, 111, 118, 128, 129, 130, 134, 136, 137, 138, 140, 144, 150, 151, 152, 153, 170, 171, 173

Brassó (city), 13, 53
Braudel, Fernand, 61
breve, 143
bread, 71
brigandage, 122
Brocquiére, Bertrandon de la, 74, 159
Buda, city, 3, 4, 12, 27, 49, 50, 54, 83, 84, 87, 90, 92, 95, 98, 99, 119, 120, 124, 143, 147, 153, 155, 156, 157, 159, 167, 171
buildings, 53, 72
bureaucracy, 29, 30
burghers, 4, 29, 37, 62, 138
Burgundian galleys, 119
Burgundy, 99
Buondelmonte, Joannes, 126
butchers, 27
Byzantine capital, 111, 155
—emperor, 22, 99, 101, 105, 106, 111
—empire, 17, 147
—envoys, 100

cabbage, 70
Caesarini, cardinal, Julian, 91, 92, 94, 95, 99, 100, 101, 102, 103, 104, 106, 108, 110, 118
Callimachus, 109
candles, 78
cannon, 47, 49, 50, 51, 52, 55, 130, 136, 143, 157, 159, 160, 161, 163, 166
capital cases, 28
—city, 159
—offenses, 30, 31
Capistrano, Giovanni, de, 152, 153, 160, 161, 164, 167, 168, 171, 173
cardinals, 43, 104, 106
card games, 38
Carpathians, 13, 17
Carpathian basin, 80

Index

carpenters, 62
Carvajal, cardinal Juan de, 124, 157, 159, 168
castles, 31, 32, 33, 37, 38, 117
catapults, 160, 163, 164
cathedral, 47, 48, 173
cahtedral chapter, 43, 47, 48, 49, 52, 118, 143
cattle, 73
cattle breeding, 74
cavalry, 95, 96, 109
Celebi, Daud, 133
Celebi, Mahmud, 98, 102
cemetery, 67
census tax, 23, 39, 58, 59, 62
Chalcocondylas, Laonikos, 6, 9, 86, 89, 130
chancellary, 26, 27, 32, 143
chancellor, 35, 44, 91
chaplain, 33, 49, 51
chapter house, 47
Charles VII of France, 5, 119
Červenka (stream), 98
chickens, 74
chief captain (of Hungary), 146, 147, 148, 150, 151, 152, 160, 170, 171, 173
Chilia (fortress), 125
choral singing, 47
Christ, 78
Christian cause, 173
—church, 64, 79
chronicler, 88, 103, 167
church, 20, 23, 26, 28, 38, 42-55, 57, 61, 65, 67, 71, 78, 142
—hierarchy, 19
—men, 25
—office, 141
—servants, 68
Cilli, Counts of, 6, 16, 64, 81, 82, 85, 100, 114, 118, 119, 120, 136, 138, 172, 173
—Barbara, 12

—Elisabeth, 134, 136, 144, 153
—family, 3
—Friedrich von, 151
—Ulrich von, 1, 2, 4, 84, 118, 129, 138, 139, 144, 146, 147, 148, 149, 151, 156, 170, 171, 172,
Cistercians, 52, 53, 68
citadel, 162, 172
city, 23, 29, 30, 35, 37, 52, 53, 54, 59, 60, 61, 62, 63, 64, 67, 70, 79, 86, 122, 135, 138, 141, 144, 149, 161, 162, 171, 172
civic consciousness, 54
civil war, 24, 83, 113, 115, 121, 145
clans, 31, 38, 63
clergy, 20, 30, 32, 42, 43, 44, 50, 51, 52, 53, 55, 79
cleric, 142, 171
clerical-county court, 45
—courts, 42, 43, 50
—institutions, 35
clerical life, 48
—lords, 45
—nobles, 44, 45
—offices, 125
—revenues, 94
climate, 61, 71, 142
cloister, 54
clothing, 37, 38, 78
clowns, 27, 28, 33
coat of arms, 8, 45
college of cardinals, 92, 95
commander, 11, 14, 15, 26, 80, 88, 109, 118, 123, 130, 138, 160, 161, 163, 173
commerce, 122
commercial center, 53
commoners, 23, 44
commune servitium, 45
communications, 51
Condolmieri, cardinal, Francesco, 94, 106, 108
condottiere, 11

Constantinople, 100, 106, 111, 147, 155, 157, 159, 160, 164, 167
conspirator, 3, 4
convent, 52
cooks, 27
coronation, 12, 19, 20, 83, 117
 —oath, 20, 147
corporate entities, 26
Corvinus (Mátyás Hunyadi), 10, 173
Council of Constance, 43
 —Basel, 11, 92, 123, 128
 —Florence, 100
count (comes), 24, 35, 39, 40, 45, 125, 172
count of Beszterce, 146
 —Temes, 84
county, 19, 24, 27, 29, 35, 38, 39, 40, 45, 112, 114, 125, 149, 156, 157
 —administrator, 39, 40
 —assemblies, 36, 39, 41
 —courts, 30, 32
court, 3, 32, 35, 36, 44, 95, 145, 149, 151, 171
 —of appeals, 29
 —of justice, 4, 18, 26, 29
 —soldier, 12
courtiers, 27
cows, 71
Cracow, 55, 82, 92, 101
crafts, 56
 —men, 27, 78, 157, 162
crown, 4, 22, 23, 29, 31, 35, 52, 64, 84, 114, 117, 121, 122, 172
crime, 39
criminal cases, 19, 71, 116
Croatia, 17, 26, 59, 63, 85, 106, 120, 129, 136, 138, 144, 147, 151
Croats, 62, 64
crop failure, 58
crusade, 91, 95, 157, 162
crusaders, 160, 161, 162, 163, 165, 167, 168, 171, 172

Crusade of Varna, 111
Csáki, György, 10
Csanádi, Ferenc, 10
Csánki, Dezső, 59
Csesznek (fortress), 36
Csupor, Demeter, 118, 136, 144
Csupor, Károly, 125
Cumans, 62, 64, 74
curia, 37, 137
currency, 101
customs duties, 23, 31, 45, 46
Czechs, 119, 122, 138, 139
Czech Hussites, 95

daily life, 70
Dalmatia, 26, 129, 147
Dan (prince of Wallachia), 122, 129
dancing, 10, 28, 53
Danube basin, 5, 20, 72, 95
 —River, 3, 15, 17, 56, 68, 79, 95, 96, 105, 115, 119, 125, 129, 130, 156, 157, 159, 160, 165, 171,
Daud Pasha, 109
dean, 143
Debrecen, 102
defeat, 111, 136, 161
defense, 65, 67, 80, 114, 116, 125, 135, 148, 152, 156, 161, 164, 166, 168, 170
demesne, 35, 68
demographic conditions, 58-60
 —disaster, 60
 —growth, 64
demons, 78, 79
depopulation, 62
desertions, 160
despot, 6, 15, 17, 80, 91, 109, 134, 137, 140, 153, 171
diet, 30, 35, 60, 64, 71, 84, 100, 101, 115, 118, 119, 120, 121, 123, 124, 125, 127, 128, 136, 137, 141, 143, 146, 147, 148, 149, 150, 152, 155, 156, 157, 166, 170, 171

Index

dignitaries, 28
diocese, 47, 48
diplomat, 44
discipline, 52
divine law (ius), 30
division of labor, 54
Dlugosz, Joannis (Longini), 5, 103, 109, 139
documents, 48, 61, 76
Dominicans, 53, 54, 55
Dominis, János, 101
Domonkos, Leslie, 62
Dömös (village), 142, 143
donation, 143
donkeys, 71
dowager, 82
Dracul, Vlad, (prince of Wallachia), 88, 95, 105, 106, 109, 113, 118, 119, 122, 123
Drágfis, 64
draft animals, 71, 96
Drava River, 56
dresses, 33
drills, 78
drinks, 33, 38
drought condition, 57
ducks, 74
dwellings, 65

East-Central Europe, 6, 89, 112, 153, 159, 173
ecclesiastical courts, 30
Edirne (Adrianople), 15, 85, 97, 100, 105, 106, 109, 122, 130, 157
education, 9, 38, 48, 49, 50, 51, 54, 55
Eger, 33, 49, 145
egregius, 35
Eizinger, Ulrich von, 146, 147, 148, 151
elders, 70
Eleanor of Portugal, 145-146
elite, 49, 51

embassy, 90
Emir of Karaman, 95
emperor, 92, 115, 116, 117, 120, 123, 124, 125, 127, 129, 140, 141, 145, 173
empire, 123, 130, 155
endowment, 48
Engel, Pál, 24, 32, 104
England, 20, 99, 119
entertainers, 32
entertainment, 54
entrepreneur, 17
envoys, 25, 99, 101, 103, 117, 118, 120, 124, 136
Eperjes (city), 84
epidemics, 79, 153, 160
Ér (stream), 73
estates, 18, 19, 29, 31, 33, 35, 37, 39, 43, 46, 53, 57, 65, 68, 78, 83, 102, 114, 117, 120, 121, 136, 140, 144, 147
Esztár (village), 73
Esztergom (city), 44, 48, 49, 85, 141, 143, 144
ethnic, 8, 62, 64
etiquette, 127
Eugene IV, pope, 91, 94, 119, 123, 142
Europe, 56, 58, 90, 98, 100, 105, 106, 108, 111, 112, 129, 130, 152, 164, 169
European, 96, 99, 102, 113, 115
—cavarly, 132
—monarchies, 19, 95
evil spirits, 78
extended family, 58

faith, 6, 52
fallow lands, 74
familiares, 14, 18, 19, 29, 30, 31, 35, 44
family castle, 9
—tree, 6

Fara, Nicholas de, 163
farm implements, 71
feasts, 79
festivals, 74, 79
feudal, 24, 40, 57, 60, 64, 94, 148
feudalism, 17
feudal armies, 8
—loyalty, 14
Feketekőrös River, 73
fiefdom, 147
field generalship, 9
fireplace, 76
Firuz bey, 151
fishing, 72
fishpond-management, 46, 72
flatlands, 73
fleet, 108
floods, 72
Florence, 33, 99, 146
Florentine, 64, 94, 100
food, 33, 38, 53, 61, 74, 96, 97
flour, 71
fodder, 74, 97, 164
foot soldiers, 89
—wear, 78
foreign envoys, 100
—policy, 101
—relations, 25
fortifications, 162, 171
fortress, 9, 19, 27, 31, 32, 33, 36, 38, 90, 98, 102, 103, 105, 117, 132, 139, 150, 153, 159, 160, 161, 162, 163, 166, 167, 168, 171, 172, 173
foundries, 157
Fraknói, Vilmos, 126, 142
France, 20, 99
Franciscan, 9, 53, 54, 166, 167, 168
Frangepán (Frankopan), Bertalan, 16, 64
freebooters, 138
frescoes, 79
friars, 54, 162, 167, 168, 171

Friedrich III of Habsburg, 1, 16, 83, 90, 91, 92, 94, 95, 100, 103, 113, 116, 120, 123, 124, 125, 127, 141, 145, 146, 163, 173
frontier district, 172
fruits, 71, 72
Fügedi, Erik, 53, 58
furnishings, 38, 76, 78
furniture, 32, 78
Futak (village), 103, 171

Gabriel of Verona, 157
Galambóc (Golubac) (fortress), 80, 92, 151
galleys, 94, 100, 102, 103, 106, 108, 163
Gallipoli, 100
Gara (fortress), 53
Garai, László, 2, 3, 36, 84, 100, 114, 117, 120, 127, 139, 140, 141, 144, 145, 147, 150, 151, 153, 170, 173
Garázda family, 10
gardens, 37, 67
geese, 74
general mobilization, 13, 27, 39, 40, 116, 149, 156
Genoa, 99, 128
Genoans, 108, 130
gente Hungarus, 64
geographic conditions, 68, 70
Gerébi family, 85
Germans, 29, 62, 63, 64, 171
Germany, 91, 94, 168
Geszti, János, 159
gold mines, 14
Golden Bull, 20
Gömör county, 139
grain, 71, 73, 74
—yields, 57, 60
grazing lands, 67, 68
grand vizier, 98
grass steppes, 74
great lords, 5, 18, 24, 25, 27, 29,

31, 32,33, 38, 39, 40, 41, 43, 82,
111, 113, 1135, 152, 153
Great Plain, 56, 59, 68, 72, 74, 115,
144, 145, 157
Greece, 100
Greeks, 63, 168
Gyál (village), 62
Győr (city), 16, 83, 125
Győrffy, Gyorgy, 58
Gyulafehérvár (Alba Iulia), 87

Habsburg, 1, 173
Hainburg (city), 92, 124
Halas (town), 14
Halecki, Oscar, 105
Halics, 103
Halil Pasha, 132
harvest, 156
hatchets, 78
Hátszeg (village), 9, 55
Hatvan (town), 90
hay, 76
heads of households, 59
heavy cavalry, 81, 88, 89, 132, 133
 —plows, 71
Hédervári, László, 144
Hédervári, Lőrinc, 81, 113, 114, 115, 119, 120, 121, 127, 134
Hedvig (Jadwiga), 81
Hellespont, 94, 99, 100
herald, 38
Herceg Rafael, 101, 126
heretics, 167, 168
Heves county, 63
Hévjó (village), 73
highlands, 81, 84, 85, 115, 138, 144, 150
highways, 52
hoes, 71, 78
hogs, 74
holydays, 33
Holy Crown, 22, 30, 36, 83, 84, 117, 123, 127, 141, 142

—kings, 140
—Roman, emperor, 5, 16, 20, 22, 95, 114, 125
—empire, 12, 155, 157
—See, 126
—Virgin of Mount Olive order 142
—year, 140
Hóman, Bálint, 24
honey, 78
horsemeat, 74
horsemen, 88, 149
horse racing, 28, 32
horses, 40, 70, 74, 76, 110, 128, 133, 165
hospes, 57
households, 7
houses, 37, 52, 53, 57, 65, 67, 71, 73, 76, 138, 144
Hunyad county, 6
Hunyadi brothers, 12, 13, 16, 84
—János, Jr., 12, 15
—László, 1, 2, 3, 4, 10, 134, 140, 147, 170, 172
—Mátyás, 2, 3, 4, 5, 10, 24, 26, 134, 144, 153, 173
Hunyadvár (Hunadoara), 14, 55
hunting, 28, 33, 74
Hussites, 3, 12, 17, 81, 96, 136, 147
hygiene, 70

immigrants, 5, 13
immigration, 58
immunities, 26
imperial army, 85, 89, 153
income, 51, 62, 85
income of bishops, 45-46
—canons, 49
indulgences, 157
infantry, 81, 130, 132
infidel, 88
inheritance, 20, 31

inns, 38
inquilinus, 62
inquisitor, 167
internal peace, 83
interregnum, 22, 24, 25
Ishak Pasha, 86, 97
Italian middlemen, 121
 —Renaissance, 9
 —states, 99, 103, 105, 155
islands, 153
Ivanics, Pál, 88

jacquerie of 1437, 87
Jakó, Zsigmond, 73
Jalomitsa River, 122
janissaries, 89, 109, 110, 130, 132, 161, 162, 163
Jantra River, 108
Jazig (Jász), 62
Jenibazar (town), 106
Jews, 23, 63
Jiškraz, Jan of Brandisa, 3, 6, 81, 83, 84, 85, 95, 100, 113, 115, 116, 117, 122, 138, 139, 140, 144, 145, 146, 147, 150, 152
jousting, 28, 32
judges, 18, 23, 27, 28, 29, 39, 40
judicial courts, 45
judicial decisions, 19
judicial system, 28, 101
jurors, 19, 122
justice, 19, 30

Kačaniki Pass, 132
Kálmán, king, 141
Kalocsa (city), 44, 48
Kamonyai, Simon, 86
Kanizsai family, 16, 18, 36
 —László, 81, 160
Kapusi, Bálint, 137, 142, 143
Karácsonyi, János, 42
Karadsa, Taji Pasha, 109, 160, 161
Karaman, 130

Karynthia, 123
Kasim Pasha, 98
Kasimir of Poland, 12
Kassa (Košice) (city), 54, 84, 116, 138
Khan, 165
Khitman, 97
King of Hungary, 5, 10, 12, 16, 18, 23, 25, 27, 30, 31, 32, 38, 39, 40, 52, 61, 62, 64, 71, 78, 81, 82, 83, 84, 85, 90, 92, 96, 97, 98, 99, 100, 101, 102, 103, 104, 105, 106, 110, 112, 113, 115, 116, 118, 125, 127, 128, 142, 145, 149, 150, 152, 153, 156, 170, 171, 172, 173
King of Poland, 81, 148
Kingdom of Hungary, 5, 6, 8, 13, 17, 24, 31, 35, 37, 43, 49, 52, 54, 55, 58, 59, 80, 82, 85, 90, 91, 92, 94, 95, 111, 113, 114, 117, 120, 122, 124, 127, 134, 135, 136, 140, 141, 143, 144, 145, 146, 147, 148, 149, 150, 151, 152, 153, 155, 163, 167, 168, 170, 171, 173
kingship, 19, 20, 22, 38, 114, 119
kitchens, 76
kniazi, 63
Kniazevac (town), 97
knights, 14, 106, 172
Komádi (village), 73
Kolozsmonostor (Cluj Manastur), 52
Komorowski, Peter, 136, 138
Körmöc (city), 139
Korógi (Korógy), János, 160
Kőröshegy (village), 50
Kőrös-Maros Rivers, 56
Kosovo-Polje, 130, 132, 133, 134, 135, 136, 137, 140
Kőszeg (fortress), 116
Kottannerin, Helene, 83

Index

Kraiburg, Bernard von, 165, 166, 167
Krain, 123
Kroja (fortress), 130
Kruševac (fortress), 151
Kučevo (fortress), 104
Kunovica Pass, 97

laborers, 62
Ladislas of Naples, 42
Lambert, Friedrich, 171
lambs, 74
landholders, 40, 62
landholding patterns, 68
landlords, 29, 33, 50, 51, 57, 59, 61, 64, 65, 71, 79
Lasocki, Nicholas, 92, 126
László V, 1, 5, 6, 8, 15, 20, 22, 27, 82, 83, 84, 94, 95, 100, 115, 116, 117, 118, 119, 120, 123, 124, 127, 138, 139, 141, 145, 146, 148, 149, 153, 155, 156, 157, 167, 173
Latin language, 9, 33, 47, 55, 121
Laubersdorf (town), 124
lawbreakers, 23
laws, 29, 30, 39, 42, 62
laws of 1351, 31, 39, 57
lawsuits, 26, 29, 41, 45
lay religious society, 54
laymen, 54
 —overseers, 52
 —society, 52
Lazarević, Stepan, 6, 9, 80
Lendvai-Bánfi, István, 130
lector, 48, 54
legislator, 23
Leithe River, 17
Léka (town), 36
Lelesz (monastery), 52
lentils, 70, 71
Lépes, György, 86, 87
Leškovac (fortress), 97

lesser noblemen, 8, 37-41, 44, 57, 63, 65, 79, 101, 114, 115, 120, 121, 122, 127, 134, 135, 140, 141, 146, 148, 149, 156
levies, 19, 25, 27
library, 37
Lichtensteins, 171
life expectancy, 58
light cavalry, 81, 88, 133, 151
lightweight plow, 71
limes, 81
literature, 54
Little Plain, 56
livestock, 73
Lőcse (city), 84
Lodomerici, Nicholas, 116
Long Campaign, 96, 98, 99, 102, 105, 108, 111, 112
"long village," 67
looting, 88, 105, 108
lord chief justice, 28, 30, 121, 144
lords, 17, 18, 30, 35, 39, 45, 48, 57, 61, 62, 64, 70, 78, 95, 99, 106, 110, 114, 115, 116, 117, 120, 129, 140, 143, 146, 148, 156, 157
lord's castle, 19
Losonc (city), 145
Losonci, Dezső, 13, 85
 —Bebek, 129
lowlands, 70
loyalty, 18
lucrum camerae, 19, 23, 124, 128

Macedonia, 130, 132
Macsó (Mačva), 10, 26, 121, 166
magic, 70, 78
magister, 10, 48
magnificus, 32
Magos (Mogos), 6
Makkai, László, 72, 74
Malča (village), 97
Mályusz, Elemér, 24, 41, 49, 59, 63

managers, 18
manor, 57
manorial courts, 30
manure, 76
manuscripts, 48
Mánya (village), 62
Marcali, Imre, 81, 129
marginal lands, 61
Maritsa River, 97
market, 67
 —towns, 41, 59, 60, 61, 62, 64, 65, 67, 74, 79, 122, 149
Maros River, 86, 157
Marosvásárhely (town), 14
Maróti, János, 10, 18
marriages, 70, 74
martial law, 149
marshes, 72
mass, 47, 50, 53, 79, 172, 173
Marxist historians, 54
master of stables, 26
mead, 78
Medgyes (town), 13
medicine, 70
medieval Hungary, 42
 —villages, 76, 79
Mediterranean, 130, 153
Mehemed II (the Conqueror), 2, 102, 144, 147, 150, 151, 153, 155, 156, 157, 159, 160, 161, 163, 164, 165, 167
mendicant orders, 53, 54, 55
mercenaries, 8, 14, 27, 31, 84, 88, 95, 100, 101, 113, 128, 129, 136, 166, 171
merchants, 25, 116, 121
Mesner, Conrad, 4
Mezid bey, 86, 87, 88
Middle Ages, 13, 57, 58, 64, 79
middlemen, 137
Mihályfalva (village), 73
Miklósy, Béla, 48
miles aulae, 8, 10, 11, 25, 27

military, 6, 11, 15, 17, 35, 40, 85, 94, 116
 —governor, 13, 14, 26, 29, 80, 84, 85, 116, 121, 135, 136, 147
 —history, 9
 —training, 9
mills, 37, 46, 71, 72
Mindszent (village), 73
mines, 23, 35
mining rights, 121
 —towns, 84
Minorities, 164, 168
mints, 122, 139
miracles, 164
mobility, 49, 51, 61, 62, 81
Mődling, 123
Moldavia, 17, 80, 88, 94, 125, 128, 147
Moldavians, 95
Moldva (fortress), 138
Molnár, Erik, 36, 58, 61
monasteries, 47, 52, 53, 54, 55, 116
Mongol invasion, 64, 100, 103
monetary base, 61
money, 61, 99, 128, 140, 149
monks, 47, 51-55, 68, 137, 141, 142, 143
monopoly, 23
Morava River, 157, 159, 165, 166
 —valley, 96, 97
Móric (village), 67, 76, 79
mortality, 58, 70
Morzsinai, 6
Moson county, 36
movable shacks, 76
Muhi (village), 65, 76
Mura-Sava Rivers, 144
Murad I, sultan, 133
Murad II, sultan, 15, 83, 86, 87, 88, 95, 96, 97, 98, 102, 104, 105, 106, 108, 109, 111, 122, 130, 132, 136, 137, 144
muskets, 129, 130, 136

Index

Muslim power, 148
Muslims, 58

Nagykőrös (town), 74
Nagyszeben (Sibiu), 6, 13, 54
Nagyvárad (Várad) (oradea) (city), 11, 23, 104, 140, 143
Nándor-Alba (Belgrade), 1
natio Hungarica, 62, 64
national, 13
 —interests, 152
natione Latinus, 64
nationes, 112
naval, 108, 111, 159, 160, 168
navies, 99, 101, 153
Nesri, 89, 160
Neukirchen, 123
Nicholas V, pope, 126, 128, 142
Nicopolis, 105, 106, 108, 119
Nis, 96
nobiles iobbagiones ecclesiae, 45
nobles, 8, 13, 14, 23, 24, 25, 26, 28, 29, 30, 31, 35, 36, 37, 38, 39, 40, 41, 45, 49, 57, 61, 64, 68, 70, 74, 100, 115, 116, 120, 122, 125, 126, 146, 148, 149, 155, 171
noble vassal, 18
non-nobles, 18
notary, 33, 47
Novobrdo, 150, 151

oats, 70, 71
Obilić, Milos, 132
obligations, 19, 61
offices, 43, 49
officers, 96, 98, 111
officials, 23, 29, 35, 45, 124, 149
oil, 78
oláh (Vlach), 64
old (religious) orders, 52, 53, 54
onions, 70
Oppeln (city), 100
Orbovai, László, 144

Orsova (city), 105
Ország, Mihály, 116, 121
orthodox, 8, 100, 108
Osmanli, 162
Ottoman army, 86, 88, 89, 94, 97, 108, 110, 151, 157, 159, 160, 161, 163, 164, 165
 —artillery, 88
 —camp, 161, 163
 —campaign, 126, 128, 152, 155
 —cavalry, 89, 168
 —commander, 87
 —empire, 5, 13, 86, 89, 90, 91, 99, 112, 114, 123, 124, 125, 128, 130, 135, 136, 137, 140, 144, 150, 153, 154
 —lines, 162, 168
 —menace, 82
 —power, 99
 —raids, 114, 118, 122, 149
 —sailors, 161
 —ships, 160
 —soldiers, 89, 97
 —threat, 116, 129, 137, 148
 —troops, 137
Ottoman Turks, 5, 112
Ottomans, 6, 12, 13, 15, 17, 54, 58, 80, 85, 86, 87, 88, 89, 90, 91, 92, 95, 96, 98, 100, 101, 102, 103, 104, 105, 106, 109, 110, 111, 112, 113, 122, 126, 127, 128, 130, 132, 133, 136, 137, 147, 148, 149, 150, 151, 152, 153, 156, 157, 159, 162, 163, 168
 —wars, 14, 92, 94, 101, 140, 143, 168, 173
Otto (Prince of Bavaria), 171
overpopulation, 60
oxen, 76
Ozora (village), 10

Palatine, 2, 25, 26, 28, 30, 84, 125
Palatio, 109

Paleologue, John, 99
Pálóci, László, 81, 121, 144
—Simon, 144
Pannonhalma (monastery), 52
Pannonius, András, 11
pans, 76
papacy, 42, 92, 94, 95, 123, 128, 143
papal curia, 136, 141
—envoy, 148
—legate, 156
parish, 43, 48, 49, 50, 71
—priest, 43, 48, 49, 50, 51, 55, 62
parliament, 25
pasha, 88, 163
pastures, 74
patent, 6, 15, 28, 117, 142
patria, 13, 15
patriot, 5, 152
patron, 14, 24
patronage, 35, 43, 79, 142, 143
Paulist order, 54, 55, 142
peace agreement, 94, 103
peace of Szeged", 104
peas, 70, 71
peasant, 14, 29, 30, 31, 35, 37, 38, 39, 41, 44, 50, 51, 56-79, 87, 101, 110, 116, 133, 140, 149, 157, 167
—menu, 76
—revolt, 12, 13, 60
Pécs (city), 49, 54
Pelbárt of Temesvár, 78
"people's" army, 87
Pelsőci, Imre, 116, 127, 129
—László, 129
Perényi family, 81, 111
perpetual baron, 5, 36
personalis presentia, 30
personal justice, 28
Pest (city), 115, 155, 157
Pest county, 63
Peter the Flagbearer, 162
Peter (prince of Moldavia), 125, 137, 148

Petrec (village), 108
Philipponi, Bernard, 142
Philippopolis, 97, 106
Piccinnino, Nicola, 11
Piccolomini, Aeneas Sylvius, 92, 115, 147, 173
picket line, 86
Pilis county, 63
Pirot (city), 97
plague, 60, 64, 153, 163
Plankenstein, 148
plows, 68
Podiebrad, Georg of, 5, 12, 119, 146, 148
Poland, 33, 84, 91, 94, 96, 100, 113, 124, 168
Poles, 57
Polish, 95, 101, 102
—army, 12, 139
—contingent, 101
—lords, 99, 103
—king, 83
—nobles, 99
political nation, 18, 22
—power, 6, 17, 144
politician, 5, 11, 138
ponds, 73
pontiff, 146
pope, 43, 92, 99, 100, 103, 111, 118, 123, 125, 126, 128, 129, 130, 137, 140, 142, 145, 148, 152
population, 53, 60
populi et iobbagiones nobilium, 57
populi nobilium, 57
pork, 74
porta, 58, 59, 63, 149
pots, 78
Pozsega county, 36
Pozsony (Bratislava), 6, 36, 81, 85, 90, 116, 117, 139, 146, 147
praedialis, 44, 45
praedium, 44
Prague, 5, 12, 148

Index

precious metal, 23
precipitation, 56
prebenda, 50
prelates, 18, 24, 26, 28, 32, 42, 43, 44, 45, 46, 50, 81, 115, 118, 120, 140, 148
Premonstratensians, 52, 53, 68
prerogatives, 29
presentia regia, 28
priests, 47, 49, 78, 79
primate of Hungary, 19
primeval forest, 60
primogeniture, 35
prince, 122, 128, 137, 142
prince of Bosnia, 137
—Burgundy, 152
—Milan, 4
—Wallachia, 137
prior, 44, 49
prisoner, 98
Pristina (village), 132
private army, 11, 14, 26, 31, 33, 44, 70, 80, 84
—property, 68
privileged orders, 18, 22, 24, 30, 31, 84, 146
privileges, 26, 31, 32, 44, 50, 57, 64, 67
proceres, 35, 36
Prochaska, Antony, 109
prods, 78
propaganda, 164
Provadia, 108
provisions, 96, 164
provost, 143
Ptoczek, Henry, 12
punches, 78

quadrivium, 47
quarrels, 79
queen, 25, 26, 84, 85, 90, 91, 92
queen Erzsébet, 12, 81, 82, 83, 89, 91, 92, 117, 118, 143

Radul, 6
Ragusa (Dubrovnik), 17, 86, 95, 97, 132
raiders, 58, 87
raids, 79, 80, 86, 96, 150
ramparts, 162
"random" (disorganized village, 67
reading, 47, 50
realm, 41, 42, 43, 44, 53, 65, 82, 83, 94, 99, 101, 114, 120, 122, 125, 126, 127, 134, 138, 141, 145, 147, 148, 150, 152, 156, 170
realpolitik, 127
rebellion, 42
regency, 102, 120, 121, 122, 123, 128, 135, 141, 146, 170
regent, 5, 22, 23, 27, 36, 43, 81, 113, 134, 136, 141, 142, 143, 145, 146, 147, 170, 171,
regnum, 17, 22, 23, 27, 28, 30, 36, 41, 42, 82, 116, 117, 136
reeds, 76
religious, 13, 42, 54
Renaissance culture, 5, 10, 173
Renaissance king, 169
requisitioning, 165
retainers, 18, 19, 24, 25, 27, 29, 30, 32, 35, 39, 44, 114, 124
revenues, 19, 23, 48, 51, 52
riverine resources, 56
rivers, 72
rhetoric, 54
robbery, 19
roads, 51, 122
Roman, 79, 81
Roman Catholic Church, 5, 8, 18, 41, 49, 55, 95, 100, 153
Romanian, 6, 64
Roman Pannonia, 59
Rome, 33, 53, 94, 125, 126, 140, 143, 153, 159
Rosenberg, Henrik, 171

Rozgonyi, György, 116
 —István, 85
 —Rajnáld, 129, 160, 172
 —Simon, 81, 84, 95, 101
rules of succession, 20
Rumeli, 98, 109, 160
Ruthenians, 63
royal administration, 26-27
 —authority, 30, 40, 100, 150
 —cityies, 115, 124
 —council, 23, 24-26, 27, 36, 43, 44, 82, 95, 99, 100, 102, 103, 108, 113, 114, 115, 116, 117, 119, 120, 121, 123, 124, 125, 127, 128, 134, 136, 137, 138, 140, 141, 142, 143, 144, 145
 —court, 19, 25, 26, 27, 28, 32, 33, 39, 65, 90, 100, 139, 142, 148, 170
 —courts of justice, 45
 —decrees, 39, 43, 149
 —demesne, 23, 32, 37, 38
 —fortresses, 24
 —grants, 14
 —judges, 26
 —justice, 28-30
 —palace, 4
 —patents, 147
 —patronage, 43, 49, 143
 —power, 24
 —seal, 26, 27
 —prerogatives, 22, 23, 25, 143, 152
 —stables, 144, 173
 —revenues, 23, 35, 101, 116, 120, 121, 122, 124, 147, 149
 —retinue, 8, 26, 28, 172
 —treasury, 3, 14
rye, 70

sacraments, 50
saint, 22, 164
sainthood, 168
salaries, 51, 116, 126, 150

salt, 14, 23, 26, 72, 78, 121
Salzburg, 165
Saneck (town), 151
Sanuto, Marino, 128
Sáros, 84
Sárrét, 73
Sárvár (town), 36
Sava River, 56, 159, 162
Saxons (of Transylvania), 23, 29, 49, 59, 62, 63, 88, 157
schism, 43
schismatic, 42, 167
Schlick, Casper, 92
schools, 38, 47, 48, 53, 55
Scolari, Philippo degli, 10, 64
scrpers, 78
scythes, 71
seal, 48
Sebeskőrös River, 73
secret chancellary, 27
secular overseers, 54
Selmec (bánya) (city), 50
Serbia, 15, 80, 98, 129, 132, 133, 150, 151, 155
Serbian despot, 129
 —fortresses, 102, 104, 109
Serbians, 9, 85, 91, 92, 95, 96, 102, 132, 151, 159, 160, 168
serf-plots, 35, 61, 62, 67, 68, 120
serfs, 18, 19, 37, 40, 44, 57, 60, 61, 65, 67, 116
sermon, 78
servants, 32, 33, 78
servientes, 62
settlements, 37, 53, 57, 59, 62, 64, 65, 67, 68, 79
Sforza, Francesco, 11
sharpeners, 78
sheep herding, 56, 74
ships, 157, 165, 166
sickles, 71
Siebenbürgen, 63
siege, 168, 171
 —guns, 159, 164, 167

Siklósd (town), 67
Sigismund of Luxemburg, 6, 8, 10, 11, 12, 22, 24, 26, 27, 33, 42, 43, 65, 80, 118, 121, 142, 143, 148
Silesia, 12, 74
silver mines, 150, 151
Simontornya, 36
Sinkovics, István, 19, 33
sipahis, 86, 88, 89, 109, 110, 133, 163
Sitnica River, 132
Skanderbeg (George Kastriota), 102, 105, 106, 108, 111, 130, 133, 153
Slavic, 63
Slavonia, 17, 26, 59, 63, 85, 106, 118, 120, 129, 136, 144, 147
Slavs, 64
Slovakia, 12, 61
Slovaks, 62, 63
Slovenes, 64
Slivnitsa River, 98
social groups, 49
social mobility, 8, 25, 48, 55
 —reformer, 17, 40
 —status, 8, 31, 44
Sofia, 97, 106, 130, 132, 151
soldiers, 8, 9, 10, 11, 14, 17, 40, 44, 88, 89, 95, 96, 98, 102, 106, 108, 110, 112, 117, 128, 143, 156, 164, 172
Somogy county, 36, 50, 63, 74
Somogyvár, 53
Sopron (city), 50, 83
Sopron county), 68
Sorba (Srba), 6
sorcery, 78
South Slav, 6
sovereign, 125, 171, 173
spade, 71
Spain, 99
stags, 74
state, 5, 14, 42, 57, 85, 114, 150
 —budget, 23

statesman, 111
stave, 78
St. Christopher, 79
St. George Square, 4
St. István, 19, 20, 21, 84, 140, 143
St. László, 140
St. Michael, 50
Sternbergs, 12, 148, 171
steward, 26
Steyrmark, 123
Stoianovich, Traian, 79
straits, 94, 108
strategy, 111
stratification, 62
straw, 76
streams, 72
students, 48, 54
studies, 47
studium, 47, 48, 54
Styria, 120
succession, 16, 81
Sumla, 106, 108
superpatriot, 83
superstition, 70, 79
swamps, 57, 60, 65, 67, 68, 72, 88
swine, 74
swordsmen, 149
Sylvester II, pope, 143
Szabadka (Subotica) (city), 14
Szabó, István, 58, 68, 70
Szalánkemén (Slankamen) (town), 160
Szakolca (fortress), 139
Szakolcai, Pongrác, 116
Szapolyai family, 18
Szászsebes, 13
Széchi, cardinal Dénes, 16, 83, 117, 125, 126, 127, 144, 147, 153
Széchi, Tamás, 16, 85, 129
Szeged (city), 53, 54, 74, 103, 104, 134, 135, 136, 137, 157
Székelyhida, 73
Székely, János, 116, 129, 133
 —Tamás, 121, 138, 141

Székelys, 10, 23, 29, 63, 65, 88
Székesfehérvár, 19, 49, 83, 84, 115, 120, 140
Szendrő (Smederevo) (fortress), 13, 15, 80, 86, 92, 97, 134, 136, 140, 150, 151, 155, 159, 164
Szentgyörgyi and Bazini, counts of, 35, 36
Szentimre (Sintimbru), 87
Szentkirály (fortress), 145
Szentmiklósi, Pongrác, 113, 139
Szentpéteri, Imre, 29
Szepesség, 29, 84, 150
Szilágyi, Erzsébet, 4, 10, 171
 —László, 10
 —Mihály, 10, 159, 160, 167, 170, 171, 172
Szilágyis, 14
Szörény (Severin), 13, 14, 26, 80, 85
Sztropka, Gregory, 111
Szűcs, Jenő, 64

Tabor, 12
Tagliacozzo, Giovanni da, 162
Talafus, 84
Tamási, Henrik, 111
Tata (town), 80
taxes, 18, 19, 23, 31, 40, 45, 58, 59, 65
Teleki, József, 104, 115
Temes county, 14, 156
Temesvár (Timisoara) (city), 3, 53, 173
Teutonic Knights, 94
Thallóczi, Frank, 81, 106, 129
Thallóczi, Zovan, 85
Thanksgiving, 99
three-field system, 71
throne of Hungary, 16, 81, 28
Thuróczi, Joannis, 5, 6, 9, 10, 18, 109, 167
tillable acreage, 61
tilling, 56, 57, 60, 67

Tisza River, 56, 59, 68
Titel (village), 15
tithe, 38, 49, 51, 65, 71, 100, 116
Tobias, Norman, 164
tolls, 31, 46
Tokaj, 74
Tolna county, 36, 63
topography, 67
Topolnista River, 97
Továnkut (village), 14
towns, 52, 53, 54, 60, 65, 152
trade, 99, 126
traders, 74
Trainan:s Grate, 97
Transdanubia, 59
Transylvania, 3, 6, 10, 12, 13, 14, 23, 29, 49, 56, 59, 63, 65, 67, 73, 80, 84, 85, 86, 87, 102, 114, 115, 116, 121, 122, 127, 135, 147, 149, 157
transhumance, 56
traveller, 38, 61
treason, 4, 23, 125
treasurer, 26, 121
treasury, 121, 140, 156
Trencsén (fortress), 149
Trencsén county, 63
tribes, 31, 63
trivium, 47
Trnava (village), 150
troops, 99, 157, 160, 163, 166
truce, 100, 102, 103, 104, 105, 124, 137, 140
Turgoviste, 123
Turkhan Pasha, 97, 133
Turkish, 9
Turks, 165
Túrmező (village), 29
Twartko, Stepan, 15, 137

Udvarhely county, 67
Ujdombró (fortress), 144
Ujlak (village), 171

Index

Ujlaki, Miklós, 2, 10, 33, 81, 83, 84, 85, 95, 97, 115, 116, 117, 119, 120, 121, 127, 139, 140, 144, 145, 150, 151, 171
Unam eademque nobilitas, 37
Ungor, Peter, 10
university, 47, 51, 54, 55
urban centers, 64
 —communities, 52
 —developments, 122
 —population, 54
Üsküb, 157
utensils, 33, 73

Vác (town), 143
Vág River, 113, 116, 149
Vajdahunyad (fortress), 6, 9
Valkó county, 36
Varna, 106, 108, 109, 110, 111, 112, 132, 134
Vas county, 36, 84
Vásárhely (town), 53
Vaskapu (village), 88
vassal, 17, 18, 27, 64, 102, 153
vegetables, 71
Venetian diplomats, 45
Venetian wars, 11
Venerio, Leonardo, 94
Venetians, 100, 108, 130
Venice, 33, 94, 99, 100, 103, 123, 128, 155
Veszprém (town), 16, 48
Veszprém county, 84
vicar, 44, 50, 115, 116
vice-count, 39
viceory, 20
Vidin, 14, 105
Vienna, 5, 15, 123, 146, 149, 151, 153, 155, 156, 164, 170
Viennese mountains, 124
Világosvár, 102, 104
village, 19, 36, 50, 53, 56, 57, 59, 60, 61, 64, 65, 67, 68, 70, 72, 76, 78, 86, 88, 108

village churches, 79
 —judges, 19, 58, 62
 —network, 65
vines, 73
vineyards, 4, 51, 62, 68
Vingárt family, 10, 85
virtue, 33
Visconti, Philippo, 11
Visegrád (fortress), 83
Vitéz, János of Zredna, 4, 11, 64, 115, 118, 126, 128, 143, 144, 147, 150, 171
Vitovecz, Johannes, 85, 118
Vlachs, 23, 29
voivode, 26
voluntarism, 18
Vöröstorony Pass, 86
Voyk (Woyk), 6, 8, 9
Vrana (abbey), 121, 144, 151

wages, 51, 62, 121
wagon-fortress, 108, 110
Wallachia, 6, 8, 13, 17, 80, 86, 88, 90, 94, 95, 97, 105, 118, 122, 128, 147, 148
Wallachian prince 113, 123, 129
Wallachians, 9, 59, 62, 63, 64, 87, 88, 95, 106, 122, 129, 133, 149
Wallachian wars, 8
Wavrin, Waleran de, 118, 119
wax, 78
weak, government, 82
Weber, Max, 17
Wenzel, Gusztáv, 58
West, 95, 99, 102, 122, 128
western envoys, 99
Western Europe, 54, 55, 60, 64, 65, 74, 95, 99
western monarchs, 101, 111, 119, 122
western powers, 138
wheat, 70, 71
Wienerneustadt, 123, 146
wine, 28

wine production, 74
wine trade, 35, 74
witchcraft, 78
Wladislaw I (III of Poland), 8, 22, 24, 81, 82, 83, 84, 85, 86, 89, 90, 91, 92, 94, 95, 96, 97, 99, 100, 101, 103, 104, 106, 110, 113, 115, 117, 118, 121, 126, 142, 143, 152
woman regent, 82
wool suits, 33
writing, 47, 50

yields of grain, 71

Zagreb (city), 85
Zagreb county, 116, 138
Zala county, 36, 63, 84
Zaránd county, 102
Zimony (Zemun) (village), 160
Zlatista Pass, 106
—River, 97
Zólyom county, 63
Zólyomi, Benedek, 136
Zotikos, 109
Zsaka (village), 73

EAST EUROPEAN MONOGRAPHS

The *East European Monographs* comprise scholarly books on the history and civilization of Eastern Europe. They are published under the editorship of Stephen Fischer-Galati, in the belief that these studies contribute substantially to the knowledge of the area and serve to stimulate scholarship and research.

1. *Political Ideas and the Enlightenment in the Romanian Principalities, 1750–1831.* By Vlad Georgescu. 1971.
2. *America, Italy and the Birth of Yugoslavia, 1917–1919.* By Dragan R. Zivjinovic. 1972.
3. *Jewish Nobles and Geniuses in Modern Hungary.* By William O. McCagg, Jr. 1972.
4. *Mixail Soloxov in Yugoslavia: Reception and Literary Impact.* By Robert F. Price. 1973.
5. *The Historical and Nationalist Thought of Nicolae Iorga.* By William O. Oldson. 1973.
6. *Guide to Polish Libraries and Archives.* By Richard C. Lewanski. 1974.
7. *Vienna Broadcasts to Slovakia, 1938–1939: A Case Study in Subversion.* By Henry Delfiner. 1974.
8. *The 1917 Revolution in Latvia.* By Andrew Ezergailis. 1974.
9. *The Ukraine in the United Nations Organization: A Study in Soviet Foreign Policy, 1944–1950.* By Konstantin Sawczuk. 1975.
10. *The Bosnian Church: A New Interpretation.* By John V. A. Fine, Jr., 1975.
11. *Intellectual and Social Developments in the Habsburg Empire from Maria Theresa to World War I.* Edited by Stanley B. Winters and Joseph Held. 1975.
12. *Ljudevit Gaj and the Illyrian Movement.* By Elinor Murray Despalatovic. 1975.
13. *Tolerance and Movements of Religious Dissent in Eastern Europe,* Edited by Bela K. Kiraly. 1975.
14. *The Parish Republic: Hlinka's Slovak People's Party, 1939–1945.* By Yeshayahu Jelinek. 1976.
15. *The Russian Annexation of Bessarabia, 1774–1828.* By George F. Jewsbury. 1976.
16. *Modern Hungarian Historiography.* By Steven Bela Vardy. 1976.
17. *Values and Community in Multi-National Yugoslavia.* By Gary K. Bertsch. 1976.
18. *The Greek Socialist Movement and the First World War: the Road to Unity.* By George B. Leon. 1976.
19. *The Radical Left in the Hungarian Revolution of 1848.* By Laszlo Deme. 1976.
20. *Hungary between Wilson and Lenin: The Hungarian Revolution of 1918–1919 and the Big Three.* By Peter Pastor. 1976.

21. *The Crises of France's East-Central European Diplomacy, 1933-1938.* By Anthony J. Komjathy. 1976.
22. *Polish Politics and National Reform, 1775-1788.* By Daniel Stone. 1976.
23. *The Habsburg Empire in World War I.* Edited by Robert A. Kann, Bela K. Kiraly, and Paula S. Fichtner. 1977.
24. *The Slovenes and Yugoslavism, 1890-1914.* By Carole Rogel. 1977.
25. *German-Hungarian Relations and the Swabian Problem.* By Thomas Spira. 1977.
26. *The Metamorphosis of a Social Class in Hungary During the Reign of Young Franz Joseph.* By Peter I. Hidas. 1977.
27. *Tax Reform in Eighteenth Century Lombardy.* By Daniel M. Klang. 1977.
28. *Tradition versus Revolution: Russia and the Balkans in 1917.* By Robert H. Johnston. 1977.
29. *Winter into Spring: The Czechoslovak Press and the Reform Movement 1963-1968.* By Frank L. Kaplan. 1977.
30. *The Catholic Church and the Soviet Government, 1939-1949.* By Dennis J. Dunn. 1977.
31. *The Hungarian Labor Service System, 1939-1945.* By Randolph L. Braham. 1977.
32. *Consciousness and History: Nationalist Critics of Greek Society 1897-1914.* By Gerasimos Augustinos. 1977.
33. *Emigration in Polish Social and Political Thought, 1870-1914.* By Benjamin P. Murdzek. 1977.
34. *Serbian Poetry and Milutin Bojic.* By Mihailo Dordevic. 1977.
35. *The Baranya Dispute: Diplomacy in the Vortex of Ideologies, 1918-1921.* By Leslie C. Tihany. 1978.
36. *The United States in Prague, 1945-1948.* By Walter Ullmann. 1978.
37. *Rush to the Alps: The Evolution of Vacationing in Switzerland.* By Paul P. Bernard. 1978.
38. *Transportation in Eastern Europe: Empirical Findings.* By Bogdan Mieczkowski. 1978.
39. *The Polish Underground State: A Guide to the Underground, 1939-1945.* By Stefan Korbonski. 1978.
40. *The Hungarian Revolution of 1956 in Retrospect.* Edited by Bela K. Kiraly and Paul Jonas. 1978.
41. *Boleslaw Limanowski (1935-1935): A Study in Socialism and Nationalism.* By Kazimiera Janina Cottam. 1978.
42. *The Lingering Shadow of Nazism: The Austrian Independent Party Movement Since 1945.* By Max E. Riedlsperger. 1978.
43. *The Catholic Church, Dissent and Nationality in Soviet Lithuania.* By V. Stanley Vardys. 1978.
44. *The Development of Parliamentary Government in Serbia.* By Alex N. Dragnich. 1978.
45. *Divide and Conquer: German Efforts to Conclude a Separate Peace, 1914-1918.* By L. L. Farrar, Jr. 1978.
46. *The Prague Slav Congress of 1848.* By Lawrence D. Orton. 1978.
47. *The Nobility and the Making of the Hussite Revolution.* By John M. Klassen. 1978.
48. *The Cultural Limits of Revolutionary Politics: Change and Continuity in Socialist Czechoslovakia.* By David W. Paul. 1979.
49. *On the Border of War and Peace: Polish Intelligence and Diplomacy in 1937-1939 and the Origins of the Ultra Secret.* By Richard A. Woytak. 1979.
50. *Bear and Foxes: The International Relations of the East European States 1965-1969.* By Ronald Haly Linden. 1979.

51. *Czechoslovakia: The Heritage of Ages Past.* Edited by Ivan Volgyes and Hans Brisch. 1979.
52. *Prime Minister Gyula Andrassy's Influence on Habsburg Foreign Policy.* By Janos Decsy. 1979.
53. *Citizens for the Fatherland: Education, Educators, and Pedagogical Ideals in Eighteenth Century Russia.* By J. L. Black. 1979.
54. *A History of the "Proletariat": The Emergence of Marxism in the Kingdom of Poland, 1870-1887.* By Norman M. Naimark. 1979.
55. *The Slovak Autonomy Movement, 1935-1939: A Study in Unrelenting Nationalism.* By Dorothea H. El Mallakh. 1979.
56. *Diplomat in Exile: Francis Pulszky's Political Activities in England, 1849-1860.* By Thomas Kabdebo. 1979.
57. *The German Struggle Against the Yugoslav Guerrillas in World War II: German Counter-Insurgency in Yugoslavia, 1941-1943.* By Paul N. Hehn. 1979.
58. *The Emergence of the Romanian National State.* By Gerald J. Bobango. 1979.
59. *Stewards of the Land: The American Farm School and Modern Greece.* By Brenda L. Marder. 1979.
60. *Roman Dmowski: Party, Tactics, Ideology, 1895-1907.* By Alvin M. Fountain, II. 1980.
61. *International and Domestic Politics in Greece During the Crimean War.* By Jon V. Kofas. 1980.
62. *Fires on the Mountain: The Macedonian Revolutionary Movement and the Kidnapping of Ellen Stone.* By Laura Beth Sherman. 1980.
63. *The Modernization of Agriculture: Rural Transformation in Hungary, 1848-1975.* Edited by Joseph Held. 1980.
64. *Britain and the War for Yugoslavia, 1940-1943.* By Mark C. Wheeler. 1980.
65. *The Turn to the Right: The Ideological Origins and Development of Ukrainian Nationalism, 1919-1929.* By Alexander J. Motyl. 1980.
66. *The Maple Leaf and the White Eagle: Canadian-Polish Relations, 1918-1978.* By Aloysius Balawyder. 1980.
67. *Antecedents of Revolution: Alexander I and the Polish Congress Kingdom, 1815-1825.* By Frank W. Thackeray. 1980.
68. *Blood Libel at Tiszaeszlar.* By Andrew Handler. 1980.
69. *Democratic Centralism in Romania: A Study of Local Communist Politics.* By Daniel N. Nelson. 1980.
70. *The Challenge of Communist Education: A Look at the German Democratic Republic.* By Margrete Siebert Klein. 1980.
71. *The Fortifications and Defense of Constantinople.* By Byron C. P. Tsangadas. 1980.
72. *Balkan Cultural Studies.* By Stavro Skendi. 1980.
73. *Studies in Ethnicity: The East European Experience in America.* Edited by Charles A. Ward, Philip Shashko, and Donald E. Pienkos. 1980.
74. *The Logic of "Normalization:" The Soviet Intervention in Czechoslovakia and the Czechoslovak Response.* By Fred Eidlin. 1980.
75. *Red Cross, Black Eagle: A Biography of Albania's American School.* By Joan Fultz Kontos. 1981.
76. *Nationalism in Contemporary Europe.* By Franjo Tudjman. 1981.
77. *Great Power Rivalry at the Turkish Straits: The Montreux Conference and Convention of 1936.* By Anthony R. DeLuca. 1981.
78. *Islam Under the Double Eagle: The Muslims of Bosnia and Hercegovina, 1878-1914.* By Robert J. Donia. 1981.

79. *Five Eleventh Century Hungarian Kings: Their Policies and Their Relations with Rome.* By Z. J. Kosztolnyik. 1981.
80. *Prelude to Appeasement: East European Central Diplomacy in the Early 1930's.* By Lisanne Radice. 1981.
81. *The Soviet Regime in Czechoslovakia.* By Zdenek Krystufek. 1981.
82. *School Strikes in Prussian Poland, 1901-1907: The Struggle Over Bilingual Education.* By John J. Kulczychi. 1981.
83. *Romantic Nationalism and Liberalism: Joachim Lelewel and the Polish National Idea.* By Joan S. Skurnowicz. 1981.
84. *The "Thaw" In Bulgarian Literature.* By Atanas Slavov. 1981.
85. *The Political Thought of Thomas G. Masaryk.* By Roman Szporluk. 1981.
86. *Prussian Poland in the German Empire, 1871-1900.* By Richard Blanke. 1981.
87. *The Mazepists: Ukrainian Separatism in the Early Eighteenth Century.* By Orest Subtelny. 1981.
88. *The Battle for the Marchlands: The Russo-Polish Campaign of 1920.* By Adam Zamoyski. 1981.
89. *Milovan Djilas: A Revolutionary as a Writer.* By Dennis Reinhartz. 1981.
90. *The Second Republic: The Disintegration of Post-Munich Czechoslovakia, October 1938-March 1939.* By Theodore Prochazka, Sr. 1981.
91. *Financial Relations of Greece and the Great Powers, 1832-1862.* By Jon V. Kofas. 1981.
92. *Religion and Politics: Bishop Valerian Trifa and His Times.* By Gerald J. Bobango. 1981.
93. *The Politics of Ethnicity in Eastern Europe.* Edited by George Klein and Milan J. Reban. 1981.
94. *Czech Writers and Politics.* By Alfred French. 1981.
95. *Nation and Ideology: Essays in Honor of Wayne S. Vucinich.* Edited by Ivo Banac, John G. Ackerman, and Roman Szporluk. 1981.
96. *For God and Peter the Great: The Works of Thomas Consett, 1723-1729.* Edited by James Cracraft. 1982.
97. *The Geopolitics of Leninism.* By Stanley W. Page. 1982
98. *Karel Havlicek (1821-1856): A National Liberation Leader of the Czech Renascence.* By Barbara K. Reinfeld. 1982.
99. *Were-Wolf and Vampire in Romania.* By Harry A. Senn. 1982.
100. *Ferdinand I of Austria: The Politics of Dynasticism in the Age of Reformation.* By Paula Sutter Fichtner. 1982
101. *France in Greece During World War I: A Study in the Politics of Power.* By Alexander S. Mitrakos. 1982.
102. *Authoritarian Politics in a Transitional State: Istvan Bethlen and the Unified Party in Hungary, 1919-1926.* By William M. Batkay. 1982.
103. *Romania Between East and West: Historical Essays in Memory of Constantin C. Giurescu.* Edited by Stephen Fischer-Galati, Radu R. Florescu and George R. Ursul. 1982.
104. *War and Society in East Central Europe: From Hunyadi to Rakoczi—War and Society in Late Medieval and Early Modern Hungary.* Edited by János Bak and Béla K. Király. 1982.
105. *Total War and Peace Making: A Case Study on Trianon.* Edited by Béla K. Király, Peter Pastor, and Ivan Sanders. 1982
106. *Army, Aristocracy, and Monarchy: Essays on War, Society, and Government in Austria, 1618-1780.* Edited by Wayne S. Vucinich. 1982.
107. *.The First Serbian Uprising, 1804-1813.* Edited by Wayne S. Vucinich. 1982.

108. *Propaganda and Nationalism in Wartime Russia: The Jewish Anti-Fascist Committee in the USSR, 1941–1948.* By Shimon Redich. 1982.
109. *One Step Back, Two Steps Forward: On the Language Policy of the Communist Party of Soviet Union in the National Republics.* By Michael Bruchis. 1982.
110. *Bessarabia and Bukovina: The Soviet-Romanian Territorial Dispute.* by Nicholas Dima. 1982
111. *Greek-Soviet Relations, 1917–1941.* By Andrew L. Zapantis. 1982.
112. *National Minorities in Romania: Change in Transylvania.* By Elemer Illyes. 1982.
113. *Dunarea Noastra: Romania, the Great Powers, and the Danube Question, 1914–1921.* by Richard C. Frucht. 1982.
114. *Continuity and Change in Austrian Socialism: The Eternal Quest for the Third Way.* By Melanie A. Sully. 1982
115. *Catherine II's Greek Prelate: Eugenios Voulgaris in Russia, 1771–1806.* By Stephen K. Batalden. 1982.
116. *The Union of Lublin: Polish Federalism in the Golden Age.* By Harry E. Dembkowski. 1982.
117. *Heritage and Continuity in Eastern Europe: The Transylvanian Legacy in the History of the Romanians.* By Cornelia Bodea and Virgil Candea. 1982.
118. *Contemporary Czech Cinematography: Jiri Menzel and the History of The "Closely Watched Trains".* By Josef Skvorecky. 1982.
119. *East Central Europe in World War I: From Foreign Domination to National Freedom.* By Wiktor Sukiennicki. 1982.
120. *City, Town, and Countryside in the Early Byzantine Era.* Edited by Robert L. Hohlfelder. 1982.
121. *The Byzantine State Finances in the Eighth and Ninth Centuries.* By Warren T. Treadgold. 1982.
122. *East Central European Society and War in Pre-Revolutionary Eighteenth Century.* Edited by Gunther E. Rothenberg, Bela K. Kiraly and Peter F. Sugar. 1982.
123. *Czechoslovak Policy and the Hungarian Minority, 1945–1948.* By Kalman Janics. 1982.
124. *At the Brink of War and Peace: The Tito-Stalin Split in a Historic Perspective.* Edited by Wayne S. Vucinich. 1982.
125. *The Road to Bellapais: The Turkish Cypriot Exodus to Northern Cyprus.* By Pierre Oberling. 1982.
126. *Essays on World War I: Origins and Prisoners of War.* Edited by Peter Pastor and Samuel R. Williamson, Jr. 1983.
127. *Panteleimon Kulish: A Sketch of His Life and Times.* By George S. N. Luckyj. 1983.
128. *Economic Development in the Habsburg Monarchy in the Nineteenth Century: Essays.* Edited by John Komlos. 1983.
129. *Warsaw Between the World Wars: Profile of the Capital City in a Developing Land, 1918–1939.* By Edward D. Wynot, Jr. 1983.
130. *The Lust for Power: Nationalism, Slovakia, and The Communists, 1918–1948.* By Yeshayahu Jelinek. 1983.
131. *The Tsar's Loyal Germans: The Riga German Community: Social Change and the Nationality Question, 1855–1905.* By Anders Henriksson. 1983.
132. *Society in Change: Studies in Honor of Bela K. Kiraly.* Edited by Steven Bela Vardy. 1983.
133. *Authoritariansim in Greece: The Metaxas Regime.* By Jon V. Kofas. 1983.
134. *New Hungarian Peasants: An East Central European Experience with Collectivization.* Edited by Marida Hollos and Bela C. Maday. 1983.

135. *War, Revolution, and Society in Romania: The Road to Independence.* Edited by Ilie Ceausescu. 1983.
136. *The Beginning of Cyrillic Printing, Cracow, 1491: From the Orthodox Past in Poland.* By Szczepan K. Zimmer. 1983.
137. *Effects of World War I. The Class War After the Great War: The Rise of Communist Parties in East Central Europe, 1918-1921.* Edited by Ivo Banac. 1983.
138. *Bulgaria 1878-1918. A History.* By Richard J. Crampton. 1983.
139. *T. G. Masaryk Revisited: A Cirtical Assessment.* By Hanus J. Hajek. 1983.
140. *The Cult of Power: Dictators in the Twentieth Century.* Edited by Joseph Held. 1983.
141. *Economy and Foreign Policy: The Struggle of the Great Powers for Economic Hegemony in the Danube Valley, 1919-1939.* By György Ránki. 1983.
142. *Germany, Russia, and the Balkans: Prelude to the Nazi-Soviet Non-Aggression Pact.* By Marilynn Giroux Hitchens. 1983.
143. Guestworkers in the German Reich: The Poles in Wilhelmian Germany. By Richard Charles Murphy. 1983.
144. *The Latvian Impact on the Bolshevik Revolution.* By Andrew Ezergailis. 1983.
145. *The Rise of Moscow's Power.* By Henryk Paszkiewicz. 1983.
146. *A Question of Empire: Leopold I and the War of the Spanish Succession, 1701-1705.* By Linda and Marsha Frey. 1983.
147. *Effects of World War I. The Uprooted: Hungarian Refugees and Their Impact on Hungarian Domestic Policies, 1918-1921.* By Istvan I. Mocsy. 1983.
148. *Nationalist Integration Through Socialist Planning: An Anthropological Study of a Romanian New Town.* By Steven L. Sampson. 1983.
149. *Decadence of Freedom: Jacques Riviere's Quest of Russian Mentality.* By Jean-Pierre Cap. 1983.
150. *East Central European Society in the Age of Revolutions, 1775-1856.* Edited by Béla K. Király. 1984.
151. *The Crucial Decade: East Central European Society and National Defense, 1859-1870.* Edited by Béla K. Király. 1984.
152. *The First War between Socialist States: The Hungarian Revolution of 1956 and Its Impact.* Edited by Béla K. Király, Barbara Lotze and Nandor Dreisziger. 1984.
153. *Russian Bolshevism and British Labor, 1917-1921.* By Morton H. Cowden. 1984.
154. *Feliks Dzierzynski and the SDKPIL: A Study of the Origins of Polish Communism.* By Robert Blobaum. 1984.
155. *Studies on Kosova.* Edited by Arshi Pipa and Sami Repishti. 1984.
156. *New Horizons in East-West Economic and Business Relations.* Edited by Marvin A. Jackson and James D. Woodson. 1984.
157. *Czech Nationalism in the Nineteenth Century.* By John F. N. Bradley. 1984.
158. *The Theory of the General Strike from the French Revolution to Poland.* By Phil H. Goodstein. 1984.
159. *King Zog and the Struggle for Stability in Albania.* By Bernd J. Fischer. 1984.
160. *Tradition and Avant-Garde: The Arts in Serbian Culture between the Two World Wars.* By Jelena Milojković-Djurić. 1984.
161. *The Megali Idea and the Greek Turkish War of 1897.* By Theodore G. Tatsios. 1984.
162. *The Hungarian Jewish Catastrophe: A Selected and Annotated Bibliography.* By Randolph L. Braham. 1984.
163. *Goli Otok—Island of Death [A Diary in Letters].* By Venko Markovski. 1984.
164. *Initiation and Initiative: An Exploration of the Life and Ideas of Dimitrije Mitrinovic.* By Andrew Rigby. 1984.
165. *Nations, Nationalities, Peoples: A Study of the Nationality Policies of the Communist Party in Soviet Moldavia.* By Michael Bruchis. 1984.
166. *Frederick I, The Man and His Times.* By Linda and Marsha Frey. 1984.
167. *The Effects of World War I: War Communism in Hungary.* By György Peteri. 1984.

168. *PNA: A Centennial History of the Polish National Alliance of the United States of North America*. By Donald E. Pienkos. 1984.
169. *The Slovenes of Carinthia*. By Thomas M. Barker and Andreas Moritsch. 1984.
170. *The Saga of Kosovo: Focus of Serbian-Albanian Relations*. By Alex N. Dragnich and Slavko Todorovich. 1984.
171. *Germany's International Monetary Policy and the European Monetary System*. By Hugh Kaufmann. 1985.
172. *Kiril and Methodius: Founders of Slavonic Writing*. Edited by Ivan Duichev. 1985.
173. *The United States and the Greek War for Independence, 1821-1828*. By Paul C. Pappas. 1985.
174. *Joseph Eötvös and the Modernization of Hungary, 1840-1870*. By Paul Bödy. 1985.
175. *Jewish Leadership during the Nazi Era: Patterns of Behavior in the Free World*. Edited by Randolph L. Braham. 1985.
176. *The American Mission in the Allied Control Commission for Bulgaria, 1944-1947: History and Transcripts*. Edited by Michael M. Boll. 1985.
177. *The United States, Great Britain, and the Sovietization of Hungary, 1945-1948*. By Stanley M. Max. 1985.
178. *Hunyadi: Legend and Reality*. By Joseph Held. 1985.
179. *Clio's Art in Hungary and in Hungarian-America*. By Steven Bela Vardy. 1985.
180. *Slovakia 1918-1938: Education and the Making of a Nation*. By Owen V. Johnson. 1985.
181. *Ilija Garasanin: Balkan Bismarck*. By David MacKenzie. 1985.
182. *Medieval Buda: A Study of Municipal Government and Jurisdiction in the Kingdom of Hungary*. By Martyn C. Rady. 1985.
183. *Eastern Europe in the Aftermath of Solidarity*. By Adam Bromke. 1985.
184. *Istvan Tisza: The Liberal Vision and Conservative Statecraft of a Magyar Nationalist*. By Gabor Vermes. 1985.